D1310833

Biographical Directory
of the Governors
of the United States
1983–1988

Biographical Directory
of the Governors
of the United States
1983–1988

Marie Marmo Mullaney

Meckler

Westport • London

Library of Congress Cataloging-in-Publication Data
Mullaney, Marie Marmo.
   Biographical directory of the governors of the United
States, 1983–1988.

   Bibliography: p.
   Includes index.
   1. Governors—United States—Biography—Directories.
2. Governors—United States—Election.   I. Title.
JK2447.M86   1989   353.9'131'025[B]   89-2273
ISBN 0-88736-177-3 (alk. paper)

British Library Cataloguing in Publication Data
Biographical directory of the governors of the United
   States, 1983–1988.
   1. United States. Governors, history—Biographies
   Collections
   I. Mullaney, Marie Marmo
   973'.09'.92

   ISBN 0-88736-177-3

Meckler Corporation, 11 Ferry Lane West, Westport, CT 06880.
Meckler Ltd., Grosvenor Gardens House, Grosvenor Gardens, London SW1W
   0BS, U.K.

Printed on acid free paper.
Printed and bound in the United States of America.

CONTENTS

Prefatory Note vii

PREFATORY NOTE

Time was when the archetypal American governor was caricatured and lampooned as "good-time Charlie," a good 'ole boy beholden to the courthouse crowd and bereft of any real executive power. Those days are gone forever. The last 25 years have witnessed a remarkable transformation in the office of the governor, so much so that political observers have called this current crop of officeholders a new political elite, part of a kind of "Governors Club" that bears close watching. Indeed, the cohort of statehouse leaders included in this volume boasts some of the most talented and innovative reformers since the heyday of the Progressives earlier in this century.

Whereas Washington was once viewed as the mecca for ambitious pols and would-be movers and shakers, that image has changed somewhat. The statehouse, not Capitol Hill, has become an increasingly attractive magnet as state government has more and more come to be seen as a path to real influence and power. With the conservative clarion to turn power and responsibility back to the states, the Reagan revolution has been at least partly responsible for the change. With the federal government less financially able and less ideologically willing to solve social problems, states more than ever have become "laboratories" for the development of solutions to pressing national concerns. It was precisely such an emphasis on pragmatism, activism, and innovation that became the hallmark of Massachusetts Governor Michael Dukakis' 1988 Presidential bid. "Whether we agree with you or not," Arkansas Governor Bill Clinton once told President Reagan, "we all admit you've made us more important."

The result has been the emergence of a new generation of leaders, committed to the challenges of state government, who are working to revitalize not only their own states but their national party programs as well. The best and the brightest young stars of both parties include within their ranks numerous representatives of the nation's gubernatorial corps— Arkansas' Bill Clinton, New Jersey's Tom Kean, New York's Mario Cuomo, and Virginia's Gerald Baliles. In both parties, governors and former governors were leading players in the race for the 1988 Presidential and Vice-Presidential nominations: Babbitt, Clinton, Dukakis, and Cuomo for the Democrats, and Deukmejian, DuPont, Thompson, Sununu, and Alexander for the Republicans. The election itself saw numerous members of the Governors Club make the trek to Washington: Virginia's Chuck Robb to the Senate, New Hampshire's Sununu to the White House as

Chief of Staff, and Pennsylvania's former Governor Dick Thornburgh to the Justice Department as Attorney General, retaining the position to which he had been named by Ronald Reagan. Moreover, state governors are taking the lead in remaking national parties. New Jersey's Tom Kean has become a national spokesman for Republicans eager to widen party ranks to include more minority and blue collar voters, while Arizona's Bruce Babbitt and Virginia's Chuck Robb have put forth a new centrist vision for Democrats that blends traditional party goals of civil rights and social justice with fiscal restraints and limits on the size of government.

Nowhere is the change more apparent than in the New South, which in the last decade has witnessed the emergence of a new breed of progressive governor. Elected without the traditional courthouse crowd and coming into office with a mandate for change, men like Clinton of Arkansas, Roemer of Louisiana, Mabus of Mississippi, and Wilkinson of Kentucky are changing the face of the Old Confederacy as they call for comprehensive economic development programs, a sincere commitment to social and racial justice, educational improvement, and increased social spending.

Yet the story of the American governorship in these years is not all sweetness and light. The years 1983–1988 were marred by tragedies both personal and political: Toney Anaya's (D-N.Mex.) fall from grace, Bill Sheffield's (D-Alsk.) impeachment, and Evan Mecham's (R-Ariz.) impeachment, conviction, and removal from office. With the 1988 verdict of the State Senate, Mecham became the first U.S. governor to be impeached and removed from office in 59 years.

A final note on demographics: This cohort of chief executives remains a homogeneous lot—overwhelmingly white, Protestant, and male. There have, however, been a few breakthroughs in the traditional political elite. The elections of Toney Anaya (D-N.Mex.) and Bob Martinez (R-Fla.) testify to the growing regional clout of Hispanic Americans, while in 1986 Hawaii's John Waihee became the state's first governor of native Hawaiian ancestry. Women continued to join the ranks of the nation's chief executives, as Martha Layne Collins (D-Ky.), Madeleine M. Kunin (D-Vt.), Kay Orr (R-Neb.), and Rose Mofford (D-Ariz.) acceded to the governorship. Nebraska made history in 1986, becoming the first state to nominate a woman as the gubernatorial candidate of both major political parties. Black Americans, however, have yet to break the color barrier that has kept them from state executive mansions in the twentieth century. Yet these years have seen some progress. In the California campaigns of 1982 and 1986, Los Angeles Mayor Tom Bradley came very close to achieving his dream of becoming the nation's first elected black governor, while in 1986 Bill Lucas of Michigan became not only the first black to win the Republican nomination for governor of Michigan, but also the first black since Reconstruction to win the GOP nomination for governor anywhere.

Insofar as it reflects larger social, economic, and cultural trends, the study of American gubernatorial politics provides revealing and fascinating insights into American life as we head toward the twenty-first century.

Marie Marmo Mullaney
Caldwell College
March 1989

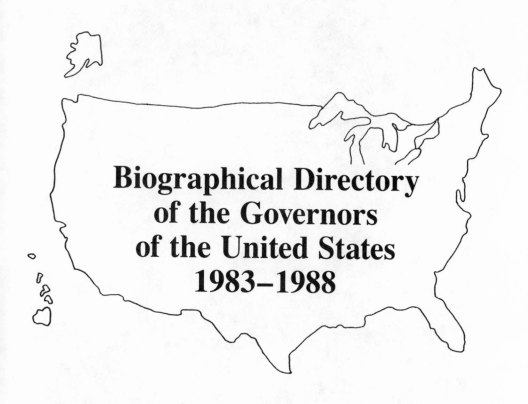

Biographical Directory
of the Governors
of the United States
1983–1988

George Corley Wallace (Courtesy of governor's office)

ALABAMA

WALLACE, George Corley, 1963–1967, 1971–1972, 1972–1979, 1983–1987

Born on August 25, 1919 in Clio, Alabama, the son of George C. Wallace, a farmer, and Mozell Smith Wallace. A Methodist, Wallace married Lurleen Burns on May 23, 1943. The couple had four children: Bobbi Jo, Peggy Sue, George Corley Jr., and Janie Lee. Lurleen Wallace died on May 7, 1968 while serving her own term as governor of Alabama. Wallace married a second time to Cornelia Ellis Snively on January 4, 1971. Snively was the niece of former Alabama Governor James E. Folsom. The pair separated in 1977 and were divorced in 1978. He married a third time to Lisa Taylor, the daughter of a wealthy Alabama coal mine operator, on September 9, 1981. Almost 30 years his junior, Taylor and her sister had had a country singing act that entertained prospective Wallace voters at rallies during the late 1960s. The couple lived apart since 1986 and divorced in 1987, Wallace's second failed marriage in less than 10 years. His 38-year-old wife cited incompatibility in filing for divorce.

Wallace attended Barbour County High School and received an LL.B. from the University of Alabama in 1942. He was admitted to the Alabama bar that same year. Wallace served in the United States Army Air Force from 1942 to 1945, achieving the rank of flight sergeant. Alabama's assistant attorney general from 1946 to 1947, he was also a member of the Alabama House of Representatives from 1947 to 1953. Wallace was a judge for the Third Judicial District of Alabama between 1953 and 1958, and had a private law practice in Clayton, Alabama from 1958 to 1962. He is a member of the American Legion, the Veterans of Foreign Wars, the Disabled American Veterans, the Masons, the Moose, the Elks, and the Modern Woodmen of the World.

Following an unsuccessful campaign for governor in 1958 as a racial moderate, Wallace became a staunch segregationist and won the governorship in 1962. He defeated Jim Folsom to win the Democratic nomination, and received 303,987 votes in the uncontested general election. Wallace was sworn into office on January 14, 1963. During his first administration Wallace barred the enrollment of blacks at the University of Alabama, promising to preserve "segregation forever." President John F. Kennedy then ordered the Alabama National Guard to active duty, and forced state officials to comply with federal court orders dealing with integration. Wallace eventually became known as the nation's premier foe of integration.

Constitutionally prohibited from succeeding himself in office, Wallace attempted to amend the Alabama constitution to allow him to do so. His efforts failed, and he left office on January 16, 1967. Nevertheless, Wallace's wife Lurleen had been elected governor in November 1966, and her husband served as a $1.00-a-year special assistant, an arrangement which allowed him to make most of the important executive decisions. When she died in office on May 7, 1968, Lurleen Wallace was succeeded by Alabama's lieutenant governor, Albert P. Brewer.

Wallace was the unsuccessful American Independent party candidate for president in 1968, although he won 13.6 percent of the vote nationally, the strongest third party candidacy since 1924. In the 1970 Alabama Democratic gubernatorial primary election, Wallace trailed the incumbent Brewer; however, he captured the runoff primary, and was elected to a second gubernatorial term in the general election on November 3, 1970. Wallace received 634,046 votes, compared with National Democratic party of Alabama candidate John L. Cashin's 125,491 and Independent A.C. Shelton's 75,679. He was inaugurated on January 18, 1971.

As a candidate for the 1972 Democratic presidential nomination, Wallace had received more popular votes in the primaries than anyone else at the time he was gunned down in a Maryland shopping center in May. The assassination attempt by Arthur Bremer, Jr. left Wallace permanently paralyzed from the waist down. As a result of his wounds, he relinquished his duties as chief executive to Lieutenant Governor Jere L. Beasley on June 4, 1972; by July 7, however, he had recovered sufficiently to reassume the office. Because of a 1968 amendment to the Alabama Constitution which allowed governors to succeed themselves, Wallace was eligible to run for re-election in 1974. He won 83 percent of the vote in the general election on November 5, 1974, receiving 497,574 votes against Republican Elvin McCary's 88,381.

Barred by law from seeking a third consective term in 1978, Wallace considered running for the Senate seat being vacated by Alabama's retiring veteran Senator John Sparkman. To that end, the Legislature even passed a bill guaranteeing him police protection after he left the statehouse. Wallace's surprise decision not to seek the Senate, confirmed in June 1978 after a second seat became available with the death of Alabama's other Senator, James B. Allen, moved political commentators to write his political obituary. Both supporters and opponents interpreted his action as being tantamount to permanent retirement from electoral politics.

In retirement, Wallace worked for the University of Alabama in Birmingham as a director of development for Rehabilitative Services. There was also some discussion concerning the possibility of endowing a chair at one of the state universities, to enable him to teach law, political science, or government.

Yet the man who has been called a compulsive campaigner ultimately found political life irresistible, and in May 1982 he announced his candidacy for an unprecedented fourth term as governor of Alabama. Running on a tax-cutting platform, he directed his campaign toward "the little man" in a state suffering from a 14.5 percent unemployment rate. Wallace's opponents for the Democratic nomination were Lieutenant Governor George McMillan, who perceived himself as Alabama's best hope for a progressive, "New South" image, and Joe McCorquodale, speaker of the Alabama House for eight years, who was supported by farmers, bankers, big business, big land owners, and timber and forest product interests. Since no candidate received 50 percent of the vote as required by state law (Wallace polled 44 percent to McMillan's nearly 30 percent and McCorquodale's 25 percent), Wallace and McMillan took part in a runoff election.

The runoff campaign tested not only political alignments, but also cultural styles and social classes. McMillan, a liberal lawyer from Mountain Brook, Birmingham's richest white suburb, depicted himself as a New South progressive. Claiming that Wallace represented the "politics of the past," he charged that poor leadership when either George or Lurleen Wallace controlled state government for all but six of the last 20 years had caused Alabama to miss much of the Sun Belt prosperity experienced by other states in the Southeast. Essentially, McMillan attempted to put together an urban coalition of blacks and middle and upper class whites, a novel political approach in Alabama.

Wallace, on the other hand, made much of his experience, and attacked McMillan's liberal views on some issues. He called for victims' rights in criminal cases, including monetary restitution by those convicted, and condemned "tax loopholes for the rich." Adopting a populist theme, he characterized the election as a battle between the "little people" and the wealthy. Pledging to combat a national economic trend in which "the rich get richer and the poor get poorer," Wallace campaigned heavily in blue-collar neighborhoods and towns where steel mills and auto plants had closed. In a stunning about-face that drew nationwide publicity, Wallace openly courted the black vote, which constituted about 25 percent of the electorate. In actions viewed skeptically by many, he also repudiated his former racist sentiments, acts, and statements, saying that his attacks had never been against blacks directly but against interference by the federal government in state affairs.

Wallace won the runoff by a margin of 51.5 percent to 48.5 percent, in a showing that demonstrated the strong rural-urban cleavages in Alabama politics. He captured both his usual rural strongholds in predominantly white counties and several counties in which blacks represented the majority. The former segregationist even got up to 40 percent of the vote in urban black precincts in Montogmery. Indeed, black leaders conceded that he received minority votes because blacks were helped by education and job programs Wallace had sponsored before he left office in 1978.

In the general election Wallace played an unfamiliar role as a liberal versus the ultraconservative Emory Folmar, the Republican mayor of Montgomery. A millionaire shopping center developer, Folmar advocated tough police tactics and supported the tenets of the "Moral Majority." The outcome was never in doubt. Wallace forged a populist coalition of blacks, labor unions, and poor whites. Speaking out for children, the jobless, the elderly and infirm, he attacked public utilities, banks, and "rich Republicans." Promising an era of economic growth by arguing that his international stature could attract business to the state, Wallace won 58 percent of the vote. His victory in 1982 and the way he won was seen by political observers as a symbol of the vast changes that have transformed the South during the last 20 years.

In his fourth and final term as governor, Wallace seemed unable or unwilling to spend needed time with legislators and administrators. Alabama remained a low-skill, mostly low-wage state that continued to have trouble competing with those southern neighbors traditionally more friendly to business. Illnesses linked to his paralysis sent him to the hospital for extended periods. In the spring of 1985 published reports speculated that the governor's ill health would soon force him to resign his office. Suffering from intense pain, Wallace underwent special spinal surgery in July 1985, with the hope that this would restore both his physical health and political vitality. For a time after the operation, Wallace publicly ruminated on the possibility of seeking an unprecedented fifth term as governor. Had he decided to run, aides admitted that his biggest task would have been convincing voters that his health had truly improved. Some polls indicated that he stood little if any chance for success. Age, longevity, and failing health made him the target of critics who said that Alabama, like other states in the region, had to move toward a more progressive, younger governor with a New, rather than Old South, image.

Trailing many of his prospective opponents in the polls, Wallace made an emotional announcement in April 1986 that he would indeed be stepping down at the conclusion of his fourth term. In increasingly poor health, he was frequently confined to bed. In addition to the pain associated with his paralysis, he was suffering from eye trouble, poor hearing, and urinary tract problems. Since leaving office in January 1987, he has worked for the Montgomery office of Troy State University in a job involving fund-raising and promotion.

George Wallace will be remembered as one of the most enduring figures in Southern politics, the only one of the region's governors whose career spanned the entire sweep of the civil rights era. Yet historians will also remember him as much more than a purely regional phenomenon. He made runs for the White House in 1968, 1972, and 1976. Of these campaigns, Wallace has said that they created the climate for a fellow Southerner, Jimmy Carter, to be elected president. As a national spokesman for the social, political, and economic discontent of working class whites in many eastern and midwestern states, he believes he made a unique contribution to American politics by being the "people's instrument" in bringing about "much of the change in American political thought." His calls for the "little people" to join his crusades against the intrusions of government bureaucrats, the federal courts, and the Eastern press rang true with many voters, and may well be seen as the wellsprings of the conservative resurgence of the 1980s.

Bibliography: Lester A. Sobel, ed., *Facts on File Yearbook, 1963* (New York, 1964); Lester A. Sobel, ed., *Facts on File Yearbook, 1972* (New York, 1973); "Democrats: Who's Almost Who," *Newsweek* (Oct. 7, 1974); Congressional Quarterly, Inc., *Guide to U.S. Elections* (Washington, D.C., 1975); Roy Glashan, *American Governors and Gubernatorial Elections, 1775–1975* (Stillwater, Minn., 1975); *The New York Times:* 4–22–77; 6–19–77; 4–21–78; 5–17–78; 5–18–78; 6–22–78; 1–16–79; 9–10–81; 5–23–82; 9–3–82; 9–8–82; 9–26–82; 9–29–82; 9–30–82; 10–3–82; 11–3–82; 8–29–85; 9–13–85; 4–6–86; 6–7–87; Michael Barone *et al.*, eds., *The Almanac of American Politics, 1978–1984* (New York and Washington, D.C., 1977–83); "Fresh Faces in the Mansions," *Time* (Nov. 15, 1982).

Guy Hunt (Courtesy of governor's office)

HUNT, Guy, 1987–

Born on June 17, 1933 in Holly Pond (Cullman County), Alabama, Hunt is the son of William Otto Hunt and Frances Orene Holcombe Hunt. A member of the Mt. Vernon Primitive Baptist Church, he married the former Helen Chambers on February 25, 1951. They have four children: Pam, Sherrie, Keith, and Lynn.

Hunt graduated from Holly Pond High School in 1950 with intentions of embarking on a career in farming. He was president of the Holly Pond chapter of the Future Farmers of America, and later became president of the Cullman County Future Farmers of America. He served in the U.S. Army during the Korean War, in the 101st Airborne Division and in the 1st Infantry Division, and was awarded the Certificate of Achievement for Outstanding Performance of Military Duty.

He began his political career in 1964 when he was elected probate judge of Cullman County. Re-elected in 1970, he chose not to seek re-election in 1976, although he remained active in state Republican politics. A supporter of Ronald Reagan's presidential ambitions from the mid-1970s, he was the state chairman of Reagan's presidential campaign in 1976, as well as chairman of the Alabama delegation to the Republican National Convention in Kansas City in 1976. He repeated these roles during Reagan's victorious run for the White House in 1980. His support was rewarded with a presidential appointment as state executive director of the Agricultural Stabilization and Conservation Service (ASCS) under the U.S. Department of Agriculture, a position he held from 1981 to 1985, when he resigned to prepare for the 1986 gubernatorial race.

Alabama politics changed dramatically in 1986 when legendary incumbent George Wallace announced that he would be retiring from the statehouse at the conclusion of his fourth term. Attention quickly focused on who would lead the state into the post-Wallace era. Almost all political observers assumed it would be a Democrat, since Alabama is a heavily Democratic state that had not had a Republican governor since 1874. Hunt was given little or no chance of victory. In fact it was widely assumed that he was in the race simply to "show the flag" for the party, after several better known Republicans had chosen not to run. Hunt had already lost badly once before: in the 1978 campaign he was defeated by Democrat Fob James, 551,886 votes to 196,963.

The 1986 Republican primary was so small and quiet that it attracted less than 33,000 voters. Hunt won the nomination easily, beating businessman Doug Carter. As had long been standard in traditional Southern politics, all assumed that the next governor of Alabama would be whoever won the Democratic primary. That primary, however, turned into a tumultuous battle that badly split the state's Democratic party and paved the way for Hunt's eventual victory. The two leading contenders were Attorney General Charles R. Graddick, a former Republican, and Lieutenant Governor Bill Baxley, a moderate-to-liberal figure in state politics. The campaign stirred racial tensions more overtly than had any other race in years. Graddick chose to spurn the sizable black vote in Alabama, appealing instead to the conservative white vote that had carried the state for Ronald Reagan in 1984. Baxley drew on Wallace's populist coalition of blacks and more liberal whites, as well as union members and public employees. Although Graddick narrowly defeated Baxley in the June 24, 1986 Democratic runoff (50.3 percent to 49.7 percent), a panel of federal judges stripped him of the nomination because he had violated state and federal voting laws by illegally encouraging Republicans to ignore Democratic party rules and cross over to vote for him in the runoff. As attorney general, Graddick had issued an opinion the day before the election saying such crossover voting was legal. A black couple sued in federal court, accusing Graddick of violating the Voting Rights Act by misusing his office to court Republican voters in order to dilute the strength of black votes. Ruling on the suit, the judges ordered the state Democratic party either to name Baxley the winner or hold a new election.

State party leaders decided to name Baxley as their nominee, concluding that it was illegal Republican ballots that had provided Graddick with his razor-thin margin of victory. When Alabama's Supreme Court refused to order a new Democratic gubernatorial runoff, Graddick threatened to run as an independent write-in candidate in the fall election. Although the deep divisions in the Democratic party aided Hunt's candidacy, the specter of Graddick's third-party challenge haunted Hunt's campaign in the early months, for both men were aiming their appeals at the same pool of white conservatives and traditional Republicans. When Graddick chose to end his candidacy, Hunt—who had been given no chance of winning—suddenly had a very good chance.

In the campaign Baxley tried to portray Hunt as unqualified, running ads playing on his lack of a college degree and describing him (a lay Baptist preacher, chicken farmer, and Amway distributor) as a former vacuum cleaner salesman. Hunt was also forced to deny allegations that he had been made to step down from his federal agricultural job in Alabama because he had solicited campaign contributions from government employees.

Hunt based his campaign on the need to create a business climate "second to none," and pledged a range of initiatives to attack waste in government, to revise state laws governing lawsuits for personal injury and property damage, and to improve the state's public school system. He said the task of creating new and better jobs would be the "foundation of his administration," and he spoke of a "philosophical partnership" between conservatives, regardless of party.

Hunt's 56 percent to 44 percent victory over Baxley in the November 4, 1986 election made him the first Republican governor of Alabama since

David Peter Lewis, who served from 1872 to 1874. Political commentators, however, attributed it solely to the bitter and divisive battles among Democrats in their struggles to choose a successor to George Wallace. Hunt's victory appeared to be a lone phenomenon, without discernible coattails or broader effect, since he propelled no local Republicans into office with him.

Surrounded by Democrats in every major executive, legislative, and administrative office, Hunt—it was widely predicted—would be "eaten alive" by the legislature. Moreover, political scientists noted that the executive authority of the Alabama governor's office ranks only in the middle or lower range among states. Interposed between the governor and department heads in many cases are elective boards, and without the cooperation of the legislature, the governor has "only his appointive powers and his powers of public persuasion." Yet Hunt and the Democratically controlled legislature have some conservative attitudes in common. Shared views on taxes, spending, and the need to create a more stable economic climate may produce opportunities for cooperation. Such cooperation is urgent, for the state faces grim financial choices. In the last years of the Wallace administration, the governor and legislature were propping up the state's operating budget with one-time non-recurring revenue acts. An unpopular choice between spending cuts or tax increases loomed as the first great policy test of Hunt's tenure. One of his first acts as governor was to commission a study of the budget to look at state services such as human resources, Medicaid, and mental health facilities.

In his inaugural address, Hunt pledged to put to rest the forces that have divided the nation since the Civil War, and promised a "color blind" administration. Yet within his first month in office he fought bitterly with an influential group of black Democrats who assailed his appointments record, which included only one black out of 23 Cabinet-level appointments.

Hunt has also proposed sweeping changes in the way public colleges are governed, prompting a clamorous debate about how much power the governor should have in setting educational policy. Hunt defended his proposals by claiming they represented a "minimum change" that would ensure better coordination of academic programs and better use of state tax dollars for higher education. His critics, however, say the changes would give the governor too much power at the expense of colleges and universities that do not have much political clout. Hunt also favors eliminating duplicative courses in the state university system, and has called for improvements in teacher-education programs.

Bibliography: Alabama Magazine 51 (Jan.–Feb. 1987); biographical information courtesy of governor's office; *The Chronicle of Higher Education:* 10–22–86; 11–12–86; 1–13–88; *The New York Times:* 6–29–86; 8–3–86; 9–4–86; 10–2–86; 10–3–86; 10–8–86; 10–25–86; 11–1–86; 11–5–86; 11–6–86; 1–20–87; 2–13–87.

William Jennings Sheffield (Courtesy of the Alaska State Archives)

ALASKA

SHEFFIELD, William Jennings, 1982–1986

Born on June 26, 1928 in Spokane, Washington, Sheffield moved to Alaska in 1953. A Presbyterian, he is a widower with one daughter, Deborah.

Trained as a radio broadcast engineer at DeForest Training School in Chicago and a member of the United States Army Air Corps from 1946 to 1949, Sheffield is founder and chairman of the board of Sheffield Enterprises, a hotel management firm that owns 10 hotels in Alaska and Canada's Yukon Territory. Combining his business talents with a sense of civic involvement, he has been president of the Alaska Visitors Association and that state's Chamber of Commerce; he is also a former national director of the United States Jaycees. Sheffield was chairman of the state March of Dimes, the state Cancer Society, the Easter Seal Telethon, and the St. Jude's Children's Hospital Telethon. His political activities include membership on the Anchorage City Planning Commission (1960–63) and the Anchorage Charter Commission (1976), service to the Foundation Board of the University of Alaska, chairmanship of the Alaska State Parole Board, and election as a delegate to local, state, and national Democratic party conventions.

Sheffield's business ventures had made him a millionaire, and in seeking the Alaska governorship in 1982 he broke all state records by spending more than $1 million, much of it his own money, to win the Democratic nomination against a field of five other candidates. Nevertheless, his primary victory was a narrow one. Sheffield defeated his closest challenger, Fairbanks lawyer Steve Cowper, by only 260 votes.

In the general election Sheffield's opponent was insurance agent Tom Fink, an outspoken conservative and former speaker of the Alaska House of Representatives, who had won the Republican nomination by defeating the favored candidate, Lieutenant Governor Terry Miller. Campaigning in the remote bush country, Sheffield picked up much support in small villages usually ignored by politicians. Alaska's voters were also impressed by his business experience. Most important to his victory was his popular stand on two hotly contested political issues: a proposal to spend $2.8 billion to move the state capital from Juneau to Willow, 580 miles away, and an attempt to repeal a law that allowed rural Alaskans to take fish and game for subsistence. The attempt to move the capital aroused considerable opposition in southeastern Alaska, while the debate on hunting and fishing rights took on racial overtones, since residents of the Alaska bush were more likely to be Alaska natives. Sheffield opposed both measures, while Fink did not. Sheffield also seemed to personify the kind of entrepreneurial success typical of Alaska politicians and respected by the electorate. The keynote of his administration, he promised, would be an open and businesslike approach to government.

Midway through his term, however, Sheffield became the focus of legal investigations that cast a pall on his governorship and foreshadowed the end of his political career. A Juneau grand jury began investigating his role in negotiating a shady office deal. The actual charge was that he had pressured state agencies to lease $9.1 million in office space to a supporter who helped settle his campaign debts. The lease was cancelled after the state attorney general ruled it was "tainted with favoritism," but an inquiry ensued, focusing on what one attorney called "the ultimate issue of accountability." The grand jury's final report suggested that the governor might have perjured himself in testimony before them. It took an unusual step, however: instead of indicting Sheffield for perjury, the jury issued a public report calling for immediate impeachment proceedings, the first impeachment action in Alaskan history and the first in the nation for nearly 50 years.

After month-long televised hearings by the Alaska State Senate in the summer of 1985, a consensus emerged to exonerate Sheffield. By a vote of 12–8, the senate concluded that there was no "clear and convincing evidence" that Sheffield had lied to a grand jury when he testified about his part in the leasing of the offices. His supporters also narrowly defeated a resolution critical of his conduct.

Despite his exoneration, political pundits quickly concluded that the inquiry had been "fatal" to Sheffield's political prospects. While many felt he would seek re-election to vindicate himself, most observers felt he had little chance of success. Sheffield was dogged not only by problems of image but also by signs of voter moodiness over the economy. Throughout the 1970s and into the 1980s economic growth in the state had been rapid, as taxes and royalties collected from Prudhoe Bay oil passed through the state treasury and into economic development, business, and consumer goods. The decline in oil prices throughout the 1980s, however, cut into the state's royalties, and caused oil income to drop. With less money available, state spending slowed and business activity was off.

Sensing victory, a big field of Republican candidates soon began lining up to challenge Sheffield. Most prominent among them was Dick Randolph, a one-time Republican state legislator who became the most successful campaigner the Libertarian party has had in Alaska. Randolph announced he was becoming a Republican again to campaign against Sheffield. Saying that under Sheffield "scandals and grand juries" had become "the rule rather than the exception," Randolph reminded voters that Sheffield had faced criticism over his fund-raising tactics, and over switching funds appropriated for other uses to pay for the renovation of the governor's mansion in Juneau.

Within the ranks of his own party, Sheffield was challenged by Steve Cowper, a Fairbanks lawyer and former state legislator who had lost to Sheffield by only 260 votes in the 1982 Democratic gubernatorial primary. Despite spending twice that of his major rival, Sheffield lost the August 26, 1986 primary to Cowper by a 2–1 margin, making it the first time in a statewide race in Alaska that the biggest spender lost. Sheffield cited the state's sinking economy as the reason for his defeat. With his loss, Sheffield became the first incumbent governor to lose in a primary of his own party since 1978, when Massachusetts Governor Edward King defeated incumbent Michael Dukakis for the Democratic gubernatorial nomination.

Steve Cowper, the man who dethroned Sheffield, went on to win the November 1986 general election and succeed Sheffield as governor of Alaska.

Bibliography: Michael Barone *et al.*, *Almanac of American Politics 1984* (New York and Washington, D.C., 1983); *U.S. News and World Report* (October 4, 1982); *Newsweek* (Aug. 5, 1985); *The New York Times:* 7–6–82; 11–4–82; 7–14–85; 8–3–85; 8–4–85; 8–11–85; 11–6–85.

Steve Cowper (Courtesy of governor's office)

COWPER, Steve, 1986–

Born on August 21, 1938 in Petersburg, Virginia, Cowper grew up in Kinston, North Carolina. He received a B.A. from the University of North Carolina in 1960 and an LL.B., also from the University of North Carolina, in 1963. He served in the U.S. Army in 1960 and in the U.S. Army Reserve from 1959–1965. He also spent three years as a maritime lawyer in Norfolk, Virginia.

Cowper moved to Alaska in 1968, when he began his political career as assistant district attorney for Fairbanks and rural Alaska, a post he held from 1968–1969. He pursued other interests as well: he was a partner in a Bethel air taxi and cargo business, a political columnist, and author of the script for a highly acclaimed documentary on the history of Alaska lands.

In 1974, Cowper, a Democrat, won the first of two terms in the Alaska House of Representatives. In office from 1974 to 1978, he served as chairman of the House Finance Committee 1977–1978; chairman of the Steering Council on Alaska Lands, 1978; a member of the Subsistence Committee, 1977–1978; and a member of the Alaska Advisory Committee for the Law of the Sea Conference, 1978.

He has also held numerous business and professional positions: research diver with the Marine Research Team, 1975–1976; a newspaper reporter in Vietnam, 1970; and an instructor at Tanana Valley Community College, 1980.

His first attempt at statewide political office came in 1982. Despite a narrow loss in the Democratic gubernatorial primary to William Sheffield, the man who went on to win the general election and become governor of Alaska, Cowper persisted in his drive for the statehouse. His quest for his party's nomination was aided by the political troubles of incumbent William Sheffield. Sheffield had been badly bruised by state senate hearings during the summer of 1985 on whether he should be impeached on charges of having designed specifications for state office space to benefit a longtime friend and political contributor. Sheffield denied any wrongdoing, and the legislature did not bring formal impeachment charges, but the televised hearings capped three years of controversy over Sheffield's conduct in office. The incumbent was also plagued by a rocky state economy. Plunging oil prices cut the state's income from petroleum taxes and royalties by two-thirds, forcing cuts of $1 billion in the state budget and causing oil companies to cut jobs. Despite being outspent by his opponent, Cowper won the August 26, 1986 Democratic gubernatorial primary by a 2–1 margin.

Cowper faced Republican State Senator Arliss Sturgulewski of Anchorage in the November 1986 general election. To win her party's nomination, Mrs. Sturgulewski led a field of seven that included former state Governor Walter Hickel. In the campaign, Cowper stressed economic recovery and redevelopment. He focused on the special development problems of rural Alaska, the need to seek new markets aggressively, and the potential benefits of sharing the state's demonstrated skills in cold-weather engineering and construction, telecommunications, and energy technology. Cowper won the governorship with 48.9 percent of the vote; Sturgulewski gained 43.9 percent, while third-party candidate J. Vogler of the American Independent party captured 5.7 percent.

In his inaugural address, Cowper called for unity in trying to solve the state's billion-dollar gap between income and spending. With the state continuing to be battered by troubles in the oil industry, he proposed re-establishing the state income tax, abolished in 1979 amid a flood of oil money. Despite the fact that the state has neither a sales nor income tax, Cowper's proposal to raise $183 million with the new tax aroused bitter opposition. He also proposed that the Alaska Permanent Fund, a part of the state's income from its vast Arctic oilfields, be tapped to pay part of the cost of state government.

As part of his economic development plan, Cowper has advocated the expansion of the University of Alaska's international study programs. He hopes to establish an International Trade Center to bring in people from the business, financial, and governmental sectors of the nations with which Alaska trades. He has also placed great emphasis on the teaching of foreign languages and culture, especially Japanese, Chinese, and Russian, in the state's public schools.

Bibliography: Biographical information courtesy of governor's office; *The Chronicle of Higher Education:* 10–22–86; 11–12–86; *The New York Times:* 1–3–86; 2–21–87; 4–6–87.

Bruce Edward Babbitt (Credit: Markow Photography)

ARIZONA

BABBITT, Bruce Edward, 1978–1987

Born on June 27, 1938, Babbitt is the son of a patrician family who came to Arizona when it was still a frontier and became wealthy by operating Indian trading posts near Flagstaff and then expanding to other interests. A Roman Catholic, he left Arizona to attend the University of Notre Dame, where he was elected student body president. Hoping to capitalize on the great mineral wealth of Arizona, Babbitt majored in geology and went on to receive an M.A. in geophysics at the University of Newcastle in England. He and his wife Hattie, who is a trial lawyer, have two children.

A mining trip to Bolivia quickly changed Babbitt's career ambitions. As he explained to a reporter, "I saw so much misery, such human deprivation while in Bolivia that I thought, how can I live in an ivory tower filled with such people problems?" While earning his law degree at Harvard, he took time off to take part in the civil rights marches in Selma, Alabama; after graduating in 1965, he joined the Johnson administration's anti-poverty drive as a civil rights lawyer. Babbitt was also special assistant to the director of VISTA from 1965 to 1967. He returned to Arizona in 1967 and became a member of the Phoenix law firm of Brown and Bain.

Babbitt entered state politics in 1974, and was elected attorney general on a platform promising to deal vigorously with land fraud, securities and insurance irregularities, bribery in business regulation, and other white collar crime. His crusading prosecution of price-fixing and other anti-trust activity reportedly endangered his life. According to court testimony, a murder contract was placed on his life by the same people who in June 1976 murdered *Arizona Republic* reporter Don Bolles, who had been investigating land fraud in Arizona. Babbitt won fame for prosecuting that case, and for winning consumer refunds in suits against companies that engaged in price-fixing practices. As attorney general, he pushed for wider criminal powers, established the first statewide grand jury, and led a spirited fight against fraud in the state's powerful and profitable land sales industry.

Babbitt became Arizona's chief executive through a partly accidental, partly tragic sequence of events. In 1977, when Democratic incumbent Raul Castro was appointed United States Ambassador to Argentina, Secretary of State Wesley Bolin succeeded to the governorship. But when Bolin died suddenly in March 1978, after less than five months in office, Attorney General Babbitt found himself Arizona's third governor within five months, the youngest chief executive in Arizona history.

Because the Republican party had grown considerably stronger in Arizona by 1978, Babbitt did not have an especially easy time of it when he sought election to his own term that year. In the general election he narrowly defeated the Republican challenger, automobile dealer and former State Senator Evan Mecham, by winning just 52 percent of the vote. He had a much easier time of it in his 1982 campaign for re-election, however, winning 62 percent of the vote over Arizona's Senate president, Republican Leo Corbet.

Babbitt won the governorship by appealing to moderate voters of both parties in conservative Arizona. Just as he had changed the attorney general's office, he took what had been a weak executive branch and put his stamp all over Arizona government. As governor, Babbitt sought to place some environmental controls on the state's growth and advocated modest increases in state government services. He acquired something of a national reputation when he was named by President Jimmy Carter to serve on a commission investigating the Three Mile Island nuclear plant accident. Drawing on his own background as an engineering student, he helped to draft a report that was widely accepted as responsible and fair. Although he began his political career as a liberal, Babbitt came to question orthodox liberal approaches to issues, especially by criticizing federal programs that required too much paperwork or gave too much control to Washington. As such, he was in the vanguard of a new breed of western Democrat: liberals who believe the government should have a strong role in civil rights, education, and health issues, but who share a certain degree of skepticism and readiness to question whether government programs are always necessary or effective solutions to social problems. When the Reagan administration announced its program of budget cuts early in 1981, Babbitt, alone among the nation's governors, suggested an alternative. At national governors' conferences, he put forth innovative proposals on the need for a new division of responsibilities between the national and state governments. As chairman of the National Governors' Association in 1985, he was one of the nation's first major Democrats to endorse President Reagan's tax simplification program.

David Osborne, the author of a forthcoming study of six innovative Democratic governors, *Laboratories of Democracy,* hailed Babbitt as a "great" governor. Political observers were impressed by how Babbitt had taken key issues for the future of Arizona—water, education, social services—and forced a Republican legislature and a conservative electorate to deal with them. With the legislature under firm Republican control in all of his nine years as governor, his major tool was the veto, which he used 114 times, more than any other governor in the history of the state.

Yet Babbitt was also not without his critics. Many labor sympathizers still chafe at his decision to call out the National Guard to quell violence in a bitter strike in the state's copper industry. Many state Democrats were also miffed that he refused to run for the U.S. Senate in 1986, with the retirement of Barry Goldwater. His reluctance, many believe, cost the party a much needed seat.

Since the Democratic party's devastating 1984 presidential race, Babbitt's star was rising in national Democratic politics. He acquired prominence among party leaders and others who believed that the Democratic party would have to re-shape itself to recapture the middle-income voters it had been losing to the Republicans. The subject of favorable reporting in *The New Republic* and *Business Week*, he emerged as one of the most conspicuous spokesmen and practitioners of "neoliberalism," a philosophy that blends traditional Democratic goals on civil rights and social justice with fiscal restraints and limits on the size of government and the interference of special-interest groups. Active in the Democratic Leadership Council, a centrist group of elected officials trying to chart new policy directions for its party, Babbitt continued to attract attention for his innovative policy ideas.

The governor chose not to run for re-election when his second term expired in January 1987. Although some observers expected him to challenge incumbent Republican Denis DeConcini for the U.S. Senate, he chose instead to embark on what he called "the darkest of dark horse bids" for the 1988 Democratic presidential nomination. In January 1987, Babbitt became the first Democrat to officially open a 1988 presidential campaign committee. Although the run was ill-fated, he drew much media attention for his intellect, candor, and pioneering proposals, and for his willingness to take courageous stands on tough issues. Promising to say "what other politicians dare not even think," he was frank about the need to increase taxes to deal with the mounting budget deficit. He also proposed a five percent national sales tax, taxing the Social Security benefits of the affluent, capping the mortgage interest deduction, cutting farm subsidies to agribusiness, and strengthening work requirements for welfare recipients. To stimulate productivity, he advocated tax incentives for businesses that included employees in profit sharing programs. His speeches also focused on the need for a universal day care system, the expansion of catastrophic health coverage for the elderly, the importance of improving relations with Mexico, and the desirability of revising present U.S. policies on international trade.

Intense and soft-spoken, Babbitt was considered by many Democrats to be a serious thinker on public policy issues but a candidate of less than compelling campaign style. Although he was receiving increasing attention in the press, he had serious shortcomings on the stump and on television. After placing fifth in a field of seven candidates in the Iowa caucuses and sixth in the New Hampshire primary, he withdrew from the race for the Democratic presidential nomination in February 1988. Nonetheless, Babbitt called the campaign "the greatest joy of my entire public life."

He is presently practicing law in Phoenix, working on issues of international trade, municipal finance and—what he's best known for—western water issues and the environment.

Bibliography: Biographical information, courtesy of governor's office; biographical information, Western Governors' Conference; Michael Barone *et al., The Almanac of American Politics, 1978–84* (New York and Washington, D.C., 1977–1983); *Newsweek,* 6–8–87; *The New York Times:* 3–8–78; 3–17–85; 11–18–86; 12–7–86; 1–8–87; 3–11–87; 6–11–87; 1–27–88; 2–19–88; *USA Today,* 6–13–88.

Evan Mecham (Courtesy of governor's office)

MECHAM, Evan, 1987–1988

Born in Duchesne, Utah on May 12, 1924. A member of the Church of Jesus Christ of the Latter-Day Saints, in which he has held many leadership positions, he is married to the former Florence Lambert. They have seven children and 17 grandchildren.

Mecham attended Altamont High School in northeastern Utah, and Utah State University before joining the U.S. Air Force, in which he served as a fighter pilot in World War II. Shot down over Germany, he spent 22 days as a prisoner of war. Upon his discharge in 1947, he enrolled at Arizona State University, majoring in economics and business management. He left the university in 1950 upon receiving a Pontiac agency franchise in Ajo, Arizona. In 1954 he moved the franchise to Glendale, Arizona, where it has remained ever since. In addition to the Pontiac agency, he has been involved in the automobile business in California and Washington State. He is also the former publisher of the American Newspaper Group, which owned weekly newspapers in Arizona, and of *The Tampa Neighbor* in Tampa, Florida.

Mecham began his political career in 1960, with election to the Arizona State Senate, where he served from 1961 to 1963. Over the next 22 years he mounted four campaigns for the governor's office and one for the U.S. Senate. All were unsuccessful. In 1978, however, he ran his most auspicious campaign, unexpectedly holding acting Governor Bruce Babbitt—seeking his own term in office—to 52 percent of the vote.

With Babbitt's retirement from office in 1987, the gubernatorial election of 1986 was a wide open affair. Launching his fifth campaign for the statehouse, Mecham won the Republican nomination by defeating Burton Barr, majority leader of the State House of Representatives. His victory over the candidate favored by state party officials was widely regarded as an upset. While Mecham was given little chance of winning the November election, a divisive split in the Democratic party paved the way for his election. The favored candidate, Democratic buisnessman Bill Schulz, had withdrawn from the race because of a family illness. When Democrats nominated State Schools Superintendent Carolyn Warner, Schulz re-entered as an independent, splitting the Democratic vote. Mecham won the three-way race with 40 percent of the vote; Warner garnered 34 percent; Schulz, 26 percent. Mecham's support was drawn largely from his own Mormon community, from fundamentalist Christians, and from the New Right.

As governor, Mecham outlined his principal goals: reducing the size and scope of government, and returning to state jurisdiction functions that he contended were granted to the states by the Constitution (e.g., the right to set speed limits on state highways). Preaching fiscal frugality, he embarked on plans to cut the state sales tax, to end drug abuse, to widen state trade, and to seek reform of the state's welfare system. He also wanted the governor's office and the State Department of Commerce to work with higher education officials to spur economic development.

Quickly, however, Mecham's positive goals were overshadowed by controversy. His rhetorical style and conservative politics provoked sharp reactions among women, blacks, homosexuals, and other minorities. In the words of one leading opponent, "never before [had] one man alienated so many people in such a short period of time."

Within a few months after taking office he moved to cut state spending and froze salaries of state employees, cancelled plans to observe the birthday of Martin Luther King, Jr. as a state holiday, demanded that schools become more accountable for their budgets, made public remarks that offended blacks, women, and homosexuals, refused to speak to a reporter he called a "non-person," and appointed an adviser on education who argued publicly that teachers should be forbidden to teach students basic facts (e.g., that the world is round) that might conflict with their parents' beliefs. He also made several other highly controversial appointments, including a state revenue director who had not filed his own income tax form on time.

Mecham's gaffes and shoot from the lip style drew the attention of the national press and television talk show hosts who frequently portrayed him as a buffoon. More serious, however, was the loss of millions of dollars of tourist revenues from cancelled conventions by at least 45 groups or associations whose membership was personally offended by some of Mecham's cutting remarks (e.g., his suggestion that working women cause divorces). Not only were leaders of the state's business community upset with Mecham, but he also alienated two other centers of power—the press and legislators in his own party. When journalists reported on problems in his administration, Mecham attacked them as biased and subversive. Yet his war on the press only prompted more scrutiny of his affairs. He angered many Republican legislators by treating them almost as adversaries, making key job appointments or drafting legislative proposals without consulting them. His actions caused a bitter and emotional rift within the state Republican party over how best to deal with the matter. With his legislative agenda lost in the emerging controversy over his philosophy and style, Republicans feared that he would do irreparable damage to one of the best financed and most powerful state political organizations in the country.

Within four months of his taking office, a group of Arizona residents established a committee to work for the governor's recall. Saying Mecham had "embarrassed Arizonans nationally" with his statements and appointments, the recall effort was given little chance of success until even more serious problems emerged: a grand jury investigation and possible impeachment charges over his failure to report a $350,000 campaign loan on either his personal or campaign finance reports. Within one year after taking office, Mecham faced both a recall election and a state investigation into his finances. By January 1988, state officials certified that more than 300,000 citizens had signed petitions demanding his recall. Refusing calls for his resignation, Mecham faced a recall election scheduled for May 17. At the same time, after a state grand jury handed up a felony indictment, the state House of Representatives decided to conduct its own investigation into his affairs. With the investigation, Mecham became the nation's first governor to face impeachment proceedings since Alaska's William Sheffield in 1985. Formal impeachment charges never followed the investigation in the Sheffield case, but Mecham's situation was different. On February 5, 1988, following a 90-minute debate in which several legislators broke down in tears, the state House of Representatives formally voted impeachment charges against him. The 46–14 vote for impeachment was far more than the required simple majority. The 23 articles of impeachment outlined details of three broad charges: (1) obstructing justice by trying to thwart an investigation into charges that an aide had made a death threat against a grand jury witness; (2) illegaly lending $80,000 in state money to his cash-strapped Pontiac dealership; and (3) concealing a $350,000 campaign loan. Throughout his 13 hours of testimony to the select committee considering impeachment, the governor insisted he was a victim of persecution by political enemies and the news media. He said he had committed no illegal acts and was guilty of no ethical lapses, and predicted he would be vindicated.

The impeachment battle polarized the state, sparking a bruising battle that fractured Arizona's powerful Republican party, raised important constitutional questions about the already scheduled recall election, and led to sharp gains in Democratic voter registration. During the six-week senate trial, Mecham took the stand to defend himself. He portrayed himself as a political outsider, who from the moment of his election had been under a concentrated attack from State Attorney General Robert Corbin and the press. He admitted only two mistakes: offending some powerful interests by moving too fast to bring about changes in government, and naiveté.

On March 30, 1988, the senate dismissed the third and most serious charge against Mecham. It did so in order to avoid prejudicing his upcoming criminal trial on the charge that he had concealed the $350,000 campaign loan. Since the evidence considered in both the senate trial and the upcoming criminal trial would have been the same, the fear was that this would have placed the governor in double jeopardy. On the night of April 4, 1988, the senate voted Mecham guilty of the remaining two charges: the vote was 21–9 on the obstruction of justice charge, and 26–4 on that involving misuse of funds. With the verdict, Mecham became the first U.S. governor to be impeached and removed from office in 59 years. (The last was Henry Johnston of Oklahoma, found guilty in 1929 of working with the Ku Klux Klan.) Secretary of State Rose Mofford, acting governor during the duration of the senate trial, succeeded Mecham as governor of Arizona the moment the gavel fell. The vote ended one-and-one-half years of political controversy that had mired the state in ridicule and criticism from the national press, politicians, and comedians.

Because the state senate didn't bar Mecham from holding office in the future, his supporters held out hope for a victory in the May 17 recall election. These hopes were quashed, however, by an April 12 ruling of the state supreme court which ordered cancellation of the election. The court ruled that the constitutionally mandated order of succession following impeachment and conviction of a governor takes precedence over the provision for recall elections. (The recall had been challenged in court by two taxpayers who contended it was no longer necessary and would be a waste of state funds.)

Mecham, the first sitting governor in the state's history to be indicted, still faced a criminal trial on six felony counts of perjury, willful concealment, and filing false documents. The governor's brother Willard, who had served as his campaign treasurer, was also indicted on related charges. State law requires elected officials to report any debt of more than $1,000 incurred or discharged from the previous year, including naming the identity of people and institutions to whom they owed money, in a report filed annually with the secretary of state. Mecham's indictment charged that he had intentionally concealed a $350,000 loan from Tempe developer Barry Wolfson, then lied about it on his campaign spending reports. Mecham didn't report the loan to the state until after it had been disclosed by the news media. He called his failure "an honest mistake," and attributed the problem to his brother's inexperience in the area of campaign financing. If convicted, the governor faced sentencing to 22 years in prison.

On June 16, 1988 a Phoenix jury acquitted both men on all counts. Vindicated, Mecham announced he was ready to go to work to clean up his "corrupt state." He planned to work with his new political action committee, Forward Arizona, to elect "an honest legislature," and he also pledged to press for a new attorney general for the state. While the acquittal left Mecham free to seek office again, he was getting no encouragement from Republican party leaders.

Bibliography: Biographical information courtesy of governor's office; *The Chronicle of Higher Education:* 11–12–86; 4–29–87; "Arizona's Holy War," *Newsweek* (Feb. 1, 1988); "Evan Mecham's Phoenix Follies," *Newsweek* (Mar. 14, 1988); "After Mecham, Mecham?" *Newsweek* (Apr. 18, 1988); *The New York Times:* 9–11–86; 1–6–87; 3–9–87; 7–7–87; 8–15–

87; 10–15–87; 10–22–87; 10–24–87; 11–1–87; 11–12–87; 11–17–87; 1–9–88; 1–10–88; 1–21–88; 1–24–88; 1–26–88; 2–6–88; 2–27–88; 3–1–88; 3–2–88; 3–17–88; 3–31–88; 4–5–88; 4–6–88; 4–13–88; 5–19–88; 6–11–88; 6–17–88; Alan Weisman, "Up in Arms: Mecham in Arizona," *New York Times Magazine* (Nov. 1, 1987).

Rose Perica Mofford (Courtesy of governor's office)

MOFFORD, Rose Perica, 1988–

Born in the small mining town of Globe, Arizona on June 10, 1922, Rose Perica was the daughter of Austrian immigrants who settled in Leadville, Colorado in 1912 and later moved to Arizona. In secondary school she was a star athlete, winning national honors in softball. She was also a prize winning typist. Mofford's feminist aspirations were roused by Ana Frohmiller, a suffragist and the first woman ever to run for governor of Arizona. Mofford came to Phoenix in 1940 to work for Governor Bob Jones in the Arizona treasurer's office. At one point she was sent to take a secretarial post at the state hospital to gather information about patient abuse. The information she gathered was sent to the State Capitol, an incident that is said to have "hooked" her on a career in public service.

Moving up through the ranks, she earned a reputation for efficiency and loyalty. In 1947 she became executive secretary to the State Tax Commission, but was discharged six years later because Commissioner Thad Mokre said, "We felt it was better to have a man in that job." After she was discharged, she was hired as executive secretary to Secretary of State Wesley Bolin. When he became governor in 1977, he appointed Mofford to be his successor as secretary of state. She ran for office on her own in 1978, 1982, and 1986, and was elected each time by large margins. Supporters commended her for her honesty, fairness, and even-tempered nature, and she was affectionately known as "Aunt Rosie" in the popular press. Working successfully with 12 governors, she had been Arizona's longtime number two, spending hundreds of days periodically standing in for traveling governors.

Her most critical stint as acting governor followed the serious political troubles of Evan Mecham. When Mecham was impeached by the state House of Representatives on February 5, 1988, she assumed control of the state government during his six-week senate trial. Because of the agony engendered during Mecham's year-long administration, she seemed almost reluctant to take over the job. Usually accessible almost to a fault, she secluded herself in her office during the impeachment vote. One of the few state Democrats who had refused to criticize Mecham during his controversial tenure, she lived up to one journalist's characterization of her as "steadfastly noncontroversial." In the immediate aftermath of the house impeachment vote on February 5, Mofford even declined to take over the title of acting governor, waiting over the weekend until she received official notification of the house impeachment vote on Monday, February 8.

Mofford was confident she could be a "healing governor." Hiring some of former governor Bruce Babbitt's top aides to head her transition team, she urged legislators to re-instate Martin Luther King's birthday as a state holiday, a move in direct opposition to Mecham's first controversial

decision in office. Although the move drew partisan reaction from legislators, with Republicans calling it a "divisive" reminder of the problems
facing impeached Governor Mecham, Mofford defended her decision,
saying the furor over the King holiday had been a "national symbol of our
disunity." She felt the reinstatement of the holiday was one of "the most
decisive things that we can do," and termed it an important part of the
healing process in Arizona. In a show of diplomacy, Mofford met with the
state's former governors, both Democratic and Republican, and put
Mecham's most controversial aide, Administrative Chief Max Hawkins,
on a paid leave of absence. Mofford also faced tough decisions while the
state legislative process was tied up with Mecham's trial. The state suffered from a $248 million budget deficit, an amount more than 50 times
greater than her annual budget for the secretary of state's office.

Mofford formally became governor on April 4, 1988, the moment the
gavel fell in Evan Mecham's senate trial. With Mecham's conviction and
removal from office, Mofford officially became the state's first woman
governor. The swearing-in ceremony in the governor's office was deliber-
ately kept low-key to avoid "rubbing salt in the wound," and exacerbating
the continuing controversy brought on by Mecham's conviction. In a
prepared statement, Mofford declared "the end of some difficult times in
Arizona," and urged residents to empty their hearts "of suspicion and
hate." An official state supreme court declaration canceling a previously
scheduled recall election as a result of Mecham's senate trial ended all
constitutional debate about the legitimacy of Mofford's succession. She is
scheduled to complete the remainder of Mecham's term of office, due to
expire in January 1991.

Mofford plans to build an administration that, in her words, will be
based on "merit and professionalism." Perceiving her role to be one of
healing and consensus building, she announced a desire to staff appointments with qualified applicants regardless of their political affiliations. At
the heart of her legislative agenda is the need to solve the state budget
crisis, and the need to decide on either a tax increase or deep cuts in
spending. Considering the state's ailing educational system, she has announced plans to encourage spending for education, even if it means
higher taxes. She also intends to launch an ambitious campaign to win a
seven-state contest for a Department of Energy supercollider contract.

Almost immediately after taking office, Mofford faced some embar-
rassing financial problems of her own, questions similar to those that had
led to the undoing of her predecessor. In late April 1988, she acknowledged that she too had not reported some land, loans, and partnerships of
her own in the financial disclosure forms that state law annually requires
to be filed by officeholders. Existence of Mofford's previously undisclosed
holdings, loans, and partnerships was discovered by the Associated Press
through interviews and records in the Maricopa County Recorder's Office,

the State Corporation Commission, and the Secretary of State's Partnership Office. Mofford attributed the errors to a confused marital situation. Married for 10 years to Captain T. R. Mofford of the Phoenix Police Department, she divorced her husband in 1967, but the couple remained close friends until his death in 1983. Mofford explained that she had undertaken most of the financial ventures on behalf of him or his estate, and therefore felt no need to report them. Others were of such a minor nature that she felt they did not warrant reporting. Filing amended financial forms, she apologized for what she called an honest mistake, and the matter came to an abrupt halt. In July 1988 she was formally cleared of any wrongdoing after an investigation by the county attorney's office.

Mofford's accession to the governorship caps a career in state government remarkable for its longevity. Folksy, fast talking, and exceedingly popular, she takes pride in her unofficial title as "grandmother of Arizona." Extremely feminine in style, she is known for her platinum beehive hairdo and heavy mascara. She often quips that she sees her career as an inspiration for other secretaries, and feels that her own experiences with being discriminated against have made her especially sympathetic to the cause of women's rights.

Bibliography: Biographical information courtesy of governor's office; "Arizona's 'Rosie' New Boss," *Newsweek* (Feb. 22, 1988); Claudia Dreifus, "The Belles of Recall," *Ms.* (June 1988); *The New York Times:* 2–7–88; 2–9–88; 2–10–88; 4–5–88; 4–6–88; 5–1–88; 7–9–88.

Bill Clinton (Courtesy of governor's office)

ARKANSAS

Born in Hope, Arkansas on August 19, 1946. A Baptist, Clinton is married to the former Hillary Rodham, a practicing attorney. They have a daughter, Chelsea.

Educated in the public schools of Hot Springs, Arkansas, Clinton received a degree in international affairs from the Georgetown University School of Foreign Service in 1968. He attended the University of Oxford as a Rhodes Scholar, and received a degree from Yale Law School in 1973. Joining the staff of the University of Arkansas Law School, he also practiced law in Fayetteville before making his first run for public office in 1974. In that Watergate year he was narrowly defeated for Congress in the Third District, holding incumbent John Paul Hammerschmidt, a Republican, to 52 percent of the vote. Afterwards, he continued to teach law; he also taught in the Criminal Justice Program at the University of Arkansas at Little Rock.

Elected Arkansas Attorney General in 1976, Clinton sued to hold down utility rates, fought against 25 cent pay phone calls, and ended bans on liquor and eyeglass advertising. Having established a reputation as an energetic and activist politician—indeed, one reporter noted that Clinton "worked like a madman"—he was elected the nation's youngest governor in 1978. After gaining 60 percent of the vote against four other candidates to win the Democratic nomination without a runoff, he went on to defeat Republican State Chairman A. Lynn Lowe in the general election by capturing 63 percent of the vote compared with Lowe's 37 percent. The campaign received national publicity. At 32, Clinton became the youngest man to be chosen chief executive of any state since Harold Stassen carried Minnesota in 1938 at the age of 31.

Boyishly handsome and charismatic, Clinton also had a rather unorthodox background for a rising politician from the deep South. He had worked as the Texas State Coordinator for George McGovern's ill-fated 1972 presidential race, and had been a staff attorney for the House Judiciary Committee before the Nixon impeachment hearings. A supporter of the Equal Rights Amendment, Clinton also seemed an anomaly because his wife Hillary, herself a lawyer, was a strong feminist who campaigned for her husband while using her maiden name. Clinton also managed to campaign successfully against a rising "Proposition 13" sentiment to cut state taxes. Instead of promising to cut taxes, he asked for new highway taxes and a $132 million spending increase to upgrade the state's school system, which was ranked 49th in quality nationwide. Explaining that he believed the citizens of Arkansas were tired of being ranked last or next to last according to major indices of social and economic welfare, he sought to accelerate the state's economic growth and to make permanent improvements in the quality of life for its residents.

During his first term Clinton established a strong record in bringing jobs to Arkansas and in selling the state's products abroad. He held down utility rates and curbed utility costs, while working vigorously to improve the state's educational system with programs to test students in basic skills, to increase opportunities for gifted children, to advance vocational education, and to increase teachers' salaries. Clinton also initiated tax cuts for senior citizens by removing the sales tax from medicine and increasing the homestead property tax exemption for the elderly. He worked to eliminate waste in government, and sponsored one of the nation's first "workfare" programs, which required that people requesting food stamps also register to work. This requirement has eliminated several thousand ineligible people from food stamp rolls. Clinton also led the way in calling for the appointment of women and minorities to cabinet-level jobs. With his activist programs and leadership style, Clinton was able to regain power for the governor's office that had been usurped by the legislature under previous administrations. For all these achievements, *Time* magazine honored Clinton in 1979, listing him as one of America's outstanding young leaders and counting him among the "50 faces to watch" in the future.

Nevertheless, Clinton had his critics. He was sometimes lampooned in political cartoons as a brat furiously pedalling a tricycle. Many thought he was more interested in national than in state politics. Conservative opponents tried to use his wife's feminism against him, and assailed him for his liberal views by charging him with support for gun control, the Panama Canal treaties, and the decriminalization of marijuana. Most of all, however, Clinton's political stature was damaged by his handling of the Cuban refugee situation. Thousands of Cuban refugees who had left or been expelled from Cuba during Fidel Castro's celebrated maneuvers of 1980 were housed at Fort Chaffee, Arkansas, and Clinton was hurt politically by his inability to force the White House to have other states shoulder some of the burden and costs. His 1980 defeat by Republican Frank White, a businessman and political novice, was widely viewed as a simple case of voter backlash against the Democratic party on both the state and national levels. White won that election by attracting 52 percent of the vote compared with Clinton's 48 percent. With his loss, Clinton became the first Arkansas governor in 26 years and only the second in this century to fail to win at least a second two-year term.

After leaving office, Clinton joined the Little Rock law firm of Wright, Lindsey, and Jennings, but astute observers knew that his political career was far from over. Indeed, he returned to the governor's mansion two years later, defeating White in his bid for re-election and becoming the first person in the state's history to be elected to a second, non-consecutive term as chief executive. This time, however, he encountered a strong challenge from members of his own party to win the Democratic gubernatorial nomination. Facing former Congressman Jim Guy Tucker and former Lieutenant Governor Joe Purcell in the primary, he was forced into a runoff when no one earned a majority in the first contest. In the second contest he defeated Purcell, 54 percent to 46 percent, to gain the Democratic nomination and the chance to run against White again.

Clinton spent much of his campaign apologizing for the mistakes of his first term. He also sought to reassure voters that, contrary to rumors, he had no national political ambitions. In terms of substantive issues, the election hinged on a record $227 million in utility rate increases approved during White's term. Public opinion surveys had consistently demonstrated that Arkansas Power and Light was one of the most unpopular institutions in the state, and Clinton capitalized on voter displeasure both with the rate increases and with White's failure to tame the "monster." The race generated an astonishingly high voter turnout (72 percent), and this time Clinton won by a margin of 55 percent to 45 percent. He identified his top priority during his second term to be putting the unemployed back to work.

In November 1984 Clinton became the first Arkansas chief executive to win a third term since Orval Faubus, when he defeated Republican newcomer Elwood Freeman by a margin of 62 percent to 38 percent.

Running for re-election in 1986, he became only the second person in the state's history to be elected to four terms as governor. To win re-nomination by his party, he faced a stiff challenge from former Governor Orval Faubus, the one-time segregationist who launched a comeback bid in the May 1986 Democratic primary. Faubus, best known for his actions in calling out the National Guard to block black students from entering Little Rock's Central High School in 1957, was making his third run for the Democratic nomination since leaving office in 1966. Faubus accused Clinton of being a friend and minion of the rich, as well as a champion of the public utilities at the expense of consumers. He accused Clinton of masterminding an unpopular rate increase for Arkansas Power and Light to help the company pay its share of the cost of the $3.5 million Grand Gulf nuclear power plant in Mississippi.

Clinton defeated Faubus and W. Dean Goldsby in the primary, and went on to trounce former Governor Frank White in the general election, garnering 64 percent of the vote to White's 36 percent. With his victory, Clinton became the only Arkansas governor in the 20th century to serve a four-year term, for a constitutional amendment in 1986 had extended the governor's term of office from two to four years.

Clinton's administration has distinguished itself in several areas, notably education, economic development, agriculture, and criminal justice.

In 1983 Clinton called the Arkansas legislature into special session to enact new standards for public schools and an increase in the sales tax to support improvements in higher and vocational education. In his view, these funds have helped put more computers in state public schools, have contributed to a rise in test scores, and have created new jobs. He has also been a strong advocate of a controversial policy that requires all school-teachers to pass a basic competency test to retain their certification. As chairman of the Education Commission of the States in 1986, he has spoken frequently and forcefully on the need to improve educational leadership in the United States.

Clinton has also introduced comprehensive economic development programs to make Arkansas competitive with other states in the quest for more and better jobs. In 1988 he signed a wide-ranging agreement with the governors of Louisiana and Mississippi to coordinate efforts to improve conditions in one of the nation's poorest regions. The agreement was intended to direct many joint efforts at the counties bordering the Mississippi River, an area scarred by high rates of poverty, unemployment, and illiteracy. The agreement calls for cooperation ranging from the search for foreign investment to highway construction to improvements in schools and health facilities.

Clinton has also worked to assist Arkansas farmers through the creation of a new Division of Agricultural Development within the Arkansas Industrial Commission, and through his work with the National Governors' Association Committee on Agriculture.

He has also supported a number of programs to improve law enforcement, help fight crime, and protect victims of crime in Arkansas. He has increased the productivity of the prison farm and industry programs.

A past chairman of the Southern Growth Policies Board, Clinton served as chairman of the National Governors' Association (NGA) in 1987, the only governor of Arkansas ever to serve in that capacity. As chairman of the NGA, he outlined a new federal welfare program that would provide child day care programs, transportation, and job training for welfare recipients. Although it would raise the cost of aiding the poor by $2 billion a year, the plan promised to save money in the long run by reducing the numbers on welfare rolls.

Clinton has increasingly attracted public attention both from his fellow governors and from the national press. In a 1986 poll conducted by

Newsweek magazine, he was selected by his fellow governors as one of the five most effective governors in the nation. Due to his heightened visibility as chairman of the National Governors' Association, he was widely expected to seek the Democratic presidential nomination in 1988. In public statements he spoke of his belief that his experiences in leading an economically troubled state had given him insights into how to solve some of the problems facing the nation. Such views notwithstanding, he surprised pundits by withdrawing his name from consideration for the nomination. In a July 1987 speech he ruled himself out of the 1988 race, citing family obligations and the desire for a "more ordinary life." Although he admitted that he hoped to run for president someday, the turmoil of Clinton's decision seemed to highlight the efforts of two-career couples like the Clintons to balance the obligations of parenting and careers.

In July 1988, Clinton gave the major nominating address for fellow governor Michael Dukakis at the National Democratic Convention that bestowed its presidential nomination upon the Massachusetts Democrat.

Bibliography: Biographical information, courtesy of governor's office; "50 Faces for America's Future," *Time* (Aug. 6, 1979); Michael Barone *et al., The Almanac of American Politics, 1980–1984* (New York and Washington, D.C., 1979–1983); "Southern Star Rising Again," *Time* (Sept. 20, 1982); "Fresh Faces in the Mansions," *Time* (Nov. 15, 1982); *New York Times Biographical Service* 9 (Nov. 1978): 1019; *The New York Times:* 12–14–78; 2–25–79; 8–5–80; 11–12–80; 1–4–82; 5–24–82; 5–26–82; 5–27–82; 6–8–82; 6–9–82; 10–28–82; 1–12–83; 11–8–84; 5–25–86; 2–18–87; 5–31–87; 7–2–87; 7–15–87; 7–16–87; 8–16–87; *The Chronicle of Higher Education:* 10–22–86; 11–12–86.

George Deukmejian(Courtesy of governor's office)

CALIFORNIA

DEUKMEJIAN, George, 1983–

Born in Menands, New York on June 6, 1928, the son of C. George Deukmejian and Alice Gairdan Deukmejian. An Episcopalian, Deukmejian is married to the former Gloria M. Saatjian. The couple have three children: Leslie, George, and Andrea.

Deukmejian graduated from Siena College with a B.A. in sociology in 1949. In 1952 he received a J.D. from St. John's University School of Law. He worked briefly for the New York State Department of Audit and Control before entering the U.S. Army. Assigned to the Judge Advocate Corps based in Paris, he served a 16-month tour of duty in France, where his major responsibilities included assisting in the settlement of claims made by French nationals against the U.S. Army.

Returning to the United States in 1955, he moved to Los Angeles. There he worked for the Land and Lease Department of Texaco before being appointed deputy county counsel for Los Angeles County. He also established a successful law practice in Long Beach. His first bid for elective office came in 1962, upon the retirement of Republican Assemblyman Bill Grant. Deukmejian served two terms in the state assembly and was named minority whip by his Republican colleagues in 1965. The following year, when the U.S. Supreme Court ordered the states to implement the one-man, one-vote provision, additional state senate seats were created in Los Angeles County. Deukmejian captured one of the new seats the same year that Ronald Reagan was elected governor of California. Thereafter he served four terms (12 years) in the senate, where he assisted Governor Reagan in moving his anti-crime program and tax-reform bills through the legislature.

In 1970, the Republicans gained control of the state senate and Deukmejian was selected senate majority leader. In 1972 he authored the death penalty initiative, which was overwhelmingly approved by California voters. In 1974 he was elected senate Republican leader and in 1977 drafted California's Death Penalty Statute. The measure was vetoed by Governor Jerry Brown, but Deukmejian led the fight to successfully override the veto in the legislature. Also in 1977 he authored the "Use a Gun, Go to Prison" law, which he later successfully defended before the California Supreme Court.

During his 16 years in the legislature, Deukmejian authored more than 180 laws including the Senior Citizens Property Tax Assistance Law, the Community Drug Abuse Act, the Career Criminal Act, and the act mandating establishment of Youth Service Bureaus.

Deukmejian first sought statewide office in 1970, when he lost the Republican nomination for attorney general. He ran again in 1978, and was elected the state's top lawyer, receiving the highest vote total for a Republican constitutional office candidate that year.

As attorney general and head of the Department of Justice, he established a Special Prosecutions Unit, a Crime Prevention Center, a School Safety Center, and strengthened the Bureau of Narcotic Enforcement. He formed a state task force centering on youth gang problems, and vigorously prosecuted consumer fraud, antitrust violations, Medi-Cal fraud, and other white-collar crimes. He also successfully argued the constitutionality of the state death penalty statute before the state supreme court.

When he launched his campaign for governor in 1982, he explained that his decision to run for the state's highest office was partially attributable to the fact that "attorneys general do not appoint judges, but governors do." He added that he was uniquely qualified based upon his experience and background to appoint the tough judges that the state desperately needed.

His opponent in 1982 was Democrat Tom Bradley, mayor of Los Angeles, who hoped to become the nation's first black governor. Deukmejian won the election by one of the narrowest margins in state history, 93,345 votes, 1.2 percent of all cast, after some experienced analysts had predicted a Bradley victory. Bradley's defeat was attributed primarily to a strong turnout by conservatives, whose election day showing may have been enhanced by the presence of a gun control measure on the ballot. Gun control opponents spent some $5 million opposing the registration proposal, which Bradley supported. Deukmejian's opposition to the measure probably contributed to his victory. Actually, Deukmejian lost the vote at the polls but won the election because of a vast and expensive Republican drive to encourage absentee ballots.

Deukmejian's popularity grew during his first term in office. Gathering around him a group of talented aides, and employing an aloof, ceremonial style in stark contrast to that of former Governor Jerry Brown, he dealt successfully and effectively with the state fiscal crisis that confronted him immediately upon taking office. Working with the legislature, he developed a fiscal rescue plan to pay off the deficit he had inherited and balance the budget without raising taxes. In addition to restoring the fiscal integrity of the state, Deukmejian also provided record increases in support for education, transportation, health care programs, and toxic waste cleanup. Over two million new jobs were created in the state, and California led the nation in new business expansion. Deukmejian also led efforts to expand the state's foreign trade, including the opening of trade and investment offices in Japan and Europe. He successfully pushed for a workfare program to reduce welfare dependency, sponsored and won passage of a Seniors Initiative to improve vital services to senior citizens, and appointed a record number of women and minorities to state government jobs.

Deukmejian's re-election victory in 1986 was seen as an over-whelming endorsement of his policies and approach. Re-elected by one of the largest vote margins in state history, and garnering a higher percentage of the vote than Ronald Reagan ever won in California, Deukmejian again faced Mayor Tom Bradley of Los Angeles. In his campaign against the popular conservative, Bradley swayed from the moderate political stance that had long been his hallmark into more visible, liberal ground. Some analysts interpreted this switch as a decision to play to his strengths with his longstanding urban constituencies, union members, Jewish, black, and Hispanic voters. Bradley advocated pay equity for women and removal from the city's pension fund portfolio of investments in companies doing business with South Africa, as well as highlighting Los Angeles' passage of a first-in-the-nation ordinance to protest discrimination against victims of AIDS. In the hostile personal race between the two rivals, Bradley accused Deukmejian of endangering children's health through failure to deal with the state's toxic waste problems, citing the governor's ties to big business as reason for his slowness to act. He also attacked the governor's integrity and character.

The state's overall economic health, however, served the incumbent well. Although Bradley could point to several economic trouble spots, notably the semiconductor portion of California's electronics industry, farming, and logging, the state's general economic condition was good. California's unemployment rate had fallen steadily, and by the time of the election a record number of Californians were at work. Although colorless and non-charismatic, Deukmejian was generally perceived as stronger on issues of genuine concern to the voters, notably control of drug abuse. His landslide victory over Bradley, 60.5 percent to 37.5 percent, was an even wider margin than most experts had predicted.

Deukmejian professed no grand goals for his second term, other than continuing the policies of his first: keeping control of the state budget, appointing a majority on the state supreme court, strengthening his workfare programs. He spurned those who in 1987 urged him to become a favorite son in the race for the 1988 Republican presidential nomination, but at the same time he set up his own organization, Citizens for Common Sense, to help him travel around the country to further his goals.

State budget problems in 1988 also worked against any aspirations for higher office. Facing a gap between state revenue and expenditures, caused largely by miscalculations of the effects of the revision of the federal tax structure, Deukmejian proposed a series of what he called "tax adjustments" to deal with the problem. The proposals were soundly condemned, even by members of his own party, who called them tax increases in disguise and reminded him of his 1986 campaign pledge not to raise taxes. Deukmejian maintained that he would do whatever was necessary to protect the state's fiscal integrity and ability to create jobs and prosperity.

Although Deukmejian's name was frequently mentioned as a possible running mate for 1988 Republican presidential contender George Bush, the governor repeatedly expressed disinterest in the position, because if elected he would be forced to turn over the reigns of state government to a Democrat, Lieutenant Governor Leo McCarthy.

Bibliography: Biographical information courtesy of governor's office; Michael Barone et al., *The Almanac of American Politics, 1984–1988* (New York and Washington, D.C., 1983–1987); *The Chronicle of Higher Education,* 11–12–86; *The New York Times:* 10–6–85; 9–15–86; 10–31–86; 11–6–86; 3–24–87; 6–3–88; 6–4–88.

Richard David Lamm (Credit: William Thach)

COLORADO

LAMM, Richard David, 1975–1987

Born on August 3, 1935 in Madison, Wisconsin, the son of A.E. and Mary (Townsend) Lamm. A Unitarian, Lamm married the former Dorothy Vennard on May 11, 1963; the couple have two children, Heather and Scott Hunter.

Lamm received a B.A. in business administration from the University of Wisconsin in 1957 and a law degree from the University of California (Boalt Hall) in 1961. In 1960 he qualified as a certified public accountant. A first lieutenant in the United States Army from 1957 to 1958, he has worked as an accountant, a tax clerk with the California Franchise Tax Board, an attorney with the Colorado Antidiscrimination Commission, and an attorney in private practice with the Denver firm of Jones, Meiklejohn, Kilroy, Kehl, and Lyons. Lamm was also associate professor of Law at the University of Denver from 1969 to 1974.

President of the Denver Young Democrats in 1963 and vice president of the Colorado Young Democrats in 1964, Lamm began his political career as a member of the Colorado House of Representatives, serving from 1967 to 1975; he was assistant minority leader of that body from 1971 to 1975. Lamm first came to statewide attention as a leader in the environmental movement that emerged in Colorado during the 1970s. With Sam Brown and David Mixner, he was one of the organizers of the so-called "anti-Olympics movement," a referendum to deny state funding for the 1976 Winter Olympics on the grounds that the Games would be too expensive, would destroy much of Colorado's environment, and would benefit only a handful of big businessmen and real estate developers. Colorado's voters agreed, and the 1976 Winter Olympic Games were held in Innsbruck, Austria. Earlier, Lamm had come to national attention as the sponsor of a liberalized state abortion law that was passed before the United States Supreme Court's *Roe v. Wade* decision dictated uniform national standards in this area.

Lamm became the leading gubernatorial contender in Colorado as the 1974 election approached. After Mark Hogan, the Democratic gubernatorial candidate in 1970, stepped out of the race, Lamm defeated the moderate state legislator Tom Farley in the primary by a margin of 59 percent to 41 percent, for the chance to face incumbent Republican John

Vanderhoof in the general election. Vanderhoof, who had succeeded to the governorship when Governor John Love took a Ford administration appointment, attacked Lamm as an outsider who would stop economic growth so suddenly that massive unemployment would result. Lamm responded that he only wanted to see limits placed on growth, and emphasized the damage that the federal government's unrestricted exploitation of surface coal and oil-bearing shale was doing to the state's environment. In the general election Lamm defeated Vanderhoof soundly, gaining 54 percent of the vote to Vanderhoof's 46 percent.

Despite his great promise, however (*Time* magazine had included him among America's top 200 leaders in 1974), Lamm's first two years in office were described as disastrous by many political observers. He was unable to get his programs through the legislature, feuded with the press, and alienated many with his somewhat abrasive personality. When the Republicans won control of both houses of the state legislature in 1976, Lamm grew more conciliatory, and began to develop the programs and policies for which he has become well known. Despite predictions that he might have trouble winning re-election in 1978, he defeated Republican Ted Strickland rather convincingly, winning 59 percent of the vote compared with Strickland's 39 percent. Having cut taxes and reduced welfare rolls during his first term, Lamm was able to pre-empt standard Republican issues, and Strickland was reduced to complaining that Lamm had appointed too many out-of-staters to top jobs. Differences of style between the two men also proved significant. As the Texas-born owner of a successful oil-related business and an occasional Baptist preacher, Strickland appealed less to Colorado voters than the well-educated, affluent, and liberal Lamm. By the end of his second term, Lamm seemed more popular and less controversial than ever, and he had little trouble winning a third term in 1982. Able to balance the requirements of economic growth with environmental protection, he trounced Republican John Fuhr, a former speaker of the Colorado House, by gaining 67 percent of the vote to Fuhr's 33 percent.

During his three terms in office, Lamm sought to administer an efficient and effective state government that was responsive to Colorado's citizens, preserve and enhance the state's infrastructure, establish a diversified economic base, improve the state's environment, and cooperate with the Western Governors' Police Office to ensure that the needs of western states were considered in the creation of federal policy. He tried to implement a comprehensive energy conservation program, improve the state's educational system, restore a meaningful executive budget through sound fiscal management, decrease crime, and improve the quality of life for all state citizens. Encouraging limited growth, Lamm favored attracting clean, high-tech industries to Colorado, and tried to combat hard economic times with austerity, hard work, and imagination. He opened his administration by recruiting professional managers from other parts of the country to run various departments of state, increased assistance to the elderly and dependent children, cracked down on shoddy nursing homes, humanized the prison system, and stopped spending to promote tourism—a dangerous industry which he claimed was growing to unmanageable and damaging proportions.

Lamm clearly changed his perspectives during his years in office. Always outspokenly liberal in cultural issues, he came to evince a mistrust of the federal government as Colorado's economy declined in the 1970s and the federal budget deficit grew. Arguing for limits to the responsibilities of government, he increasingly came to express his growing pessimism about the ability of government to solve all the problems of society. He earned national recognition and respect for his outspoken warnings and bold predictions, reaching beyond the traditional governor's domain to speak out against inequities, the trade deficit, deficit spending, U.S. immigration policies, prospects for American health care, and other issues, which he chronicled in several books: *Megatraumas, America at the Year 2000,* and *The Immigration Time Bomb.* Preaching his new "politics of limits," he attracted national attention in 1984 when he said the terminally ill have a "duty to die" and "let our kids build a reasonable life."

In the wake of such rising national attention, political observers were shocked when Lamm unexpectedly announced in 1985 that he would run neither for re-election nor for any other office in 1986. His extemporaneous announcement made at the end of his annual state of the state message ended months of speculation over whether he would run for a fourth term in 1986 or seek the Democratic nomination to the U.S. Senate if incumbent Gary Hart retired to seek the presidency. His decision was based, he explained, on his desire to raise unpopular issues without worrying about their effect on the electorate.

After his retirement from the governor's office in January 1987, Lamm began a career as a college teacher and popular lecturer. After teaching a course entitled "Hard Choices" at the University of Colorado, which focused on his evolving views on the deficit, demographics, health care, and Social Security, he was named a Montgomery Fellow at Dartmouth. His speeches as a popular lecturer have addressed his belief that government must re-focus its spending priorities and its expectations of what it can reasonably accomplish.

Bibliography: Biographical information, courtesy of governor's office; "200 Faces for the Future," *Time* (July 15, 1974); "Colorado's Lonely Long-Distance Runner," *Economist* 264 (September 17, 1977), 55; Michael Barone *et al., The Almanac of American Politics, 1978–1988*

(New York and Washington, D.C., 1977–1987); "A White-Water Governor," *Newsweek* (July 19, 1982); *Roanoke Times and World News,* 9–20–86; *The New York Times:* 3–7–81; 6–22–81; 7–12–81; 2–18–82; 9–16–82; 11–23–82; 11–28–82; 1–12–83; 4–16–83; 1–5–85; Biographical file, Colorado Historical Society.

Roy Romer (Courtesy of governor's office)

ROMER, Roy, 1987–

Born on October 31, 1928 in Garden City, Kansas. A Presbyterian, he and his wife, the former Bea Miller, have seven children.

Romer grew up in the southeastern Colorado town of Holly, where he moved with his family as an infant. He received a bachelor's degree in agricultural economics from Colorado State University, and a law degree from the University of Colorado. He also studied ethics at Yale. Prior to entering public life, Romer was an attorney in private practice, as well as a businessman. From 1942 to 1952, he engaged in dryland farming, irrigated farming, cattle and sheep ranching, and grain elevator operations in Holly, Granada, Dove Creek, and Bristol, Colorado. He has also been owner of a chain of construction equipment stores in Colorado, Virginia, and Florida. He developed a portion of Colorado's Centennial Airport, ran a flying school, and operated a ski area.

Romer, a Democrat, has a long career in public service. As a member of the State House of Representatives, 1958–1962, he served on several important committees. A member of the Joint Budget Committee, he chaired the House Judiciary Committee, the Joint House-Senate Committee on Education Beyond High School, and a legislative task force which recommended creation of Metropolitan State College. From 1962 to 1966, he served in the state senate, rising to the rank of assistant minority leader, 1964–1966. After an unsuccessful campaign for the U.S. Senate in 1966, he dropped out of public life for nearly a decade, only to return as a member of Governor Richard Lamm's administration. Chief of staff to the governor from 1975 to 1977 and again from 1982 to 1983, he also served as Colorado Agricultural Commissioner in 1975 and as state treasurer from 1977 to 1987. Few of the nation's current governors had such a long record of experience in their state capitals as did Romer when he assumed the governorship in January 1987.

Richard Lamm's decision not to seek re-election left the 1986 governor's race wide open. Running in a year when state Republican registration topped Democratic for the first time in two decades, Romer's quest to succeed his mentor was assisted by a weak Republican challenger. He was opposed by State Senator Ted Strickland, a controversial Texas native who had lost overwhelmingly to Lamm in 1978. Strickland's campaign was marked by a series of mistakes: he said America should become a "Christian centered" nation, and emphasized his strong opposition to abortion. He also ran an advertisement linking Romer with Angela Davis, the once prominent Communist agitator. When negative advertising on both sides threatened to alienate voters, Romer offered to take all his negative spots off the air; Strickland declined. In the opinion of political observers, Strickland had defeated himself with a pose voters perceived as decidedly "ungubernatorial." He lost to Romer 58 percent to 41 percent.

Romer's plans for his administration included stimulating Colorado's economy, creating new jobs, and encouraging foreign investment in the state. He also has special concerns about the quality of Colorado's educational system, including public schools as well as colleges and universities, the preservation of Colorado's quality of life and environment, and the construction of needed public improvement projects like a new Denver airport and Convention Center. He has promised to spend the state's tax reform windfall on education, highways, water projects, and economic development. One of the most controversial decisions he faced early in his term concerned the construction of a billion dollar dam that supporters said would assure the state's future water supplies and fuel growth. Opponents, on the other hand, worried about its environmental impact. Romer's critical decision to construct the dam only as a last resort was seen as a compromise.

Bibliography: Biographical information courtesy of governor's office; Michael Barone *et al., The Almanac of American Politics, 1988* (New York and Washington, D.C., 1987); *The Chronicle of Higher Education:* 11–12–86; 5–20–87; *USA Today,* 6–10–88; *The New York Times:* 7–14–87; 6–11–88.

William Atchinson O'Neill (Courtesy of governor's office)

CONNECTICUT

Born in Hartford, Connecticut on August 11, 1930; the son of Joseph and Frances O'Neill. A Roman Catholic, O'Neill married Natalie Scott Damon in 1962. The couple have no children.

Early in O'Neill's life, the family moved to East Hampton, where he attended the local schools and graduated from East Hampton High School. He later attended New Britain Teachers' College and the University of Hartford. A combat flier with the U.S. Air Force from 1950 to 1953, he returned to East Hampton at the end of his military service. His father owned a tavern there. Governor O'Neill still owns "O'Neill's Restaurant" in East Hampton, on the lower Connecticut River. He worked as a draftsman for a time, then sold life insurance.

His background is a traditionally Democratic one. When he returned from the Air Force, he got involved in local Democratic politics, serving on the East Hampton Democratic Town Committee from 1954 to 1980. After two unsuccessful bids, he was elected to the Connecticut House of Representatives as a Democrat in 1966; he was assistant majority leader for the 1971 and 1972 sessions, assistant minority leader for the next two sessions, and majority leader from 1975 through 1978. O'Neill strongly supported Governor Grasso in the 1974 election, and when John M. Bailey, the Connecticut State Democratic Chairman and former Democratic National Chairman, died the next year, Governor Grasso at first nominated O'Neill to the vacancy. O'Neill accepted, but Grasso later withdrew her support. Relations between the two were strained after that incident, and he was elected lieutenant governor in November 1978, despite Grasso's unwillingness to endorse a candidate in the primary. A conservative, O'Neill stated the view as lieutenant governor that Connecticut should not enact a state income tax.

When Grasso resigned from office on December 31, 1980 due to ill health, O'Neill assumed the governorship the same day. He steered the legislature through two special sessions, one concerning the budget and the other flood relief. O'Neill also approved an unpopular tax on incorporated businesses. It was a difficult transition for O'Neill, who claimed he felt like a caretaker.

He was elected to his own full four-year term in 1982, defeating former

State Senate Majority Leader Lewis B. Rome in the general election by 578,264 votes to 497,773. O'Neill campaigned on the theme that Connecticut had been relatively prosperous during the recession. Rome drew strong support from normally Republican Fairfield County, but he was unable to overcome the incumbent's advantage in the rest of the state.

During his first term, O'Neill established a more forceful presence, winning enactment of new programs and rebuilding the state's roads and bridges. Although derided by detractors as an amiable but uninspiring leader, O'Neill benefitted from a robust state economy that produced large budget surpluses and record tax cuts. Many Republicans said he was merely the beneficiary of an economic boom which they credited the Reagan administration with creating.

In 1986, O'Neill was challenged for re-nomination by former U.S. Representative Toby Moffett, who called the O'Neill administration "Unprofessional, unprepared, unresponsive, unimaginative, and totally uninspiring." Moffett said he would be an advocate of better programs to aid education and day care, to help laid-off workers start their own businesses, and to protect the environment. He also pledged to have an "accessible" administration that would put "professionalism over politics."

O'Neill rebuffed Moffett's challenge and was renominated by the Democratic State Convention in July 1986. Moffett received 250 delegate votes, short the 20 percent needed to force a September primary. O'Neill received 1,098 votes, 82 percent of all delegate votes cast.

In the general election, he faced Republican Julie Belaga, a 10-year state representative from Westport who had faced a three-way primary fight to win her party's nomination. As the state's first female Republican candidate for governor, she faced a difficult challenge, for the Republicans had elected only one governor in the past 32 years. Making her first bid for statewide office, she campaigned on the theme of bringing "pride and performance" to the state government. She accused the O'Neill administration of being dominated by politicians rather than professional managers, and condemned the governor for reacting to events rather than anticipating them. Attributing the state's prosperity to federal economic policies, she charged Democrats with running an administration "based on cronyism rather than excellence," and called state government "a festering sore," with frequent "embarrassments," such as the dismissal of bridge inspectors who collected extra pay for work they didn't perform. Presenting herself as a "fresh new face," she called for direct primaries for party nominations, elimination of the state's inheritance tax, and overhaul of the Departments of Motor Vehicles and Transportation to provide better services.

O'Neill stressed his leadership record, claiming that his six years of solid, steady governance had brought the state unparalleled prosperity, with high personal income and low unemployment. He also said he was more attuned to the problems of the state's cities and towns than Belaga, "a millionaire from Westport." Questioning her record in public service, he charged that she had missed 43 percent of all roll call votes during the 1986 legislative session, and had not produced "one piece of meaningful legislation" in her 10 years in the general assembly.

In the opinion of political observers, the contest featured more differences of style and personality than major disagreements on issues. Both candidates were political moderates who opposed a state personal income tax and supported the death penalty. Both opposed mandatory drug testing, and forcing suburban communities to accept low- and moderate-income housing. Neither candidate made gender a major issue.

In a sweeping re-election victory, O'Neill defeated Belaga by 168,329 votes, more than double his winning margin of 80,491 votes in 1982. The contest had set a spending record for a gubernatorial campaign in the state.

For his second term, O'Neill planned to follow "the same pattern" of his past six years in office, stressing programs to create jobs, protect the environment, and improve transportation. In the area of education, he fashioned sweeping changes. His Education Enhancement Act of 1986 raised salaries of public school teachers. The state is also recognized as one of the nation's leaders in teacher testing and improvement plans. Another noteworthy accomplishment was Connecticut's ranking among the top five states nationally in both its existing program for a clean environment and its climate for economic development. In 1987, the state created a $10 million superfund to clean up hazardous wastes, allocated $409 million to rebuild roads and bridges and to improve commuter service, and returned $1.68 billion in state revenues to cities and towns to cut local property taxes. O'Neill also called for a $6.8 million increase in state programs to help the elderly buy prescription drugs. His 1988–1989 budget included new monies for low-income housing, children's programs, and open space acquisitions.

In the face of such accomplishments, O'Neill scoffs at those who attack his style: "I'm a workhorse, not a showhorse," he explains. The low-key O'Neill is generally praised by his fellow Democrats for his legislative skills. Rarely does he find himself locked in combat with the general assembly, which is controlled by his own party.

At the end of his current term, which expires in 1991, O'Neill will have been Connecticut's governor longer than anyone since Jonathan Trumbull 2nd, who died in office in 1809, after serving more than 11 years. He has already hinted that he plans to seek a third term.

Bibliography: Biographical information, courtesy of governor's office;

The Chronicle of Higher Education: 10–22–86; 11–12–86; Michael Barone et al., *The Almanac of American Politics, 1984* (New York and Washington, D.C., 1983); *The New York Times:* 6–2–85; 11–15–85; 7–20–86; 7–27–86; 9–8–86; 9–10–86; 9–11–86; 9–21–86; 10–17–86; 10–20–86; 10–31–86; 11–5–86; 11–6–86; 2–5–87; 6–2–87; 7–7–87; 2–4–88.

Pierre Samuel DuPont, IV (Courtesy of DuPont for President campaign)

DELAWARE

DuPONT, Pierre Samuel IV, 1977–1985

Born on January 22, 1935 in Wilmington, Delaware; the son of Pierre Samuel DuPont III, an industrialist, and Jane (Holcomb) DuPont. An Episcopalian, he married Elsie Ravenel Wood on May 4, 1957. The couple have four children: Elsie, Pierre, Benjamin, and Eleuthere.

DuPont's ancestors arrived from France nearly 200 years ago, and his family became one of the wealthiest and most socially prominent in the nation. His education was impeccably upper crust: he graduated from Phillips Exeter Academy in 1952 and received a B.S.E. from Princeton University in 1956. He entered the U.S. Navy as an ensign in 1957, and obtained his discharge in 1960 with the rank of lieutenant. Poised to join the family business, the behemoth DuPont Corporation, he raised family eyebrows when he chose instead to go to Harvard Law School, from which he received an LL.B. in 1963.

Finding the practice of law unappealing, he joined DuPont as a quality control engineer. At the age of 34 he decided to run for public office. A Republican, he began his political career as a Delaware State Representative, serving from 1968 to 1970. In 1970, he was elected to the U.S. House of Representatives, where he served three terms, 1971 to 1977. In congress he was viewed as a moderate to liberal Republican.

On November 2, 1976 he defeated Sherman W. Tribbitt, a Democrat, by a vote of 130,531 to 97,480 to become governor of Delaware. He was re-elected to a second term in 1980, easily defeating William J. Goody, a Democratic legislator, by a vote of 159,004 to 64,217. He thus became the state's first chief executive in 24 years to be elected to consecutive terms.

As governor, DuPont earned a reputation as a moderate, a pragmatist and consensus builder, who endeared himself to fellow Republicans and Democrats alike. He made Delaware a model of fiscal stability and economic growth. The crowning achievement of his administration was pulling the state from its economic morass. In the five years prior to his taking office, state taxes had been increased 22 times. The state had budget deficits for four of those six years, and Delaware had the nation's highest average income tax rate at 19.8 percent. His administration resolved the state's financial crisis, bringing down repressive income taxes, balancing the budget, turning deficits into surpluses and creating new jobs in the state. Although DuPont had had a reputation as a moderate Republican, as governor he became convinced that government needed pruning, and that the private economy needed to be liberated from overgovernance to be productive.

DuPont created a favorable business climate in the state. Delaware's constitution was amended to limit spending to 98 percent of estimated revenue. Another constitutional change made it necessary to obtain a ⅗ vote of both houses of the legislature before a new tax could be imposed. Personal income taxes were lowered by 10 percent. One of his major achievements was a revision of Delaware's banking laws to encourage out-of-state banks to move their operations there. DuPont worked to broaden the state's economic base, and during his administration the state's jobless rate declined from 9.7 percent to 6.3 percent. Wilmington's growing, glassy skyline was another testament to the successes of his administration.

DuPont also helped to defeat a move to rescind Delaware's ratification of the Equal Rights Amendment, and another requiring administration officials to file financial disclosure forms.

Constitutionally ineligible to seek a third term, DuPont retired from public office in 1985, with his protégé and chosen successor Michael N. Castle following him in the governorship. Retreating to practice law with a Wilmington firm that represents DuPont Corporation interests, he left behind a physically stable state government, a growing state economy, and a well-knit public and private establishment.

Although DuPont had reportedly turned down an opportunity to run for the U.S. Senate in 1984, he retained national political aspirations. In September 1986 he launched an ill-fated bid for the 1988 Republican presidential nomination, the first Republican candidate to announce for the presidency. Saying from the outset that his campaign was "not for the fainthearted," he presented himself as a staunch conservative alternative to the frontrunner, Vice President George Bush. Throughout the campaign he battled both his image as a monied aristocrat and his reputation as an advocate of tough, controversial ideas. He urged the elimination of $20 billion in farm subsidies, proposed a "no work, no check" policy for welfare recipients, called for mandatory drug testing of all high school students, supported the creation of a private alternative to Social Security, and recommended a voucher system for education that would allow parents to send their children to the public or private school of their choice. DuPont also pledged never to raise taxes.

From the outset, his candidacy was seen as a longshot. Although he campaigned for more than 17 months and spent approximately $7.5 million, he managed to gain only 10 percent of the vote in the critical New Hampshire primary. After placing fifth of five candidates in the Iowa caucuses and fourth of five in New Hampshire, he withdrew from the presidential race on February 18, 1988. In June 1988, he formed a new political action committee, "Ideas for America's Future," that could help pay for his travels around the country to lay the groundwork for another White House bid.

Bibliography: Gerard Colby Zilg, *DuPont: Behind the Nylon Curtain* (Englewood Cliffs, N.J., 1974); Michael Barone et al., *The Almanac of American Politics, 1984–1988* (New York and Washington, D.C., 1983–1987); *Newsweek,* 6–8–87; *The National Review,* 8–28–87; *The Boston Globe,* 9–28–87; *The Washington Post,* 4–13–87; *Human Events,* 7–4–87; *The Newark (N.J.) Star Ledger:* 11–12–87; 1–24–88; 6–18–88; *The New York Times:* 1–19–77; 11–8–84; 1–16–85; 9–17–86; 7–13–87; 2–19–88.

Michael Newbold Castle (Courtesy of governor's office)

CASTLE, Michael Newbold, 1985–

Born in Wilmington, Delaware on July 2, 1939; the son of J. Manderson Castle, Jr. and Louise B. Castle. A Roman Catholic, Castle is a bachelor.

A graduate of Hamilton College (B.A. 1961) and Georgetown University Law School (J.D. 1964), Castle, a Republican, has been an attorney in private practice as well as a longtime state government official. State deputy attorney general from 1965 to 1966, he served in the state House of Representatives from 1966 to 1967, as well as in the state senate from 1968 to 1976, where he was minority leader from 1975 to 1976. He served as lieutenant governor under Governor Pierre DuPont from 1981 to 1985. As a close political ally of DuPont, Castle was given major policy jobs. On top of the part time position's duties of presiding over the state senate and Board of Pardons, he headed a study of drunken driving that led to tougher penalties and enforcement procedures. In 1984 he headed a panel that produced more than 70 proposals to improve the state's educational system, resulting in an immediate raise in teachers' salaries totaling $14 million.

Since Governor DuPont was constitutionally ineligible to run for a third term in 1984, Castle was groomed as his successor. Although he was carried along in the election by the tide of affection Delaware feels for DuPont, Castle had been an active lieutenant governor, and he campaigned hard to win the governor's office. He held a commanding lead from the start of the campaign. His opponent was former state Supreme Court Justice William T. Quillen, who had won the Democratic gubernatorial nomination against former Governor Sherman Tribbitt. Quillen was the favorite of Samuel Shipley, the state Democratic party chairman, who believed the former justice had the best chance of defeating the Republican ticket in the general election. Quillen, however, in the opinion of political observers, "showed little zest for campaigning." Castle won with 55 percent of the vote in a year when Democrats were winning most of the other state offices in Delaware. One of Castle's main assets on the road to victory was his predecessor's support, and his win was seen as a vindication of DuPont's record.

In office, Castle has continued DuPont's policies. He presides over a booming state economy with a healthy budget surplus. Two major cuts in personal income taxes, strict controls on state spending, improved management of state government, and increased state support for public schools have been the highlights of the first years of his administration. Nineteen eighty-six also saw new reforms in the state's long-term capital improvement program, with greater emphasis on long-term cost benefit analysis and more public scrutiny of projects. An administration proposal for a three-year, $130 million highway improvement program was approved by the general assembly. In both 1985 and 1986, Castle increased economic development efforts aimed at attracting financial institutions to Delaware, already a center for major banking operations, and increasing the state's role in international trade and finance.

Castle, who has taken an active role in promoting changes in Delaware's welfare system, is chairman of the National Governors' Association Task Force on Welfare Prevention. In this capacity, he has an opportunity to make a personal impact on a critical national issue.

Castle easily won re-election in 1988, defeating Jacob Kreshtool, a retired labor lawyer, with over 70 percent of the vote.

Bibliography: Biographical information, courtesy of governor's office; L.J. Davis, "Delaware Inc.," *The New York Times Magazine* (June 5, 1988); Michael Barone *et al., The Almanac of American Politics, 1986–1988* (New York and Washington, D.C., 1985–1987); *The New York Times:* 11–6–84; 11–8–84; 1–16–85.

Robert Graham (Courtesy of Senator Graham)

FLORIDA

GRAHAM, Robert (Bob), 1979–1987

Born in Coral Gables, Florida on November 9, 1936. Graham is the son of Ernest and Hilda (Simmons) Graham, a distant cousin of former President Jimmy Carter, and brother-in-law of Katherine Graham, the publisher of the *Washington Post*. A member of the United Church of Christ, he is married to the former Adele Khoury, by whom he is the father of Gwendolyn Patricia, Glynn Adele, Suzanne, and Kendall Elizabeth.

Graham received a B.A. from the University of Florida in 1959 and an LL.B. from Harvard University in 1962. He is a cattle and dairy farmer and chairman of the board of Sangra Development Corporation, a real estate development firm. Graham is also an attorney and a member of the Florida bar. In 1966 he became a member of the Florida House of Representatives. He was named by the Florida Jaycees as one of the five most outstanding young men in Florida in 1971; the same year he became a member of the state senate, and in 1972 he was chosen the outstanding first-term member of that body. Graham received an award in 1973 as the most valuable member of the senate, and an award as the second most effective senator in 1976. In 1978 he entered a field of eight Democratic hopefuls for the gubernatorial nomination. Graham took part in a runoff election against Robert L. Shevin, whose identification as a Jew from Miami hurt him in the rest of the state. After winning the primary with 54 percent of the vote, Graham faced Republican Jack Eckerd in the general election. The campaign became an expensive battle of millionaires (Eckerd owns a large retail drug chain), and Graham had to overcome the handicap of hailing from South Florida, which had never seen a local citizen become chief executive. In the end, he carried most of the counties in the state, beat Eckerd narrowly in Duval County (Jacksonville), and won by an overwhelming margin in Miami's Dade County. The final count was 1,406,580 votes for Graham and 1,123,888 votes for Eckerd.

Graham assumed office on January 2, 1979, succeeding Reubin Askew. On May 18, 1979, he signed the death warrant of John Arthur Spenkelink, who became the first person to be executed against his will since a United States Supreme Court decision had temporarily halted all executions. Graham later ordered an investigation, when it was charged that the prisoner had been abused before his electrocution. The next year

Graham called out the National Guard to quell a major riot in Miami. The governor also made an effort to work one day a month at jobs ranging from teacher and television newsman to sponge fisher and cook. This policy reportedly gave Graham a good image with the working class in Florida, and contributed to his electoral success. The beginning of America's space shuttle program returned Florida's Cape Canaveral missile complex to national prominence in 1981. The following year Graham approved a recodification of Florida's insurance laws, which had been enacted during a special legislative session.

In the 1982 gubernatorial primary Graham defeated two weak opponents, one of whom was an advocate of homosexual rights. In November he overwhelmed L.A. (Skip) Bafalis, a 10-year veteran of the U.S. House of Representatives little known outside his south Florida district. Graham enjoyed an easier victory than in 1978, taking even most northern Florida counties convincingly. He received 1,739,553 votes, while Bafalis received only 949,013.

Although Graham had been one of Jimmy Carter's most vocal supporters, he ran much better than Carter had in 1980. While Graham had been fiercely criticized for the state's handling of Cuban refugees, he benefitted from other accomplishments. Presiding over the rapidly expanding government of a rapidly expanding state, he was nonetheless able to avoid the imposition of a state income tax. Once considered a liberal, Graham established a reputation as a strong law and order man by backing capital punishment and by signing a 1978 bill that provided harsh minimum sentences for convicted drug dealers. In 1985 Graham was chosen chairman of the Southern Governors' Association.

In 1986, as Graham completed his second term in office, he chose to challenge incumbent Senator Paula Hawkins, a freshman Republican elected in the Reagan landslide of 1980. He won 85 percent of the Democratic primary vote over gay activist Bob Kunst, who criticized the governor for vetoing a bill providing funds for AIDS research. Graham painted Hawkins as a "narrow senator" with a lightweight agenda. The governor said his opponent had failed to grow in office and had limited her service in Washington to such family-oriented issues as child abuse. While he attacked Hawkins' record in Washington, he was careful not to position himself too far from Reagan administration policies, increasingly popular in Florida. He pledged support for the Nicaraguan rebels, the President's missile defense plan, and military spending.

Hawkins, on the other hand, tried to attack Graham's record, by labeling the Democrat as being against environmental issues and programs to benefit the elderly. Graham countered by citing strong support from leaders in both fields. Hawkins strove to overcome not only the liabilities of what even some members of her own party conceded was a lackluster first term, but also physical infirmity. She underwent surgery in

1986 to correct an old back injury, and her long convalescence gave Graham the opportunity to influence conservative voters. Graham, with especially strong support from young voters, held a lead in the polls from the start.

The senate race was primarily a battle of negative TV commercials. Both candidates promised to get tough with drug traffickers, and to protect Social Security, two key issues in the state.

Graham defeated Hawkins, garnering 55 precent of the vote to her 45 percent to win office as Florida's junior senator. He resigned as governor three days before the formal expiration of his term to be sworn in as senator on January 3, 1987. As senator, Graham drew national publicity for a practice he had begun during his years as governor, keeping in touch with his constituents by performing one-day stints in more than 200 different jobs. He was a serious contender for the 1988 Democratic vice presidential nomination, being considered for the second spot by nominee Michael Dukakis because of the assistance he could give the ticket in the South.

Bibliography: Biographical information courtesy of Senator Graham's office; Michael Barone *et al., The Almanac of American Politics, 1982–1984* (New York and Washington, D.C., 1981–1983); *USA Today,* 6–24–88; *The New York Times:* 9–8–85; 10–5–86; 10–29–86; 11–5–86; *The Miami Herald:* 11–8–78; 11–3–82; *The Washington Post:* 5–19–79; 8–11–79.

John Wayne Mixson (Courtesy of Governor Mixson)

MIXSON, John Wayne, January 3, 1987–January 6, 1987

Born in Coffee County, Alabama on June 16, 1922; the son of Cecil Mixson and Mineola Moseley Mixson. A Methodist, he married Margie Grace in 1974, the same year he received a B.S. from the University of Florida. Mixson served in the U.S. Navy from 1942 to 1945.

A farmer and cattle rancher, Mixson's career in state Democratic politics spanned 20 years. He began his long public service career in March 1967 by winning election to the Florida House of Representatives. He served six consecutive terms, representing districts including Jackson, Gadsden, Liberty, Washington, Holmes, and Walton counties. From 1972 to 1978 he was chairman of the House Committee on Agriculture and General Legislation, and served on the Appropriations and Rules Committees.

In 1978 he ran for lieutenant governor on a ticket with Bob Graham. Their campaign stressed the need to broaden the state's economic base by diversifying the economy. With their victory, Mixson became Florida's 12th lieutenant governor. With the reelection of the ticket in 1982, Mixson became the first lieutenant governor in state history to be elected to consecutive terms.

During his tenure as lieutenant governor, Mixson chaired a Tax Revision Commission working to make state taxes more supportive of an improved business climate. He also served as coordinator of economic development among the agencies of state government, chairman of the Florida Council on Criminal Justice, chairman of the Florida Council on Highway Safety, and chairman of the Coastal Plans Regional Commission. During his second term, he served concurrently as secretary of commerce, successfully spearheading the state's efforts to promote tourism and economic development. Under Mixson's leadership, the department assisted in the location or expansion of more than 600 businesses. The state also led the nation in the number of jobs created.

Mixson assumed the governorship when Governor Bob Graham resigned from office three days early to be sworn in as Florida's junior U.S. Senator. In the shortest gubernatorial term of office known to state historians, Mixson was sworn in as Florida's 39th governor on January 3, 1987. He held office until the formal January 6th inauguration of incoming Governor Robert Martinez. Entering office "with a brief agenda," Mixson planned a weekend administration mostly of appointments and ceremonies, as well as tending to a few necessary details of government. Among his official actions was a 90-minute Cabinet meeting that was of a largely ceremonial nature.

The three-day administration marked the pinnacle as well as the end of Mixson's political career, and he planned to retire from public life once Martinez was sworn into office.

Bibliography: Biographical information courtesy of Governor Mixson; Michael Barone et al., *The Almanac of American Politics, 1988* (New York and Washington, D.C., 1987); *The Newark (N.J.) Star Ledger,* 1–4–87; *The New York Times,* 1–4–87; Jaques Cattell Press, *Who's Who in American Politics, 1985–1986* (New York, 1985).

Robert Martinez (Courtesy of governor's office)

MARTINEZ, Robert, 1987–

Born in Tampa, Florida on December 25, 1934, the son of Serafin Martinez and Ida Carreno Martinez; a Roman Catholic, he married Mary Jane Marino in 1954. The couple have two children, Sharon and Alan.

A lifelong resident of Tampa, Martinez attended local public schools there. He earned a B.S. from the University of Tampa and a master's degree in labor and industrial relations from the University of Illinois. Martinez held a number of jobs before seeking public office. A one-time restaurant worker, he spent seven years as a classroom teacher and a total of 12 years in the field of education. During his teaching career, he helped lead a teachers' union strike against the policies of Governor Claude R. Kirk, Jr. He also served as a labor consultant specializing in the area of employee relations.

After a career in private business, Martinez was elected mayor of Tampa in 1979. He was re-elected in 1983 with 81 percent of the vote. As mayor, Martinez practiced a conservative approach to government that lowered property taxes, decreased the number of city employees, and improved the quality of life. During his tenure as mayor, the city was hailed as one of the 10 "megatrend" cities of the future in the United States, and its robust, diversified economy was seen as a model for growth. Futurist John Naisbett highlighted Tampa as one of the 10 best sites in the nation for small business growth and development.

While mayor, Martinez was a member of the U.S. Conference of Mayors, a member of the Board of Directors of the National League of Cities, and president of the Florida League of Cities. One of the political highlights of his second term in office was being chosen as a featured speaker at the 1984 Republican National Convention.

With incumbent Governor Robert Graham constitutionally ineligible to serve a third term in 1986, the governor's race was wide open. Martinez resigned as mayor of Tampa in the summer of 1986 to campaign for the governorship, an office that only one Republican had won in the last century. From the start, Martinez was seen as the party's best hope of securing the governorship. The grandson of Spanish immigrants, Martinez and the Republicans hoped to capitalize on the state's changing demographics: Republican registration had been swelled by newcomers, retirees from the Midwest and increasing numbers of naturalized Cuban exiles. Martinez drew a good share of his strength from Miami's Cuban population, which had become overwhelmingly Republican. Political observers were unclear, however, as to whether non-Hispanic Republicans outside of his Tampa Bay base would support him in a climate where cultural divisions were pronounced. Old-line Republicans had initial doubts that someone of Hispanic origin could be elected to statewide office. Martinez also had some problems with party regulars due to his late conversion to the Republican party. Since he had officially become a Republican only in 1983, his endorsement of Jimmy Carter in 1980 enabled his opponents to confront him with the fact that he had opposed the election of Ronald Reagan.

Martinez built his campaign around his experience as a public official and reputation as a strong and effective manager. A stern opponent of crime, he pledged to trim $800 million in waste from the state's $16 billion budget, and pledged no new taxes. He faced three opponents in the race for the Republican gubernatorial nomination: Lou Frey, a 52-year-old former congressman from the Orlando area; Tom Gallagher, a 42-year-old state representative from Miami; and 48-year-old conservative Chester Clem from Vero Beach. Because no candidate won a majority of the vote, a runoff election was necessary between Martinez and his leading rival, Lou Frey. Martinez missed winning the nomination in the first primary by a few thousand votes. After his narrow miss, he asked his opponent, who had previously lost bids for the governorship in 1978 and for a U.S. Senate seat in 1980, to drop out of the race in the name of party unity. Frey, however, declined. Martinez officially won the Republican gubernatorial nomination in the September 30, 1986 runoff primary, defeating Frey by a 2–1 margin. By defeating Frey, a former five-term Congressman whose name was familiar in state Republican circles, Martinez ably demonstrated his appeal both to traditional Republicans as well as to new party registrants.

Martinez was also to benefit from a divisive primary fight among Democrats. Three Democrats sought to succeed outgoing Governor Graham: former state representative Steve Pajcic, Attorney General Jim Smith, and State Senate President Harry Johnston. Smith combined name recognition as the state's chief law enforcement officer with a hefty campaign warchest: he had reportedly spent $1 million of his own money to ignite the campaign. Yet his campaign appeared disorganized and uncertain, and as he lost some of his organization and support to Johnston, a runoff primary was necessary among the Democrats as well. Although Pajcic was the eventual winner of the nomination, he had been badly bruised by his opponents' charges. Leading rival Smith had attacked Pajcic sharply, accusing the Jacksonville lawyer of voting on the wrong side of law and order issues, and of masking his liberal ideology behind a moderate image. In the general election, Pajcic continued to be dogged by the labels planted on him by his rivals for the Democratic nomination, who had accused him of being too liberal on such issues as homosexual rights and capital punishment.

The defection of conservative Democrats to Martinez was seen as central to the Republican victory. Martinez's victory with 55 percent of the vote heartened those who had worked to establish a viable two-party system in the state.

Inaugurated on January 6, 1987 as the state's 40th governor and the first elected governor of Hispanic ancestry, Martinez confronted numerous problems associated with the state's rapid growth: overcrowded roads, schools, and prisons, a strained budget, and a poor tax base unable to support the growth needs of Florida. The main issue of his administration rapidly emerged: how to pay the price of such growth?

In the first few months of his administration, Martinez showed a command over the legislative agenda. He put together a coalition of leaders of the Democratic House plus a coalition of conservative Democrats and Republicans in the state senate. Having called for budget cuts, he promptly switched direction and called for extending the state sales tax to services, a move that was expected to raise more than $1 billion for the rapidly growing state. In a dramatic and surprising policy reversal a few months later, however, he called the legislature into special session to repeal the controversial tax, which had cost him the confidence of many Floridians.

In other areas, he signed legislation creating a new gun law that drew national attention to the state. He planned to continue programs to improve higher education and to support appropriations increases for the state university system. Fighting the war on drugs also emerged as one of his top priorities, since it is estimated that 80 percent of the cocaine in use in the United States enters the country from Florida. He planned to appoint a "drug czar" and to create a task force to fight drug dealing. He has recommended options such as using the state's National Guard to locate drug shipments, requiring random drug tests for state workers, and mandating the death penalty for drug traffickers and dealers.

Bibliography: Biographical information, courtesy of governor's office; Michael Barone *et al., Almanac of American Politics, 1988* (New York and Washington, D.C., 1987); *The Chronicle of Higher Education:* 11–12–86; 9–30–87; *USA Today,* 6–23–88; *The New York Times:* 9–2–86; 9–3–86; 9–30–86; 10–1–86; 10–2–86; 10–12–86; 11–2–86; 11–5–86; 1–6–87; 5–13–87.

Joe Frank Harris (Courtesy of governor's office)

GEORGIA

HARRIS, Joe Frank, 1983–

Born on February 16, 1936 in Bartow County, Georgia, the son of Franklin Grover Harris and Frances Morrow Harris. A member of the Faith United Methodist Church, Harris married Elizabeth Carlock in 1961. The couple have a son, Joe.

Harris received a B.A. in business administration from the University of Georgia in 1958. Following active duty in the U.S. Army, he opened a concrete products business in Cartersville, Harris Cement Products, Inc., and expanded operations to Bartow and Cobb Counties. He also served as president of Harris Georgia Corporation, a diversified industrial development company.

A lifelong Democrat, Harris served 18 years in the State House of Representatives before seeking the governorship in 1982. For the last eight of those years, he was chairman of the House Appropriations Committee, a position that provided him with an intimate knowledge of the state's budgetary process. He is an acknowledged expert on state revenues and expenditures.

To gain the Democratic gubernatorial nomination in 1982, Harris defeated Savannah area Congressman Bo Ginn in a runoff election, gaining 55 percent of the vote to his opponent's 45 percent. Harris made his strong Christian views on issues and his abstemious personal behavior the centerpiece of his campaign. He pledged early and often that he would impose no new state taxes. Early in the primary race, he was attacked for being dominated by House Speaker Tom Murphy, but after winning the nomination, he was able to secure the selection of a strong Democratic state chairman, former federal Budget Director Bert Lance, thereby demonstrating his own political clout and independence.

The 1982 general election was anticlimactic, due to the continuing weakness of the Republican party in state elections. Harris defeated Republican candidate Robert H. Bell with 63 percent of the vote to his opponent's 37 percent.

Despite a lengthy career in state politics, Harris entered office a largely unknown quantity. Yet he has become a popular governor, presiding over a state with rapid economic growth, emphasizing an orderly administration, the improvement of education, and the attraction of new business. His major legislative achievement has been a $231 million education reform package, enacted in 1985, that did not call for a tax increase. Besides supporting major increases in state spending for higher education, he has also persuaded the legislature to create a statewide coordinating board for postsecondary vocational education. He also created the Georgia Research Consortium to funnel private sector funds to advance technological research and development at Georgia's institutions of higher education.

As a businessman, Harris has injected a businesslike management style and organizational principles into state government. He created the Economic Development Council of state agency and department heads to coordinate economic development at the state level. He has placed special emphasis on small and minority business development, supported the expansion of existing industry, and encouraged international trade with and investment in the state.

In the field of human services, Harris has spearheaded a successful public awareness campaign against drinking and driving, coupled with higher fines against lawbreakers. He has also backed an award-winning campaign against child abuse developed by the Georgia Department of Human Resources and the Medical Association of Georgia. He has created the Special Strike Force on Drug Suppression, combining manpower and equipment of several state agencies in the war on drug cultivation.

So popular did Harris' policies prove that he won the 1986 Democratic gubernatorial primary with 85 percent of the vote, defeating rival Kenneth B. Quarterman. In the general election, he beat Republican Guy Davis with 71 percent of the vote, carrying every one of the state's 159 counties. Expecting a Democratic sweep, state Republican leaders had earlier toyed with the idea of not even attempting to field a candidate against the popular incumbent.

In his second term, Harris has promised a campaign against illiteracy, better access to health services, and a "growth strategy" to regulate economic development.

Perceived as a serious and dignified leader, Harris has been seen by political observers as a key example of the need for ideological realignments in southern Democratic politics. He has gone to unusual lengths to distance himself from the party's national leaders, refusing to meet with either Walter Mondale or Geraldine Ferraro when they visited Georgia during the 1984 presidential campaign.

Although he is not well known beyond Georgia politics, Harris has served as chairman of the Southern Growth Policies Board, the Appalachian Regional Commission, and the Southern Regional Education Board. He also serves on various committees of the National Governors' Association: the Energy and Environment Committee; the Committee on

Transportation, Commerce, and Communications; and the Education
Task Force on School Leadership and Management.

Bibliography: Biographical information, courtesy of governor's office;
The New York Times, 6–25–85; Michael Barone *et al., The Almanac of
American Politics, 1984–1988* (New York and Washington, D.C., 1983–
1987); *The Chronicle of Higher Education,* 11–12–86; Jaques Cattell Press,
Who's Who in American Politics, 1985–1986 (New York, 1985).

George Ryoichi Ariyoshi (Courtesy of governor's office)

HAWAII

ARIYOSHI, George Ryoichi, 1974–1986

The son of a sumo wrestler, Ariyoshi was born on March 12, 1926 over a soybean curd shop in the Japanese section of Honolulu. He is the first American of Japanese ancestry to be elected governor of a state and the third chief executive of Hawaii since it gained statehood. His parents, Ryozo and Mitsue (Yoshikawa) Ariyoshi, operated a dry cleaning shop after coming to Hawaii. The president of his senior class at McKinley High in Honolulu, Ariyoshi served as an interpreter with the United States Army's Military Intelligence Service in Japan at the end of World War II. After returning to Hawaii, he attended the University of Hawaii and then transferred to Michigan State University, where he received a B.A. in history and political science in 1949 and a J.D. in 1952.

A Protestant, Ariyoshi and his wife, the former Jean Miya Hayashi, have three children: Lynn Miye, Todd Ryozo, and Donn Ryoji.

A practicing attorney, Ariyoshi entered politics as part of the Democratic machine established following World War II by former Governor John A. Burns. He was elected to the Territorial House of Representatives in 1954, and served for four years before his election to the Territorial Senate in 1958. After Hawaii achieved statehood he remained in the state senate, serving as chairman of the Health and Welfare Committee in 1959, chairman of the Ways and Means Committee from 1962 to 1964, majority leader from 1965 to 1966, and majority floor leader from 1969 to 1970. In 1962 Ariyoshi was selected as one of the top 10 legislators in Hawaii by the Kiwanis Club.

Ariyoshi was elected lieutenant governor in 1970, thus becoming the first Japanese-American to hold that position in any American state. When Governor Burns fell ill, Ariyoshi served as acting governor from October 1973 until the end of Burns' term. Upon his mentor's resignation due to cancer of the colon, Ariyoshi sought election to his own term as governor in 1974. He won his party's nomination after a stiff challenge from Honolulu Mayor Frank Fasi, a savage critic of the Burns organization and a controversial public figure. The candidate of the Democratic establishment, Ariyoshi promised to bring more dollars into Hawaii. He went on to defeat Republican Randolph Crossley, a Honolulu businessman, by attracting 55 percent of the vote in the general election. Ariyoshi compiled his heaviest margins in the so-called Neighbor Islands, where the Democratic organization had strong support from heavily unionized agricultural workers and dockers.

Although Ariyoshi had the distinction of never having lost an election, and was re-elected to the governorship in 1978 (defeating Republican John Leopold, 55 percent to 44 percent) and again in 1982, his victories were not without difficulty. In particular, the Fasi-Ariyoshi rivalry became a classic one in Hawaiian politics, and Ariyoshi's abrasive contests with the three-term mayor of Honolulu opened wounds in the state's Democratic party. Fasi again challenged Ariyoshi in the 1978 gubernatorial primary, gaining 49 percent of the vote to the governor's 51 percent, and also in the 1982 general election, when he established his own Independent Democratic party to confront the incumbent.

The two men disagreed on several issues. In 1975 Fasi condemned salary increases voted for high state officials, including the governor, and a pension bill that the legislators had voted for themselves. Hoping to capitalize on the discontent of voters and taxpayers on that instance, he had his own problems two years later when he was accused of arranging a bribe of $500,000 from a real estate developer and then collecting part of it himself. Asserting his innocence (the accusations were later dropped), Fasi accused Ariyoshi of arranging to have the charges brought to spoil his rival's chances of winning the Democratic gubernatorial nomination in 1978. The two were also on a collision course over Ariyoshi's efforts to control Hawaii's rising population. While Fasi argued that development is good, Ariyoshi was a strong believer in population control, and once proposed limiting the number of people who could move to the islands. In 1977 Ariyoshi was criticized by Fasi when he signed a bill establishing a one-year residency requirement for most state and county jobs. Although Fashi claimed the measure was unconstitutional, it was endorsed by the public employee unions which have repeatedly given Ariyoshi their electoral support. There were also contrasts in character and style between the two men. While Fasi was flamboyant and dynamic, the non-charismatic Ariyoshi frankly admitted that he was not an "image person." Documentary campaign films routinely featured little footage of him speaking, and in 1978 his campaign slogan was "quiet but effective." He was not closely associated with specific policies. When Hawaii was booming, he advocated limits on growth; when the tourist industry slumped, he claimed credit for the islands' still low unemployment rate.

Many political observers believed that the general public was disappointed with him. By his second term, there were even signs of resentment within the governor's own ethnic constituency. Some felt that he had become "just another *haole* at heart," a pejorative term applied to whites from the mainland. In 1982 Ariyoshi narrowly won his bid for a third term, gaining 45 percent of the vote in a three-man race against Fasi and

Republican State Senator D. G. Anderson. Even more humiliating was the bitter primary contest, in which his leadership ability was attacked by six members of his own party, including his own lieutenant governor, Jean Sadako King. Ariyoshi polled 53.3 percent of the vote in that election. Afterward, political observers speculated as to his political future, wondering how long he and his organization could remain in office if his victories came by such tenuous margins.

In 1986 Ariyoshi chose to retire from the governorship after serving three four-year terms. His political organization, however, remained intact, throwing its support behind Lieutenant Governor John Waihee, Ariyoshi's ultimate successor.

Ariyoshi retired as one of the nation's senior governors in terms of service. He had served as chairman of the Western Governors' Conference, president of the Pacific Basin Development Council, and vice-chairman of the Committee on Legal Affairs and chairman of the task forces on Tourism and Public Retirement Systems of the National Governors' Association. He will be remembered as a political moderate who presided over Hawaii in a sometimes painful era of transition from a plantation economy based mostly on sugar and pineapple to one dependent on tourism, urban growth, military spending, and diversified agriculture.

Ariyoshi is currently "Of Counsel" with the law firm of Kobayashi, Watanabe, Sugits and Kawashima, specializing in international business consulting.

Bibliography: Biographical information courtesy of governor's office; *The New York Times:* 4–20–74; 10–7–74; 6–23–75; 6–3–77; 6–28–77; 12–18–77; "The AJA's Fast Rising Sons," *Time* (Oct. 20, 1975); Michael Barone *et al., The Almanac of American Politics 1978, 1982, 1986* (New York and Washington, D.C., 1977–1985); National Governors' Association, *Governors of the American States, Commonwealths, and Territories* (Washington, D.C., 1983).

John Waihee (Courtesy of governor's office)

WAIHEE, John, 1986–

Born in the small plantation town of Honokaa on the island of Hawaii, on May 19, 1946, Waihee is Hawaii's fourth elected governor and the first of native Hawaiian ancestry. He and his wife, the former Lynne Kobashigawa, have two children: John and Jennifer.

Waihee holds a bachelor's degree in history and business from Andrews University in Michigan. He has also done graduate work at Central Michigan University. He was a member of the first graduating class from the William S. Richardson School of Law, University of Hawaii, 1976.

After graduating from law school, Waihee became an associate with the distinguished Honolulu law firm of Shim, Seigle, Tam, and Naito. Subsequently he assumed a career in private practice. He has also served as an administrator of community education programs in Michigan and in the Honolulu Model Cities Program, as well as program manager in the Honolulu Office of Human Resources.

His political career began with his election to the 1978 State Constitutional Convention. Serving as majority leader of the convention, he played a key role in its deliberations, helping to draft such essential components of the new document as the water code, the section on preservation of agricultural lands, the establishment of the Office of Hawaiian Affairs, and the provisions of autonomy for the University of Hawaii. Two years later, he was elected to the State House of Representatives, in which he served on the Policy, Judiciary, Consumer Protection, and Commerce Committees.

In 1982 he ran successfully for lieutenant governor, serving during the third and final term of Democrat George Ariyoshi's administration. During Waihee's term as lieutenant governor he was involved in a number of complex issues, including a major airline dispute that threatened the Hawaiian economy; development issues on Molokai; the settlement of long-standing liquor tax disputes; and tort reform.

In 1986, with Ariyoshi's retirement, the governor's race was wide open. Since the Democratic party had controlled Hawaiian government since statehood, the September 20, 1986 Democratic primary was widely regarded as one of the most pivotal in Hawaii's 27 years of statehood, with seven candidates seeking the party's nomination. Waihee ran as a protégé of outgoing Governor Ariyoshi, and as a member of that faction of the Democratic party that has controlled Hawaii since 1962. By 1986, however, there were signs that the electorate had grown increasingly dissatisfied with these so-called "Burns-Ariyoshi" Democrats, who had come under criticism for purportedly allowing businesspeople with ties to the statehouse to profit excessively from land development. Waihee, who tried to distance himself from organization Democrats by arguing he was very much his own man, was an underdog in the primary. The favorite was

Congressman Cecil Heftel, a broadcasting millionaire free of ties to the governor's office. Heftel outspent Waihee by a 4–1 margin. The third major Democrat in the race was Honolulu City Council member Patsy Mink, a liberal former six-term congresswoman and once the best known Hawaiian politician outside the state. Waihee's 46 percent–36 percent victory over Heftel (with Mink garnering 16 percent of the vote) was widely regarded as an upset, attributed by some political observers to an unfortunate "smear" campaign launched against Heftel in the last days preceding the election. Although Waihee had no part in the negative advertising blitz—launched by public employee unions and Republicans who hoped to remove the strongest Democratic candidate from contention—he was its direct beneficiary.

In the general election, Waihee opposed D. G. Anderson, a wealthy businessman and former managing director of Honolulu, who won the Republican nomination against token opposition. The Republicans argued that voters wanted change after three decades of Democratic dominance. Waihee countered by repeatedly denying that he was part of any Ariyoshi machine. Calling the politicians who had run Hawaii since statehood "the first wave," he pledged to name his own top appointees and painted his administration as "a new beginning for Hawaii." Despite his emphasis on the new, however, Waihee did enjoy the unofficial support of the Ariyoshi forces as well as the financial backing of many of the state's builders, architects, and developers, who favored the continuation of intensive development in the state. Waihee won the governorship with 52 percent of the vote.

In office, he has pledged an open government, marked by citizen involvement. He also wants to increase state support for faculty salaries and facilities at the University of Hawaii, and to expand Pacific Studies programs there.

Bibliography: Biographical information, courtesy of governor's office; *The Chronicle of Higher Education:* 11–12–86; 2–18–87; Jaques Cattell Press, *Who's Who in American Politics, 1985–1986* (New York, 1985); Michael Barone *et al., The Almanac of American Politics 1988* (New York and Washington, D.C., 1987); *The New York Times:* 9–20–86; 9–22–86.

John Victor Evans (Courtesy of Governor Evans)

IDAHO

A Democrat and former lieutenant governor of Idaho, Evans first succeeded to the governorship on January 24, 1977, when President Jimmy Carter selected then Governor Cecil Andrus to be his Secretary of the Interior. The son of David Lloyd and Margaret Thomas Evans, he was born on January 18, 1925 in Malad City, a small town in the heavily Mormon southeast corner of the state. He is married to the former Lola Daniels, and has five children and nine grandchildren.

Evans attended Idaho State University and graduated from Stanford University with a degree in business and economics. He also spent 18 months overseas as an army infantryman during World War II. He first entered public service at age 27, choosing to follow in his grandfather's footsteps, and acquired extensive experience in state government. A member of the Idaho State Senate from 1953 to 1957 and again from 1967 to 1974, he was majority leader from 1957 to 1959 and minority leader from 1969 to 1974. Evans also served as mayor of his native Malad City from 1960 to 1966, during the break in his senatorial career. While in the state senate, he was a member of the National Legislative Committee on Natural Resources; in recognition of his performance, he received the Distinguished Service Award from the Association of Idaho Cities in 1974.

First elected lieutenant governor of Idaho in 1974, Evans was elected to the Executive Board of the National Conference of Lieutenant Governors in August 1975. After succeeding to the governorship, he emphasized a long-standing interest in environmentalism and assumed a leadership role among the nation's chief executives. Elected vice chairman of the Western Governors' Conference in September 1977 and chairman in June 1978, Evans, a rancher by trade, was named chairman of the National Governors' Association Agricultural Subcommittee on Rangeland Management in September 1979.

Although political observers at first believed that he lacked former Governor Andrus' political style, Evans managed state affairs well enough to win election to his own term as chief executive in 1978, soundly defeating Republican legislative leader Allen Larsen with 59 percent of the vote. The contest marked the third time in a row that the Democrats had captured the statehouse in this increasingly Republican state, and the second time in the state's history that the voters had chosen a Mormon as governor. Helping Evans in 1978 was the decidedly unpopular position taken by Larsen on one key issue. Although both candidates were Mormons, Evans did not believe that the state should legislate Mormon rules of morality. Larsen's proposals to restrict liquor sales stirred intense opposition in a state where more than 70 percent of the voters are not Mormons. Capitalizing on a widespread fear that the Mormons "were trying to take over the state," Evans did especially well in the largely non-Mormon Idaho panhandle.

Rather conservative for a Democrat, Evans nevertheless retained protection of the environment as an important item on his agenda. One of his major controversies in office early on was a dispute with Idaho Attorney General Wayne Kidwell over whether to sue the state of Washington for seeding clouds which might otherwise drop moisture over Idaho. In his 1982 campaign for re-election, Evans faced a strong challenge from Republican Lieutenant Governor Philip Batt, a wealthy farmer, who campaigned as an opponent of farm workers' unions and a backer of right-to-work laws. Batt also criticized Evans for his support of budget cuts and a four-day work week for state employees. Evans, on the other hand, highlighted his opposition to right-to-work measures and publicly accepted union support. A folksy campaigner, Evans won, but with only 51 percent of the vote.

Evans was viewed as a popular governor who enjoyed the backing of organized labor. He faced problems in 1986, however, when upon the completion of his second four-year-term as governor, he chose to challenge Republican incumbent Steven D. Symms for the U.S. Senate. From the start, political observers realized that it would be a significant upset for a Republican to lose an Idaho Senate seat barring any major shifts of public opinion in the state. The conservative Symms, in office since 1980 and a congressman for eight years before that, benefitted from incumbency, as well as from having had good committee assignments while in the Senate—Budget, Finance, Environment, Public Works. Spending time and money to halt erosion in his political base, especially among Mormons and independent voters, he defeated Evans, 52 percent to 48 percent.

Evans completed his second term as governor on January 5, 1987, having held the office for 10 years, the second longest term of any governor in Idaho's history. A resident of Burley, Idaho, Evans is now the president of the D.L. Evans Bank, founded by his grandfather in 1904. He serves on the Burley Economic Development Commission, the Idaho Law Foundation, and the Idaho Nature Conservancy, as well as holding memberships in the Regional Board of Easter Seals and the Burley Rotary Club.

Bibliography: Biographical information courtesy of Governor Evans; Michael Barone *et al., The Almanac of American Politics, 1978, 1982, 1984* (New York and Washington, D.C., 1977–1983); *Idaho Blue Book, 1981–1982; The New York Times:* 11–1–86; 11–5–86. The file of John V. Evans is located at the Idaho Historical Society in Boise.

Cecil D. Andrus (Courtesy of governor's office)

ANDRUS, Cecil D., 1971–1977, 1987–

Born in Hood River, Oregon on August 25, 1931, the son of Hal S. Andrus and Dorothy Johnson Andrus; a Lutheran, Andrus married Carol M. May in 1949. The couple have three daughters: Tara, Tracy, and Kelly.

Andrus attended Oregon State University and served in the U.S. Navy during the Korean War. First elected to the Idaho State Senate at the age of 29, he served there with distinction from 1961 to 1966, and again from 1968 to 1970. As a legislator, he quickly established a reputation as a forceful advocate for education, the environment, and a growing economy.

After an unsuccessful race for the governorship in 1966, he came back to win that office for the Democrats in the elections of 1970 and 1974. As governor he championed the causes of improved funding for education, the creation of kindergartens, the establishment of child development centers, and the support of programs to assist the elderly. He twice led the effort to reduce property taxes and pushed the "circuit-breaker" property tax relief program for senior citizens. Andrus also spearheaded the drive to reorganize state government and was personally involved in the effort to bring new industry and jobs to Idaho. A member of the Executive Committee of the National Governors' Association from 1971 to 1972, he chaired the organization in 1976. From 1971 to 1972, he was also chairman of the Federation of Rocky Mountain States. He served as a delegate to the Democratic National Convention in 1972, 1976, and 1984.

On January 24, 1977, Andrus resigned from the governorship to become the first Idahoan ever to serve in a presidential cabinet. Named Secretary of the Interior by President Jimmy Carter, he strove for a sense of balance in the development and protection of the nation's resources. During his four-year tenure as Interior Secretary, his leadership was decisive in resolving the bitter Alaska lands dispute. That settlement protected 103 million acres of virgin public land for parks, wildlife habitat, and forest land, as well as opening up more than 250 million acres of federal land for development.

With the end of the Carter administration in January 1981, Andrus returned to Idaho to establish his own successful natural resources consulting firm. Remaining widely popular, he challenged Republican Lieutenant Governor David Leroy for the governorship in 1986. Characterizing himself as a problem solver and pledging to turn around the state's ailing economy, he won a narrow victory, garnering 50 percent of the vote to his opponent's 49 percent, a margin of just 3,500 votes. Andrus was able to carry heavily the northern panhandle of the state, hurt by layoffs in the mining and timber industries.

Inaugurated to his third term as governor on January 5, 1987, Andrus promised a progressive administration, telling the assembled crowds that "our gaze must be fixed firmly on the future; there is no looking back."

Decrying the Republican legislature's opposition to spending on education, he promised to spend much of the state's anticipated revenue windfall from federal tax reform on public education. Keeping the pledges he made frequently during his campaign, he has proposed a 10 percent increase in spending for higher education—welcome news in a state with stagnating timber, mining, and agricultural industries. In his view, the quality of a state's education system is its "most important development program."

Bibliography: Biographical information, courtesy of governor's office; Michael Barone *et al., The Almanac of American Politics 1988;* Jaques Cattell Press, *Who's Who in American Politics, 1985–1986* (New York, 1985); *The Chronicle of Higher Education:* 11–12–86; 2–18–87; *The New York Times,* 1–6–87.

James R. Thompson (Courtesy of governor's office)

ILLINOIS

THOMPSON, James R., 1977–

Born in Chicago, Illinois on May 8, 1936, the first child of James Robert Thompson, a Chicago pathologist, and Agnes Swanson Thompson of Dekalb, Illinois. A Presbyterian, he married Jayne Ann Carr of Oak Park, Illinois on June 19, 1976. Mrs. Thompson, an attorney, was formerly deputy chief of the Criminal Division, Illinois Attorney General's Office, and was employed by the Mid-America Committee of Chicago as executive vice-president and president of the committee's Foundation from November 1985 until December 1986. The couple have one daughter, Samantha Jayne.

After attending local grammar and secondary schools, Thompson enrolled in 1953 at the University of Illinois, Navy Pier, Chicago. Two years later he resided temporarily with his family in St. Louis and attended Washington University. Without receiving his undergraduate degree, Thompson entered Northwestern University Law School in 1956. He served as student editor-in-chief of the *Journal of Criminal Law, Criminology, and Police Science,* and received a law degree in 1959. After his admission to the Illinois bar, he served from 1959 to 1964 as assistant state's attorney for Cook County under Republican Benjamin Adamowski and, following the 1960 election, the Democrat Daniel Ward. Thompson argued more than 200 cases before the Illinois Supreme Court, and took the lead in prosecuting pornography cases (although he lost the Lenny Bruce case on appeal). In 1964 he presented the state's arguments before the United States Supreme Court in the case of *Escobedo v. Illinois.* By a five to four vote, the Court ruled in favor of Escobedo, thereby broadening the concept of the civil rights of suspects during police interrogations.

Thompson returned to Northwestern University as an assistant professor of Law later in 1964. He co-authored three criminal casebooks with his former mentor—Fred Inbau—and others, and was promoted to associate professor. While at Northwestern, Thompson in 1966 joined Inbau and former Chicago Police Superintendent O. W. Wilson in founding Americans for Effective Law Enforcement (AELE). Thompson served as vice president of this organiation, which has often acted as *amicus curiae* for police and prosecutors. He was a member of the committee that revised the Illinois criminal code from 1959 to 1963, and of the president's task force on crime in 1967.

Thompson left Northwestern in 1969 to accept a post under William J. Scott as assistant state attorney general for Illinois. The following year he was named chief of the Department of Law Enforcement and Public Protection, and soon thereafter he became Assistant United States Attorney for the Northern District of Illinois. In November 1971 Thompson was appointed United States Attorney, and during his almost four years in that office he earned a reputation as a prosecutor of corrupt public officials. Under his leadership, some 300 individuals were convicted of various charges of professional misconduct. The most spectacular of these convictions was that of Otto Kerner, a Federal Appeals Court judge convicted of accepting a bribe when he was governor of Illinois.

Thompson received the Republican nomination for governor in 1976, and easily defeated his Democratic opponent—Michael J. Howlett—by a vote of 3,000,395 to 1,610,258. His margin of victory was the largest in Illinois history. During his unique two-year first term, Thompson was instrumental in securing passage of a "Class X" crime law. This provided a mandatory six-year minimum sentence for those convicted of specified violent crimes.

In 1978 Illinois began holding gubernatorial elections in non-presidential years. Seeking re-election, Thompson defeated Michael Bakalis by a vote of 1,859,684 to 1,263,134. The nearly 600,000 vote margin was a record for an incumbent chief executive in Illinois. During his second term Thompson continued to balance the state budget, despite having no general tax increases with which to work.

In 1982 Thompson faced a fierce challenge from Democrat Adlai Stevenson 3rd in his bid for a third term. Stevenson, the scion of one of Illinois' leading political families, was a formidable opponent. His father had been the Democratic candidate for president in 1952 and 1956, and he himself had been elected to the U.S. Senate in 1970 to serve the unexpired term of Everett McKinley Dirksen. He was re-elected in 1974. Thompson's margin of victory—5,074 votes—was the smallest in state history (1,816.101 to 1,811,027). The outcome was not officially recognized until the Illinois Supreme Court ruled against Stevenson's request for a statewide recount. During the campaign, Thompson had presented himself as a "can-do" official, citing his popular $2.2 billion public works program and his role in persuading a Mitsubishi-Chrysler joint venture to build an automobile manufacturing plant in Bloomington.

In 1986 voters saw a rematch of Thompson's tough struggle with Stevenson. Political observers felt Thompson was vulnerable after 10 years in office, and the state's manufacturing base had been hit hard by imports. Stevenson was preparing to hammer away at Thompson for huge cost overruns on the State of Illinois Center in Chicago. He also accused him of "wheeling and dealing," and of failing to arrest the state's economic decline by buttressing dying industries rather than nurturing growth. Thompson was prepared to counter by discussing how he brought business and labor together to agree on tax reform, how he got striking Chicago teachers and the Board of Education together to reach a contract, how he froze spending, built new prisons, and set up an in-home care program for the elderly.

In the face of such planning, however, an upset in the March 1986 Democratic primary quickly altered the nature of the campaign and elevated it to one of historic dimensions. Stevenson's campaign stumbled badly when two followers of extremist Lyndon H. LaRouche, Jr., the conspiracy theorist, upset Stevenson's running mates for lieutenant governor and secretary of state. Rather than run with people whose philosophy he denounced, Stevenson refused the nomination of the Democratic party and collected nominating petitions to run instead as the head of a new party, Illinois Solidarity. Never before had anyone in Illinois history sought the fourth term Thompson was after, and never before had the Democratic party not had an official candidate for governor.

Stevenson tried to turn the campaign into a referendum on Thompson's three terms as governor. He hammered away at the incumbent over tax increases, soaring utility bills, the loss of one-quarter of the state's manufacturing jobs, and state contracts awarded to friends of the governor. Thompson attacked his challenger for spending more time criticizing him than with presenting his own vision of the state. Throughout the campaign, he often asked how Stevenson could be expected to run the state when he could not even run a winning primary campaign for his running mates. Thompson won his unprecedented fourth term by a margin of 399,220 votes. In the 1986 campaign, he was the first Republican ever endorsed for governor by the Illinois AFL-CIO. With his victory, Thompson became the nation's senior governor in continuous service.

Political observers see Thompson as the last big state governor in the liberal Republican tradition of Thomas E. Dewey and Nelson Rockefeller. Governing by accommodating the major interests in the state, he has managed to maintain effective working relations with many sectors of Illinois society and politics, including Democrats in state government who were hard hit by the criminal prosecutions he led in the early 1970s. His administration has been stamped by tough criminal justice measures, conservative fiscal policies, and substantial doses of social spending.

Goals of his fourth term include developing new uses for surplus agricultural products, major changes in state taxes, and welfare reform. He plans to continue to support increases in state spending for higher education. In a controversial 1987 decision, he vetoed a bill that would have ended teenagers' access to contraceptives at public school health clinics. The legislature had approved the contraceptive ban under intense lobbying from anti-abortion groups, the Roman Catholic Church, and the conservative Eagle Forum.

Thompson's unparalleled political achievements in Illinois have fueled much speculation about his future. In March 1987 he formally took himself out of the running for the 1988 Republican presidential nomination. In October 1987, after the failure of Robert H. Bork's nomination to the U.S. Supreme Court, Thompson's name surfaced as a possible running mate for George Bush in the 1988 presidential race, one who could potentially help Bush in areas where he was showing signs of weakness, such as the farm and rust belt. Others speculated that he would be named attorney general or Supreme Court justice in a Bush administration.

Bibliography: Biographical information, courtesy of governor's office; *The Chronicle of Higher Education,* 11–12–86; *USA Today,* 6–7–88; Michael Barone *et al., The Almanac of American Politics 1988* (New York and Washington, D.C., 1987); *The New York Times:* 8–20–85; 9–12–86; 9–19–86; 11–5–86; 1–11–87.

Robert D. Orr (Courtesy of governor's office)

INDIANA

ORR, Robert D., 1981–

Born in Ann Arbor, Michigan on November 17, 1917, of parents who were lifelong residents of Evansville, Indiana, Robert D. Orr is the son of Samuel Lowry, an industrialist, and Louise (Dunkerson) Orr. A Presbyterian, he is the brother of Samuel and Kendrick Orr. The Orr family has resided in Indiana since 1835 when Samuel Orr, a Scotch-Irish immigrant to the United States in 1833, moved to Evansville to establish a mercantile and iron manufacturing business in that Ohio River town. The Orr Iron Company in Evansville continued to be operated by the family until 1974, when it was acquired by the Shelby Steel Company.

Robert Orr grew up in Evansville, attending school there and at the Hotchkiss School in Connecticut, from which he was graduated in 1936. His education also included occasional trips abroad, one of which (in 1935) is delightfully described in James L. Clifford, *From Puzzles to Portraits: Problems of a Literary Biographer* (1970). In 1940 Orr received a B.A. in history from Yale University; he then attended the Harvard University Graduate School of Business Administration. Following America's entry into World War II, Orr enlisted in the United States Army, attending Officers Candidate School, and subsequently served on the quartermaster general's staff in the Pacific. He left the service in 1946 as a major and with a Legion of Merit decoration. In 1944 Orr married Joanne ("Josie") Wallace of Springfield, Massachusetts, who was also in the military during World War II as a Ferry Command pilot with the Women's Air Force Service Pilots. The Orrs have three children—a son, Robert D., and twin daughters, Susan and Robbin.

Following their military service, the Orrs took up residence in Evansville and joined in the management of the Orr Iron Company which, after 1948, was headed by Orr's older brother, Samuel. During the next few years Robert Orr became active in a number of other businesses in the Evansville community, specializing (with others) in the economic development of the region by buying vacant factories, refurbishing them if necessary, and then finding new owners and industrial uses for the plants. Orr was also chairman of the board of Indian Industries, a manufacturer of recreational products, and a member of the board of several other companies, incuding Hahn, Sign Crafters, Erie Investments, Sterling Brewers,

Evansville Metal Products, and Product Analysis and Research Industries, all of Evansville, and Dixson, Inc., of Grand Junction, Colorado. He played an important role in local civic affairs, serving as deacon and elder in the First Presbyterian Church of Evansville. Orr was also a member of the Rotary Club, active in the Evansville YMCA, a director of the Willard Library, vice president of Evansville's Future, Inc., and president of the Buffalo Trace Council of the Boy Scouts of America. Subsequently, Orr served as a director of the Indiana Manufacturers Association for eight years; he is a trustee of Hanover College. In 1953, when named the Jaycees' Young Man of the Year and given its Distinguished Service Award, he was an officer in 13 service organizations and a director of 12 companies.

Orr, a Republican, began his political career in a modest way, serving first as a member and then chairman of the Center Township Advisory Board in Vanderburgh County (1950–54), and then as Republican Precinct Committeeman from 1954 to 1962; from 1958 to 1960, he was treasurer of the Eighth District Republican Committee. In 1965 Orr was elected chairman of the Vanderburgh County Republican Central Committee, a position he held for six years. During this time he also launched a legislative career, winning election to the Indiana State Senate in 1968. Before his four-year term ended, however, he was named to the Republican state ticket in 1972 as Otis R. Bowen's running mate, and elected lieutenant governor of Indiana in 1972. Both Bowen and Orr were re-elected in 1976.

As lieutenant governor, Orr presided over the state senate and frequently had to cast tie-breaking votes, particularly when the state tax system was restructured in 1973. He also had primary responsibility, since Indiana's lieutenant governor also serves as Commissioner of Agriculture and Director of the Indiana Department of Commerce, for promoting state economic development and for fostering tourism programs. Orr participated regularly (not a traditional role for lieutenant governors) in Governor Bowen's staff meetings and policy discussions, and received high marks for his loyalty to the governor's programs. Endorsed by the popular Bowen to be his successor, Orr easily won the party's nomination in 1980. His campaign stressed the Bowen connection—"Let's Keep a Good Thing Going"—and resulted in a victory over Democratic candidate John Hillenbrand, II by the largest plurality in the history of the state.

Despite this auspicious beginning, Orr's first year as governor was marked by difficulties. Not only was the state in the midst of a recession, which turned what had been a comfortable surplus into a large deficit during 1982, but pent-up demands among various groups of state employees for improved wages and working conditions, unmet by Governor Bowen's property tax relief and budget austerity programs, boiled over. In addition, Orr's leadership style contrasted sharply with his predecessor's, whose departure from office was made even more poignant by the death of his wife shortly before the term ended. Moreover, his major recommendations to the Indiana General Assembly in 1981 against any tax increases (which also meant minimal increases for state workers and for public education) and for a jobs creation and general economic development program, while popular with the general public, irritated most of the 27,000 state employees and disappointed public school teachers. The generally poor economic conditions of the early 1980s, highlighted by unemployment rates which exceeded 20 percent in such automotive-related manufacturing centers as Anderson, Kokomo, and Muncie, and which reached 14 percent statewide, exacerbated the traditional needs of the state for improved mental health and correctional facilities, and for additional educational and highway maintenance and construction funding.

In 1982, following the fall general elections which resulted in continued Republican majorities in both houses of the legislature, Governor Orr confirmed Democratic charges that the projected state deficit for 1983 was in excess of $450 million. After he called the legislature into special session in December to deal with the problem, the state income tax was increased from 1.9 to three percent and the state sales tax from four to five percent. When the regular session of the legislature convened in January 1983, it appeared that the taxation issue had already been handled, but difficult new issues emerged, particularly utility reform legislation. The governor, in his 1983 state of the state message, had stressed the need for educational reforms, especially through additional instruction in mathematics, science, and the use of computers, and announced a "Decade of Excellence in Education" program. His second priority related to his long-standing interest in jobs creation and general economic development. Budget restrictions, however, meant that little could be done to deal with these problems in a decisive way.

The most explosive issue in 1983 concerned the huge increase in utility rates, particularly natural gas rates which had climbed 40 to 50 percent within the year. The utility reform bill which emerged in 1983, given Governor Orr's firm opposition to any "construction work in progress" (CWIP) expenses being passed along to consumers, contained no reference to CWIP. It did, however, expand the number of members on the state regulatory agency (the Public Service Commmission) and limited the size and frequency of allowable rate increases. As Governor Orr testified before the United States Senate Committee on Energy and Natural Resources in March 1983, the state had only limited ability to deal with the issue; Congress was the responsible body in this area, and he urged prompt action.

The Democrats had some hopes of unseating Orr in the election of 1984. Defeating challenger John K. Snyder to win the Republican nomination, he faced veteran state Senator W. Wayne Townsend in the general election. Only the second state governor constitutionally eligible to succeed himself since Indiana's 1851 Constitution was amended in 1972, Orr defeated his Democratic challenger by just over 100,000 votes out of about 2.1 million ballots cast, garnering 52 percent of the vote to his opponent's 47 percent. He ran at the bottom rather than at the top of the Republican ticket statewide. The campaign produced an interesting bit of political trivia: the first known MTV commercial for a statewide candidate was cut for Orr. The take showed the silver-haired governor walking through a roomful of youths, pointing toward the future.

Orr has made education and economic development the cornerstones of his administration. The governor's "Prime Time" program reducing class size in grades K through 3 has become a model for other states since its introduction in 1981. His "A + " Program, adopted by the 1987 general assembly, has brought accountability to public education by measuring results and rewarding performance in Indiana's public schools. The 1987 law encompasses the most comprehensive set of educational reforms ever adopted by an Indiana legislature. Emphasizing Indiana's need to compete in the world marketplace, Orr has proposed a tax increase to improve public education. Indiana's economy, once dominated by agriculture and heavy industry, has shifted in recent years and new jobs, Orr argues, demand better educated employees. His proposal includes dropping the state sales tax by ½ cent but extending it to professional and consumer services. The revenue generated—estimated at $350 million annually— would be earmarked for public education.

Orr has also encouraged foreign investment in the state. In 1988 Indiana bid for—and won—a new Isuzu/Subaru light truck and auto plant, a controversial issue due to the size of the financial incentive package put together by state officials to lure the operation to Indiana. Despite popular resentment over the plant-site bidding, Orr continued to maintain that the financial benefits of the deal outweighed the political risks.

Orr serves on the executive committee of the National Governors' Association and is a member of the National Governors' Association Committee on Transportation, Commerce and Communications, and the Committee on International Trade and Foreign Relations. He is also past president of the Council of State Governments. By appointment of President Reagan, he is a member of the Amtrak Board of Directors, representing all governors.

Despite his achievements, Orr has suffered by comparison with his predecessor, Otis Bowen, who is regarded as one of Indiana's most popular governors. Orr, who is now the nation's oldest governor, is constitutionally ineligible to run for re-election in 1988. He was succeeded as governor by Evan Bayh, son of former three-term Senator Birch Bayh. With his victory, the 32-year–old Bayh not only became the nation's youngest governor, but also ended the Republicans' 20-year hold on the state's top office.

Bibliography: Biographical information courtesy of governor's office; *Newsweek,* 5–30–88; *The Chronicle of Higher Education,* 2–18–87; Michael Barone *et al., The Almanac of American Politics, 1984–1988* (New York and Washington, D.C., 1983–1987); Jaques Cattell Press, *Who's Who in American Politics, 1985–1986* (New York, 1985); *The New York Times:* 5–7–84; 5–10–84; 11–8–84.

Terry E. Branstad (Courtesy of governor's office)

IOWA

Born in Leland, Iowa on November 17, 1946; the son of Edward Arnold Branstad and Rita Garland Branstad; a Roman Catholic, he married Christine Ann Johnson in 1972. The couple have three children: Eric, Allison, and Marcus.

Branstad received a B.A. in political science from the University of Iowa in 1969 and a J.D. from Drake University Law School in 1974. He served in the U.S. Army from 1969 to 1971, and was the recipient of an Army Commendation Medal.

Branstad first entered state Republican politics in 1968, serving as a delegate to district and state Republican conventions. He was first elected to the Iowa House of Representatives in 1972, winning re-election in 1974 and 1976. Winning the 1978 Republican nomination for lieutenant governor on the basis of his record in the legislature, he served as lieutenant governor during the last term of 14-year incumbent Robert Ray's administration, 1969–1983.

In 1982, he won the Republican gubernatorial nomination to succeed Ray. Political observers believe he won the election largely because of the personal problems of his opponent, Democrat Roxanne Conlin, who lost, in part, because she had legally avoided paying state income taxes one year. Despite Branstad's "ultra-conservative" positions on some issues— positions seen as out-of-step with those of his moderate predecessor Ray—Branstad won the election with 53 percent of the vote to Conlin's 47 percent.

Branstad won re-election in 1986, again thwarting the predictions of political observers. Most felt Branstad would suffer the consequences of a farm economy in dire straits: he himself owed more money on his family farm than its market value. Branstad, however, blamed the Reagan administration for state problems. Highlighting the fact that he had cut business taxes, he pushed for a moratorium on farm foreclosures and also advocated other programs to help farmers. In the campaign, he was also assisted by the unpopular proposals of his opponent, former state senate leader Lowell Junkins. Junkins proposed a plan to issue $400 million in bonds to stimulate new business and trade, to be paid back out of proceeds from a state lottery. Branstad launched a blistering attack on Junkins' programs, pointing out that lottery proceeds in other states had routinely dropped after the novelty of the venture had worn off. Obviously convinced by these arguments and uncertain that government could allocate money intelligently, voters gave Branstad 53 percent of the vote.

In office, Branstad has shown a knack for executive leadership and a degree of success with a Democratic legislature that few experts predicted. To deal with the farm crisis of his first term, he proposed budget cuts totalling $91 million, forcing the state government to do—in his words—what farmers and businessmen had already done, "pare back and adjust to the economic realities of today." He said the spending cuts would force layoffs but not raise taxes.

For his second term, Branstad promised big spending increases for teachers' salaries and education and more money for highways. He has proposed new programs to improve higher education and the economy at the same time. Seeking more than 10 million dollars in new funding to improve academic and research programs at the state's colleges, and one million dollars to start a work-study program for students, he has proposed that the state finance construction of a $25.1 million molecular biology building at Iowa State University.

Branstad has chaired the Midwestern Governors' Association as well as the Committee on Agriculture of the National Governors' Association. He has been a member of the NGA's Committee on International Trade, a member of its Executive Committee, and co-chairman of its Task Force on Jobs, Growth, and Competitiveness.

Bibliography: Biographical information courtesy of governor's office; Michael Barone *et al.*, *The Almanac of American Politics, 1984, 1986, 1988* (New York and Washington, D.C., 1983–1987); *The Chronicle of Higher Education:* 11–12–86; 2–18–87; *The New York Times:* 9–20–85; 9–4–86; Jaques Cattell Press, *Who's Who in American Politics, 1985–1986* (New York, 1985).

John W. Carlin (Courtesy of John Carlin)

KANSAS

CARLIN, John W. 1979–1987

Born on August 3, 1940 in Salina, Kansas, the son of John William and Hazel (Johnson) Carlin. A Lutheran, Carlin married Ramona Lenore Hawkinson in 1962. They had two children, David and Lisa, before divorcing. In 1981 Carlin married Karen Bigsby Hurley, a former member of his political staff.

A lifelong Kansan, Carlin attended high school in Lindsborg and was graduated from Kansas State University at Manhattan, where he earned a B.S. in dairy science, with honors, in 1962. While attending Kansas State, he was a member of Farm House fraternity, Phi Kappa Phi, and Blue Key.

After an unsuccessful campaign in 1968, Carlin was first elected to public office in 1970 as a Democratic member of the Kansas House of Representatives; he was re-elected in 1972, 1974, and 1976. He served as minority leader from 1975 to 1977, and as speaker of the house from 1977 to 1979, thereby becoming the first Democrat to serve in the latter position since 1912. In the house, Carlin served on the Agriculture and Livestock Committee, the Education Committee, the Ways and Means Committee, and the Commission on Higher Education. A member of the State Finance Council, he was also chairman of the Legislative Coordinating Council, the Legislative Budget Committee, and the Rural Development Committee of the National Conference of State Legislatures. Carlin was a delegate to the Democratic National Convention in 1976, and to the Democratic Mid-Term Convention in 1978.

In November 1978 Carlin was elected governor of Kansas at age 38, a victory considered an upset by most political observers. Due to the unpopularity of the incumbent Republican governor, Robert F. Bennett, there was a serious contest for the Democratic nomination, with Carlin defeating liberal Bert Chaney and former American Legion National Commander Harry Wiles to gain his party's nomination. The three men received 55 percent, 26 percent, and 18 percent of the vote, respectively. Although the Democrats hammered away at increases in spending during Bennett's term, the incumbent had managed that growth without tax increases, and political observers believed him to be a reasonably competent administrator. Carlin's victory surprised political pundits even more since Kansas is a traditionally Republican state. Nonetheless, in an election that hinged more on style than substance, Carlin's image proved more to the liking of Kansas voters. A dairy farmer and cattle sales manager from a rural county, he seemed to embody Kansas values more than the suburbanite Bennett, a lawyer from the affluent Kansas City suburbs. Carlin won by the narrow margin of only about 16,000 votes.

Once in office, Carlin immediately reneged on a campaign promise to sign a death penalty bill. Several technical reasons for rejecting the bill existed, but Carlin, in what he called "one of the toughest decisions he had to face," vetoed the bill as a matter of conscience. Rather than angering voters, however, some commentators thought his action aroused sympathy because it had demonstrated moral courage. Carlin went on to veto two other death penalty bills in the next three years.

Observers feel that Carlin grew in office after facing some early organizational problems. He achieved his greatest national attention when he came out against the binding rule sought by his fellow Carter supporters at the 1980 Democratic National Convention. One of the most controversial issues of his first term was his attempt to push a tax bill through the legislature that would take eight percent of the revenue on oil and gas produced in the state. Clyde Reed, editor of the *Parsons Sun,* called the episode "the political sensation of the decade—and longer—in Kansas." Once before, in 1957, such a severance tax was voted and promptly challenged by the courts because of a drafting error. As funds for local spending diminished, however, teachers and members of labor unions backing the severance tax were pitted against drillers and energy operating companies. Carlin supported the severance tax as a means to provide increased funding for government and proper financing for public schools, but opponents accused him of exploiting the issue for political gain. Said one critic, "He thinks that's the way to get ahead because everyone hates big oil."

In 1982 Carlin easily won the Democratic nomination for a second term, his only challenge coming from Jimmy D. Montgomery, a disc jockey. In the general election he defeated Republican Sam Hardage, a Wichita businessman, by gaining 54 percent of the vote to Hardage's 45 percent. He is the first governor of Kansas to be inaugurated to a second consecutive four-year term.

During his second term Carlin was forced to offer the Republican-controlled legislature a $51 million package of spending cuts, combined with steps to speed tax collections and others to delay aid payments to local governments. Other accomplishments included taxes on oil and gas production, more taxes on gasoline, liquor, and cigarettes, and cancellation of general assistance for 4,400 able-bodied state residents, one-third of the total enrolled. Political observers believe that the major achievements of his eight years in office were the imposition of a severance tax on oil, and the fact that he succeeded in making Kansans more export-conscious.

As governor, Carlin served as a member of the Executive Committee of the National Governors' Association, chairman of the NGA Committee on Agriculture, Chairman of the NGA Task Force on Agriculture Exports and the Subcommittee on the Environment, chairman of the Midwestern Governors' Conference, and chairman of the six-state High Plains Study Council.

Constitutionally ineligible to run for a third term, he left office upon the inauguration of his successor, Mike Hayden, in January 1987, and retired to his farming and business interests. He owns and maintains an interest in an 800-acre dairy farm near Smolan, Kansas, which was homesteaded by his family four generations ago. A member of the Kansas Holstein Association and the Holstein Association of America, he is especially interested in the farm's Holstein operation, which at one time was one of the most successful and productive herds in Kansas.

From January 1987 until May 1988, Carlin served as a visiting professor of Public Administration and International Trade at Wichita State University in Wichita, Kansas. Currently his business activities include serving as president of Economic Development Associates, an international economic development consulting firm headquartered in Topeka; vice president and partner in CMS Medical, Inc., Topeka; and partner in C & W Ranch, Inc., Smolan, Kansas.

Bibliography: Biographical information courtesy of Governor Carlin; *The New York Times:* 7–29–78; 2–22–81; 3–22–81; 6–1–81; 8–3–82; 3–5–83; Michael Barone et al., *The Almanac of Amerian Politics, 1982, 1984, 1988* (New York and Washington, D.C., 1981–1987); National Governors' Association, *Governors of the American States, Commonwealths, and Territories* (Washington, D.C., 1983).

Mike Hayden (Courtesy of governor's office)

HAYDEN, Mike, 1987–

Born on March 16, 1944 in Atwood, Kansas. A member of the United Methodist Church, he married Patti Rooney in 1968. They have two daughters, Chelsi and Anne.

Hayden attended Kansas State University, receiving a B.S. in wildlife conservation in 1966. He then entered the military, serving in the U.S. Army from 1967 to 1970, including 13 months in Vietnam where he was promoted from second to first lieutenant. For his actions as a platoon leader and company commander he was heavily decorated, awarded the Soldiers Medal, two Bronze Stars, and the Army Commendation Medal, among others.

Upon completion of his military service, he returned to Kansas and enrolled at Fort Hays State University, where he taught biology on a graduate assistantship and worked toward an M.S. in biology, which he received in 1974. Hayden explains that he entered politics because of environmental concerns. An ardent hunter and fisherman, he "soon figured out that the people who make the real decisions regarding the environment were politicians."

A Republican, Hayden served in the Kansas House of Representatives from 1972 to 1986, leading his colleagues as speaker from 1983 to 1986. As a legislator, Hayden was known as a tough negotiator.

The 1986 Kansas governor's race was wide open due to the constitutional ineligibility of retiring two-term incumbent John Carlin to seek re-election. Despite being far outspent, Hayden won a seven-candidate primary to gain his party's nomination, carrying most of the state's rural areas and small towns. He was weakest in urban areas, where he ran second to Larry Jones, a business leader.

The 1986 gubernatorial campaign was one of the year's tightest and most hotly contested races. It was also a contest that presented one of the sharpest contrasts between competing candidates.

Hayden faced Lieutenant Governor Thomas R. Docking, a Democrat from a famous Kansas political family. His father Robert had served as the state's governor from 1967 to 1975, as had his grandfather George from 1957 to 1961. Both earlier Dockings were popular, fiscally conservative governors whose well-known political slogan—maintaining budgets that were "austere but adequate"—was adopted by their political heir apparent. Docking criticized Hayden for urging an embargo on grain sales to South Africa, but was put on the defensive when Hayden called on him to sell his stocks in companies that do business there.

The election was a close one. Kansas, although predominantly Republican in registration figures, has had Democratic governors for nearly 20 of the last 30 years. Although his victory with 52 percent of the vote was not large, Hayden was able to win the governorship despite his party's nationwide association with the crisis on the farms.

One of Hayden's priorities for his governorship has been improving the quality of state higher education: he plans to create a statewide governing board for community colleges and technical schools, and to change the state financing formula so colleges won't lose state funds when enrollment fluctuates.

Bibliography: Biographical information courtesy of governor's office; Michael Barone *et al., The Almanac of American Politics 1988* (New York and Washington, D.C., 1987); *The Chronicle of Higher Education,* 11–12–86; *The New York Times,* 9–23–86.

John Young Brown, Jr. (Credit: Office of the Governor, Kentucky)

KENTUCKY

BROWN, John Young Jr., 1979–1983

Born in Lexington, Kentucky on December 28, 1933, the son of John Y. Sr., a noted Kentucky political figure and often-defeated candidate for the United States Senate, and Dorothy (Inman) Brown. A Baptist, Brown has three children by a previous marriage—John Y. III, Eleanor Farris, and Sandra Bennett. In 1979 he married Phyllis George of Denton, Texas, who was Miss America of 1971 and drew national attention as a national television commentator on professional football. Brown has one son, Lincoln Tyler, by his second marriage.

Brown received his B.A. from the University of Kentucky in 1957, and was graduated from the University of Kentucky Law School in 1960. He later became president of Kentucky Fried Chicken and together with the chain's founder, Colonel Harland Sanders, earned a fortune in one of the first and most successful fast-food businesses. In 1971 Brown became owner of Ollie's Trolley, Inc., of Louisville, Kentucky, a fast-food business that operated from mockups of trolleys. In 1972 and 1973 he first experienced politics as chairman of the Democratic Party's National Telethon. Brown was briefly a part-owner of the Boston Celtics professional basketball franchise in 1978, during a lackluster period in that illustrious team's history. He had previously owned the Buffalo Braves of the National Basketball Association.

In 1979 Brown entered Kentucky's gubernatorial race promising to run the state like a business and to root out political corruption. He defeated Harvey Sloane in the Democratic primary. Financing the campaign with the aid of his estimated $20 million fortune, Brown faced former Governor Louis B. Nunn in the general election. The campaign was personal and bitter. Brown attacked Nunn for enacting a two-cent sales tax measure while chief executive. Nunn retaliated by conducting "Operation Undercover," which attempted to link Brown to Las Vegas gambling, organized crime, and a former employee who had been convicted of smuggling marijuana. In the end, Brown carried most of the state, losing only in the heavily Republican southcentral region. The final vote was 558,088 for Brown and 381,278 for Nunn.

Brown's flamboyant lifestyle came into question soon after he took office. He was criticized for holding expensive parties, including one aboard a yacht moored off Manhattan during the 1980 Democratic National Convention. Shortly after Brown was inaugurated, the state lost a suit in the United States Supreme Court over the location of its boundary with Ohio. Later in his administration Brown sought unsuccessfully to revise Kentucky's constitution to permit consecutive gubernatorial terms. Although he admitted that he was not likely to be re-elected, two of his cabinet members underwrote a $150,000 bank loan to finance an advertising campaign. In 1982 Kentucky drastically revised its strip-mining law and enacted a provision limiting late, non-therapeutic abortions to hospitals. The latter piece of legislation was declared partly unconstitutional by a federal court.

A series of political troubles overtook Brown in his final year in office, problems that eroded his image as a reform politician and raised questions about his personal life. In Miami, a federal grand jury began looking into his withdrawals of large sums of cash from a Florida bank. Brown, who admitted the money was for gambling debts, was reported to have lost as much as $1 million in a single sitting in Las Vegas. He was further embarrassed when one of his closest friends and former business associates became the center of a federal investigation of illegal drugs and gambling. Finally, Brown found himself under mounting public pressure to explain his abrupt dismissal of Neil J. Welch, a former FBI special agent who was recruited by the governor in 1980 to shape up the state's law enforcement agencies. Welch was in the midst of a crackdown on state banking fraud when he was dismissed.

Brown's term in office expired in December 1983. In 1982, state voters had refused to change the constitution to allow him to run for a second consecutive term.

Despite his political problems, however, Brown's political career was far from over. In May 1983 he was the prime mover behind a national telethon for the Democratic National Committee. Raising more than $1.5 million dollars from Kentucky Democrats to guarantee the production costs of the program, he was honored as "Democrat of the Year" for his fundraising efforts. Although he had hinted that he was considering a dark horse bid for the 1984 Democratic presidential nomination, he chose instead to seek the Democratic nomination for the U.S. Senate, challenging Kentucky incumbent Walter D. Huddleston for the nomination. While Huddleston's campaign attacked Brown's freewheeling and flamboyant way of life, Brown countered that Huddleston was beholden to special-interest groups because of the campaign contributions he had received from several political action committees. Late in the primary campaign, however, Brown inexplicably withdrew his name from consideration, citing his need for further recuperation from heart surgery he had undergone eight months earlier. The former governor had never received much more than 40 percent support ratings from voters in pre-election polls.

In February 1987, Brown announced that he was again a candidate for the governorship. Saying he felt it was his "duty" to run, he promised a "war on education and jobs." Although Brown went into the June 1987 Democratic primary as the overwhelming favorite, he was defeated in a surprising upset by Wallace Wilkinson, a self-made millionaire who was making his first bid for public office. A total of five candidates vied for the nomination in a race called the "dirtiest campaign in memory." Brown, it seems, was hurt by the negative advertising of Lieutenant Governor Steve Beshear, a former attorney general, who sought to make Brown's image a liability. Using TV ads attacking Brown's lavish way of life and contending that Brown would raise taxes, Beshear suggested that Brown wanted to be governor only to restore his public visibility. Wilkinson, on the other hand, attacked both men for attacking each other, and charged both of them with wanting to raise taxes. Voters warmed to Wilkinson's low key, anti-establishment approach, and went on to select him as Kentucky's next governor in the general election.

Kentucky voters will remember Brown and his wife for having brought glitter to a state not accustomed to being considered glamorous.

Bibliography: The Courier-Journal (Louisville): 5–30–79; 11-7-79; *The Washington Post,* 4–3–81; *Newsweek,* 6–8–87; *The New York Times:* 4–29–83; 6–13–83; 6–26–83; 10–2–83; 10–9–83; 3–16–84; 3–18–84; 5–29–84; 5–30–84; 9–3–85; 2–21–87; 5–27–87; Michael Barone *et al., The Almanac of American Politics 1988* (New York and Washington, D.C., 1987).

Martha Layne Collins (Courtesy of governor's office)

COLLINS, Martha Layne, 1983–1987

Born in Bagdad, Kentucky on December 7, 1936; the daughter of Everett L. Hall and Mary Taylor Hall. In 1959 she married Bill Louis Collins, a dentist and banker. The couple have two children, Stephen and Marla.

Collins graduated from the University of Kentucky in 1959, where she won several beauty titles and was the first Kentucky Derby Queen. She worked for 12 years as a home economics and mathematics teacher before getting involved in politics at the grassroots level in 1971. She played a major role in Wendell Ford's 1971 gubernatorial campaign and in Walter Huddleston's first bid for the U.S. Senate. Her climb through the ranks took her from precinct committeewoman to the state's National Democratic committeewoman. Along the way, she served on the State Democratic Central Executive Committee and as Democratic Party Secretary.

In her first bid for elective office in 1975, Collins was elected clerk of the Court of Appeals, a post that has since been abolished. She guided the clerk's office efficiently through a time of the most far-reaching changes in the history of the state's judicial system.

In 1979 she was overwhelmingly elected the state's lieutenant governor, winning by a decisive margin of more than 200,000 votes. As lieutenant governor, Collins served as acting governor on numerous occasions, and was the first lieutenant governor in the state's history ever to serve in the governor's Executive Cabinet. She also served as president of the senate, where she won the respect of her senate colleagues for her firm and effective leadership. The nation's lieutenant governors recognized that leadership ability in 1982 when they unanimously elected her chairman of the National Conference of Lieutenant Governors, the first woman ever to serve in that post. In 1981 she had served as vice-chairman of the group.

Upon the completion of Governor John Y. Brown's term, Collins entered the May 24, 1983 Democratic primary race to succeed him. Her opponents included Louisville Mayor Harvey Sloane, a physician, whom Brown had defeated for the 1979 Democratic gubernatorial nomination, and Dr. Grady Stumbo, former head of the State Department of Human Resources, who benefitted from a last minute endorsement by Brown.

In the primary, Collins was accused by her rivals of being too "soft" to be governor, In response, she stressed a tough anti-crime program and highlighted her willingness to order executions under the state's death penalty law.

Without dominant issues or a clear leader, the race was extremely close. Collins managed a very close victory over Sloane, by a margin of less than 3,500 votes out of 650,000 cast. As a central Kentucky native, she benefitted from the strong support of thoroughbred horse breeding and racing interests.

Her opponent in the general election was State Senator Jim Bunning, a former Detroit Tigers and Philadelphia Phillies star player, one of four men to pitch no-hit games in both the National and American leagues. He had also worked as an investment banker with a Cincinnati concern. Returning to his native Kentucky after 17 years in major league baseball, he was elected to the state legislature in 1979, after serving as a city councilman in his hometown of Fort Thomas. Representing Campbell County in the state senate, he had pursued a philosophy of fiscal restraint, taking a hard line on spending and resisting efforts to raise taxes. He ran on a platform of fiscal austerity, limited government, and deregulation of business. Collins stressed her integrity and knowledge of the needs of different areas of the state, and also repeatedly emphasized that she was a native Kentuckian. As lieutenant governor, she had visited hundreds of thousands of state residents and toured all 120 of the state's counties. Although she was endorsed by feminists, Collins opposed abortion except in cases of rape or incest, and seldom voiced her support for the ERA publicly.

In the opinion of political observers, both candidates were criticized for being lackluster and vague on the issues of economic development and education reform. Neither had executive experience, in or out of government. Since Kentucky is an overwhelmingly Democratic state, there were few sharp differences between the candidates on issues. In televised debates, Bunning accused Collins of being a practitioner of patronage with little knowledge of government. One of the most important issues of the campaign was a much discussed state proposal to ban labor contracts that require union membership as a condition of continued employment. Bunning said he would not fight vigorously for the bill, but would sign it, while Collins equivocated. Saying it was a legislative issue, she chose not to commit herself.

The choice for Kentucky voters came down to the question: Did they want a woman or a Republican for chief executive? Collins won decisively, garnering 54.6 percent of the vote to Bunning's 44.2 percent. She made a strong showing throughout the state, including western and eastern regions where some analysts had thought voters would reject the candidacy of a woman.

With her victory, Collins became the state's first woman governor, the only woman to serve among the nation's current crop of governors, and only the third woman in the nation's history to be elected governor without succeeding her husband in that position. She also became the highest ranking elected woman in the Democratic party nationally. As such, she received nationwide attention, being named chairperson of the 1984 Democratic National Convention in San Francisco and receiving serious consideration by Democratic presidential candidate Walter Mondale for the vice presidential slot on the 1984 ticket.

Improving education was one of her major goals for Kentucky.

Among her chief accomplishments was legislation that made kindergarten mandatory and the establishment of an internship program for beginning teachers. She was also responsible for the passage of important new remedial programs, and for "an academic receivership act" which allowed the state to step in and assume control when a local school district failed to meet certain academic standards.

The Collins administration was also responsible for creating thousands of new jobs in the state. In December 1985 the Toyota Motor Corporation announced it would build an $800 million plant in Georgetown, near Lexington and Frankfort, that would eventually employ 3,000 people. Since the Toyota announcement, more than 87 foreign and domestic companies announced plans to locate in Kentucky, bringing with them investments of $600 million.

The Collins administration also scored historic successes in other areas: increasing funding for the state's flourishing arts community; establishing a business development program for Kentucky's growing crafts industry; setting up the Governor's Literary Commission, recognized as one of the nation's finest; and creating one of the nation's fastest growing athletic competitions, the Bluegrass State Games.

In 1986 Collins was selected chairperson of the National Governors' Association Task Force on Drug and Substance Abuse, and she launched an intensive statewide effort to stop drug abuse called "Champions Against Drugs."

Constitutionally limited to one term in office, she stepped down from the governorship in December 1987.

Bibliography: Biographical information, courtesy of governor's office; Michael Barone *et al., The Almanac of American Politics 1988* (New York and Washington, D.C., 1987); Jaques Cattell Press, *Who's Who in American Politics, 1985–1986* (New York, 1985); *The New York Times:* 5–23–83; 5–25–83; 5–26–83; 10–14–83; 11–6–83; 11–9–83; 11–10–83; 12–14–83; 5–20–84.

Wallace G. Wilkinson (Courtesy of governor's office)

WILKINSON, Wallace G., 1987–

Born in Liberty, Kentucky on December 12, 1941. A self-made millionaire, Wilkinson got his start in business with a second-hand bookstore in Lexington. The business grew, and he invested the profits, diversifying on a large scale. His real estate and business holdings came to include farms, coal mines, a flying service, and two banks.

In a remarkable rise from political obscurity, Wilkinson, making his first bid for public office, won the Democratic gubernatorial nomination in the May 26, 1987 primary. Waging a state-of-the-art media campaign in which he spent $6.3 million, he described himself as a "conservative Democrat" and placed an anti-establishment message at the heart of his campaign. His lack of a political history enabled him to run a campaign that cut across ideological boundaries. Speaking repeatedly against "politics as usual," he promised to bring as much economic success to Kentucky as he had to his own business career. Casting himself as the candidate of new ideas, he proposed the establishment of a state lottery in lieu of raising taxes. The proposal proved especially popular in parts of the state along the border of Ohio, which already had a lottery of its own.

In a surprising upset, Wilkinson soundly defeated four other major candidates for the Democratic nomination: former Governor Julian Carroll; Dr. Grady Stumbo, a member of Governor John Brown's Cabinet who, as a coal miner's son, built his campaign around a folksy, "down home" image; Lieutenant Governor and former Attorney General Steven Beshear and former Governor John Y. Brown. For much of the campaign, the race was a contest between Beshear and Brown who attacked each other unsparingly. The campaign also transformed the state into a lucrative showcase for media consultants. Beshear sought to tarnish Brown's image, using TV ads to attack Brown's extravagant lifestyle and to suggest that he planned to raise taxes. He also hinted that Brown wanted to be governor only to return to the public spotlight. For most of the campaign, the major issue was Brown, and whether he had the drive and motivation to serve a second term: he had dropped from public view after he left office in 1983. Wilkinson painted Brown as part of the history of mediocrity in Kentucky, that had it leading the nation in unemployment and trailing in educational achievement. He assailed both Brown and Beshear for their dirty tactics, and accused both of them of wanting to raise taxes.

Brown was the frontrunner for much of the campaign, while Beshear had the support of key Democratic groups, including most of the state's union leaders and the state teachers association. Wilkinson's victory was all the more striking since he had registered only 5 percent in public opinion polls conducted early in the race. Relying on a TV and media blitz, he promised to change the way politics was conducted in Kentucky.

What was also noteworthy about his victory was that he seemed to have picked up most of his support in the final week of the campaign. Voters, in the opinion of political observers, had grown weary of the negative campaign waged by Wilkinson's opponents, and placed little credence in their charge that he was unknown and untested. Their negativism opened the way for his surprising win, with 35 percent of the primary vote. Brown, by contrast, drew only 25 percent. Remaining totals were: Beshear, 18 percent; Stumbo, 14 percent; Carroll, seven percent. Three minor candidates shared the remaining one percent.

According to political observers, the returns indicated that the power of local politicians to deliver votes was at an all-time low. This proved a further vindication of Wilkinson, who had run against the courthouse crowd.

From the time of his dramatic victory in the primary, Wilkinson remained far ahead in public opinion polls, and until the final weekend of the campaign regularly urged audiences to give him the biggest margin of victory in state history. His Republican opponent was John Harper, a respected state legislator from a heavily Democratic district near Louisville who was bidding to become the first Republican elected governor in 20 years. The Republicans' chances of victory were sharply reduced when Larry Forgy, a politically active lawyer who was thought to be the strongest potential nominee, dropped out of the race at the beginning of 1987. Harper entered the Republican primary only after his withdrawal. To his credit, he had experience as a candidate able to come from behind in tough races, winning his first election in 1984 in a district where Democrats outnumbered Republicans 9–1. His campaign, however, was poorly financed from the start. He was able to raise less than $250,000 compared with the $4 million Wilkinson had amassed since the primary. Harper called the size of the Democratic warchest "obscene," and ridiculed Wilkinson's lottery proposal. He claimed his opponent was planning to eliminate the right of counties to remain dry, and to start a chain of state liquor stores—a charge Wilkinson hotly denied. While Wilkinson vehemently ruled out a tax hike, Harper admitted he could not be so optimistic, a reversal of the usual Democratic and Republican positions on this issue. Although neither candidate had much experience in education policymaking, Wilkinson promised to make education a priority in his administration.

Wilkinson won the election resoundingly with 65 percent of the vote, giving him the highest victory margin ever recorded in a gubernatorial race in state history. He was inaugurated on December 8, 1987.

Bibliography: Michael Barone *et al.*, *The Almanac of American Politics 1988* (New York and Washington, D.C., 1987); *The Chronicle of Higher Education:* 9–23–87; 11–11–87; *Newsweek*, 6–8–87; *The New York Times:* 5–26–87; 5–27–87, 11–1–87; 11–3–87; 11–4–87.

David C. Treen (Credit: Executive Department, Louisiana)

LOUISIANA

TREEN, David C., 1980–1984

Born on July 16, 1928 in Baton Rouge, Louisiana, the son of Joseph Paul and Elizabeth (Speir) Treen. A Methodist, Treen married the former Dolores ("Dodie") Brisbi of Metairie, Louisiana in May 1951. They have three children—Jennifer Treen Neville, David Conner Treen, Jr., and Cynthia Treen Lunceford.

Educated in the public schools of East Baton Rouge, Jefferson, and Orleans parishes, Treen was graduated from Fortier High School in New Orleans in 1945. He majored in history and political science at Tulane University, where he was president of his freshman class and a member of the Honor Board; he received a B.A. in 1948. In 1950 Treen was graduated with honors from Tulane University Law School. There he was a member of ODK (a national leadership fraternity), Phi Delta (a legal fraternity), and the Order of the Coif (a legal scholastic fraternity). He was also the winner of a Junior-Senior Moot Court competition. After a short stint from 1950 to 1951 as an associate attorney with the New Orleans firm of Deutsch, Kerrigan, and Stiles, Treen served two years of active duty as a first lieutenant with the United States Air Force. Stationed in Wichita Falls, Texas, and London, England, he also acted as a defense counsel and a prosecuting counsel while in the Air Force. Treen then resumed his legal career as vice president and legal counsel of the Simplex Manufacturing Corporation in New Orleans from 1952 to 1957. He was also an associate attorney with Beard, Blue, and Schmitt, and subsequently a partner in the firm of Beard, Blue, Schmitt, and Treen from 1957 to 1972.

Chairman of the Republican Executive Committee of Jefferson Parish between 1963 and 1967, Treen made unsuccessful runs for the United States Congress in 1962, 1964, and 1968, each time against the long-time incumbent Democrat Hale Boggs. His percentage of the popular vote increased each time, from 32 percent to 44 percent to 49 percent respectively, as Boggs' support of civil rights legislation weakened his popularity among Louisiana voters. Treen also made an unsuccessful gubernatorial race in 1972, losing to Democrat Edwin Edwards, who polled 57 percent of the vote to Treen's 43 percent. Although Treen did well in Jefferson Parish and in the predominantly Protestant northern part of the state, Edwards won large enough majorities in so-called "Cajun country" and among the state's black voters to secure his election. Treen, however, was elected to the United States Congress later that same year, defeating J. Louis Watkins by polling 54 percent of the vote. The first Republican elected to Congress from Louisiana in the twentieth century, Treen drew his greatest support from Metairie, the high-income suburb in Jefferson parish just west of New Orleans. He was re-elected to subsequent terms in 1974, 1976, and 1978, defeating Charles Brisbaum in 1974 with 59 percent of the vote and David Scheuerman in 1976 with 73 percent of the vote. He ran unopposed in 1978.

In congress, Treen was chairman of the Republican Study Committee and a member of the Executive Committee of the Republican Congressional Campaign Committee. He was also a member of the House Select Committee on Intelligence, the Ad Hoc Select Committee on the Outer Continental Shelf, the Merchant Marine and Fisheries Committee, and the Armed Services Committee. He served on subcommittees on military personnel, investigations, the coast guard and navigation, the merchant marine, and oceanography. Treen had a conservative voting record in congress.

Political observers knew that Treen had long had his eyes on the Louisiana governorship. In 1979 he led a field of nine candidates (all Democrats except himself) in the open primary held to determine a successor to the popular outgoing Governor Edwin Edwards, who was constitutionally ineligible to seek a third term. The hotly contested, $20 million race attracted the largest voter turnout in Louisiana's history, and was considered by experts to be the most expensive non-presidential campaign in American history. Treen led all candidates with 22 percent of the vote. His rivals (all Democrats) were Public Service Commissioner Louis Lambert (21 percent), Lieutenant Governor James E. Fitzmorris (20 percent), Secretary of State Paul Hardy (17 percent), House Speaker E. L. ("Bubba") Henry (10 percent), and State Senator Edgar G. Mouton, Jr. (nine percent). Three others shared one percent of the vote. According to Louisiana's election law, the two top vote-getters in the primary, regardless of their party affiliation, were eligible to face each other in the general election. Here Treen was helped by in-fighting among his Democratic opponents. Observers had predicted that Lieutenant Governor Fitzmorris would face Treen in the general election, but when Lambert pulled ahead by a few thousand votes, Fitzmorris charged voter fraud and election irregularities. The integrity of the free-spending Lambert was attacked by members of his own party. As a candidate he had little potential for unifying state Democrats, and most of the other Democrats originally in the race, even those with decidedly liberal reputations, endorsed Treen in the general election.

In the runoff between Treen and Lambert, the vote divided sharply along racial and economic lines. Lambert, who tried to portray his opponent as the candidate of the "silk-stockinged" and privileged, presented himself as a modern-day Harry Truman, and drew strength from a state-wide Democratic coalition of blacks, rural populists, and organized labor. Treen, on the other hand, ran as a conservative, pledging to veto any effort to repeal Louisiana's "right to work" law, which outlaws the union shop. Others were wary of Treen because of his membership during the early 1960s in the Louisiana States' Rights Party, which included some avowed segregationists in its ranks. Nonetheless, Treen's reputation for honesty and integrity appealed to many voters. He promised to give the state a politically independent "elections integrity commission" and proposed campaign spending laws. His decision to disclose his own personal finances had few precedents in the state.

Despite President Jimmy Carter's last-minute support of Lambert, the election was a cliffhanger. Treen won by a margin of only 9,871 votes out of the nearly 1.4 million votes cast. He drew his greatest support in the affluent white suburban parishes and in the other sizable towns of the state. Treen's election in a state where Democrats outnumber Republicans 18–1 drew national attention, and seemed to be a harbinger of growing Republican strength in the once solidly Democratic South. With his victory, Treen became the first Republican chief executive of Louisiana in the twentieth century. (Louisiana's last Republican governor had been William Pitt Kellogg, a carpetbagger from Vermont, who held office from 1873 to 1877.)

Once in power, Treen announced that the way had been cleared for an out-of-court settlement of a seven-year-old federal integration lawsuit against Louisiana's 17 public colleges and universities. He also supported a historic reapportionment plan that created, for the first time in state history, a congressional district with a majority of black residents. A backer of the Reagan administration, he signed a bill that required students in public schools to be taught both Biblical and scientific explanations of human evolution; approved legislation that gave Louisiana $35 million to fight the erosion of almost 50 square miles of its coast each year; and began the search for a solution to the state's environmental ills. He served as chairman of the National Governors' Association Subcommittee on Oil and Gas, and was also chairman of the Interstate Oil Compact Commission.

Treen was seen as the leader of a "good government" movement that had been growing up in white middle class suburbs, and was conceded to have been a competent, honest governor. Yet he was never viewed as an especially effective administrator, and his administration had a decidedly lackluster cast. The image hurt him badly when he ran for re-election in 1983, when his opponent was the flashy and flamboyant former Governor Edwin Edwards, who was seeking an unprecedented third term. The victim of the national recession and the state's declining oil and gas revenues, Treen courted blacks and other minorities with promises of economic advancement through free enterprise and better education. He also promised an honest administration—a direct reference to Edwards' questionable financial and business dealings while governor. Yet Treen himself acknowledged that he seemed dull in comparison to Edwards, a severe liability in Louisiana where voters appreciate personal style as much as political substance. In a race tagged as the most expensive in state history, Treen lost to Edwards by a margin of 62 percent to 36 percent, failing to carry even those parts of the state usually considered to be Republican strongholds.

With his defeat, Treen retired to his private law practice. In July 1987, President Reagan nominated him to a post on the U.S. Court of Appeals for the Fifth Circuit.

Bibliography: Michael Barone *et al., The Almanac of American Politics, 1978, 1982, 1986* (New York and Washington, D.C., 1977–1985); *The New York Times:* 10–29–79; 11–1–79; 12–8–79; 12–10–79; 10–10–80; 4–18–81; 7–22–81; 8–22–81; 8–26–81; 11–22–81; 11–27–81; 4–18–82; 8–10–82; 11–28–82; 3–1–83; 8–6–83; 9–25–83; 10–23–83; 10–24–83; 12–15–83; 3–10–85; 7–23–87.

Edwin Washington Edwards (Courtesy of governor's office)

EDWARDS, Edwin Washington, 1972–1980, 1984–1988

Born in Marksville, Louisiana on August 7, 1927, the son of Clarence W. and Agnes (Brouillette) Edwards, who were French-speaking sharecroppers. A Roman Catholic, Edwards married Elaine Schwartzenburg on April 5, 1979. He is the father of Anna Edwards Hensgens, Victoria Elaine, Stephen Randolph, and David Edwin.

After serving in the Naval Air Corps during World War II, Edwards received an LL.B. from Louisiana State University School of Law in 1949. In private practice with a Crowley, Louisiana law firm from 1949 to 1964, he first entered public service when he was elected as a Democrat to the Crowley City Council in 1954. He was re-elected to a second term in 1958. Edwards first captured statewide attention when he ran for the state senate in 1963. Surprising the experts, he defeated the president *pro tem* of the senate, an incumbent of 20 years. As a floor leader in the senate, Edwards played an active part in the passage of key legislation. Following the death of Seventh District Congressman T.A. Thompson in an auto accident in 1965, Edwards defeated four other candidates to win election to the United States House of Representatives. He remained in Congress for almost seven years, winning re-election in 1966, 1968, and 1970. Edwards served on the Public Works, Judiciary, and Internal Security committees. The Democratic Whip for the Louisiana and Mississippi delegations for four years, he played a key role in increasing United States exports of Louisiana farm products. He was also considered by experts to have a rather liberal voting record for a congressman from the Deep South.

Edwards bested 17 other candiates to win the Democratic nomination for governor in 1971, and narrowly defeated State Senator J. Bennett Johnston of Shreveport in the primary runoff by a vote of 584,262 to 579,774. In February 1972 he defeated Republican David Treen in the general election, gaining 57 percent of the vote to Treen's 43 percent. As a French-speaking Cajun, Edwards won by an especially wide margin in the "Cajun country" along the Gulf of Mexico, outside New Orleans in the bayou country south of Alexandria, and west of the Mississippi River. He also gained a majority of the black vote.

Inaugurated on May 9, 1972, Edwards became Louisiana's first French-speaking chief executive in more than a century, and one of the state's few public officials to have served at the city, state, and national levels. He was fortunate to inherit a state that had put racial issues behind it, a state ready to reap the benefits of economic prosperity as the price of oil rose. In 1973 Edwards called a special "energy crisis session" of the Louisiana Legislature, which doubled the severance tax on natural gas and changed the levy on oil from a volume to a value basis, thus adding $169 million a year to the treasury. He also received a measure of national attention as a spokesman for the oil industry. Graced with a special ability to dominate the legislature, Edwards was considered to be a highly successful administrator in his first term and had little trouble winning re-election in 1975. That election was the first to be conducted under a new open primary law which the governor himself had engineered. The new system required candidates from all parties to enter an October primary. If any candidate polled 50 percent of all votes cast for the office, that candidate was elected; if not, the top two candidates faced each other in a runoff election. Thus, Edwards faced five primary opponents in 1975, all Democrats—Robert G. Jones, Wade O. Martin, Jr., Ken Lewis, A. Roswell Thompson, and Cecil M. Pizzi. He gained 62 percent of the vote to Jones' 24 percent and Martin's 12 percent. The other candidates split the remaining two percent.

Edwards eventually came to dominate state politics as had no governor since the legendary Huey Long. Major achievements of his administration included the calling of a state constitutional convention and an addition to the natural gas tax to finance health, education, and prison improvement. His tenure was also marked by the creation of a plan to simplify state aid to local governments, the establishment of tough policies to fight crime and to aid law enforcement, and the construction of an intrastate highway connecting north and south Lousiana. Edwards represented the state on numerous multi-state commissions and committees. Chairman of the Interstate Oil Compact Commission and state co-chairman of the Ozarks Regional Commission, he was host governor for the 1975 National Governors' Conference held in New Orleans. A member of the Energy Committee of the Southern Governors' Conference, Edwards also served on the Committee on Natural Resources and Environmental Management of the National Governors' Conference. He was a member of the National Governors' Conference Task Force on Foreign Trade and Tourism, and has served on the NGC's Rural and Urban Development Committee.

One of the most colorful governors Louisiana has ever had, Edwards won widespread popularity because of his ability to appeal to and to work well with various social groups. His popularity stood him in good stead when charges of scandal surfaced in 1976, charges that as a member of Congress he had received gifts from Korean government agent Tongsun Park. Later, in 1980, he was one of 13 Louisiana public officials subpoenaed to appear before a federal grand jury investigating allegations of bribery in connection with a major federal undercover investigation in the Southwest. Despite such problems, however, political observers consider Edwards to have been one of the most popular and strongest chief executives in state history, and during his years in office he received national attention as a spokesman for the New South. He nominated Jerry Brown for president at the 1976 Democratic Convention, and there were even rumors that he might be offered the vice presidential nomination that year.

Political observers predicted that he would easily have won a third term had he been constitutionally eligible to run again in 1979. Barred from serving a third consecutive term, he went back to his private law practice until he could run again in 1983, when he won overwhelmingly. He proved his appeal by overwhelming the incumbent Republican Governor David C. Treen by a margin of 62 percent to 36 percent in the October election, thereby becoming the state's first chief executive to be elected to three terms.

The historic campaign was the most expensive in state history, with Edwards outspending Treen by more than a 2–1 margin. Treen, while a competent and honest executive, seemed dull in comparison to the flamboyant Edwards, and himself acknowledged that this was a liability in Louisiana, which has a long tradition of embracing colorful and charismatic leaders. While Treen based his campaign on character issues, promising an honest administration, Edwards offered effective leadership. Frank about his image problems, he pledged to take steps to see that his actions in office did not carry even the appearance of impropriety. He also said he would seek to increase the state income tax, and would ask the legislature to approve $200 million in raises for teachers, school personnel, and state employees. He pledged to appoint a representative number of women, blacks, Hispanics, and the disabled to state government posts.

Although Edwards had long been considered one of the ablest administrators in state history, his third term was beset by problems. Louisiana's economy continued to suffer from oil industry problems, and Edwards strained to overcome the revenue drain caused by the oil glut and the slumping production of oil and natural gas. With a moribund economy and a deficit riddled treasury, the state led the nation in many negative indicators, including unemployment (which rose to a high of 14 percent) and the high school dropout rate (48 percent). Edwards found himself faced with one of the lowest job approval ratings of any incumbent in the nation.

He also continued to be dogged by accusations of scandal and wrongdoing. In March 1985 he was indicted by a federal grand jury on charges of conspiracy and racketeering, alleging that he and associates plotted to use his influence to acquire and sell hospital building certificates that netted them $10 million. His first trial in December 1985 ended in a mistrial; his second, in May 1986, in an acquittal.

Controversy continued to follow him, however. He was also the subject of a federal probe concerning his involvement with Texaco, and the sale of state land in northeastern Louisiana to campaign contributors. In October 1986 he testified before a grand jury investigating allegations that state pardons were being sold. His appearance brought to 11 the number of grand juries that had looked into his activities since 1975.

His third term also saw some successes, however. He was credited with rescuing the financially plagued 1984 New Orleans World's Fair by providing $18 million in loans and guarantees, and with helping the Saints football team stay in New Orleans. A survey by the National Women's Political Caucus found that his administration led the nation in the number of female appointments to cabinet-level positions.

Although Edwards had been considered the favorite to succeed retiring Senator Russell Long on Capitol Hill, he chose instead to seek re-election for an unprecedented fourth term in 1987. Counting on the coalition that had always supported him—the Cajun vote in his home base, blacks, and labor—he denounced his opponents as enemies of the weak, needy, elderly, and black. At the center of his campaign were proposals for a state lottery and a casino in New Orleans to buttress state revenues. Casino gambling, he predicted, would cure the state's economic ills, generate 50,000 new jobs and $325 million in public revenue, as well as make New Orleans a resort center. Nonetheless, the proposals drew sharp criticism, denounced by one challenger in colorful, emotional language: "I don't want my children to grow up to be pit bosses and call girls in a casino."

Edwards' opponents in the state's unusual open primary were: Congressman Billy Tauzin, a Democrat serving his fourth term; Republican Bob Livingston, a congressman and former prosecutor; Secretary of State James H. Brown, who waged a campaign as a reformer, and Congressman "Buddy" Roemer, a conservative Democrat from northern Louisiana. The theme of all challengers was that the flamboyant Edwards was not the governor to lead the state through difficult economic times.

Under the state's unique system, candidates of all parties run together in the primary. If no one wins a majority, a runoff is held between the top two vote getters, regardless of party.

The October 24 primary was seen as an historic turning point in state politics. Edwards' second place finish to Roemer (28.5 percent to 31 percent) marked the first time he had ever lost an election. Roemer, who had the support of most of the state's leading newspapers, had run TV ads denouncing the Edwards' administration as a "sinkhole of dirty corrupt politics." He ran as a "revolutionary" who promised "A Revolution for Louisiana," and as a reformer who disdained contributions from political action committees and who disclosed the names of all financial supporters. According to political analysts, voters knew little about Roemer himself, but were "swept up in a sea of change and voted for the candidate they perceived as being the greatest change from the political system." Bumper stickers appearing throughout the state attested to the prevalence of such sentiments. Frankly and candidly, voters declared themselves for "ABE"—Anybody But Edwards. The fact that Roemer carried a substantial number of parishes in Edwards' home base of southern Louisiana indicated that sentiment for change was pervasive. With practically no public officials supporting him, Roemer won with a coalition of college-educated, affluent, under-55 voters tied into his congressional base in northern Louisiana.

In the opinion of political analysts, Edwards had lost his long-time constituency; the state's economic troubles had most affected his traditional supporters—minorities and blue-collar workers. Although blacks continued to vote largely for Edwards, their low turnout seemed to indicate disillusionment about the possibility of change in the system. Poll-takers noted that Edwards' statewide support began to erode even before his much publicized trials. The 1984 tax increases mandated by the state's economic malaise cost him the votes of the white middle class. Political writer John Maginnis called Edwards a "sort of a good-times governor," whose administration could not survive hard times.

Even more surprising than Edwards' second-place finish was his reaction to his showing. Although a runoff between Edwards and Roemer, as the primary's two top finishers, was scheduled for November 21, 1987, Edwards astounded friends and enemies alike with his post-primary concession to Roemer. After two other major candidates had indicated they would back Roemer in the runoff, Edwards chose not to continue with the contest.

His concession brought Buddy Roemer to the governorship, and marked the start of a new era of Louisiana politics. Elected without any of the traditional courthouse gang, black or white, Roemer came into office with both a clean slate and a mandate for change. After Roemer's inauguration on March 14, 1988, Edwards retired to his private law practice, a symbol of an old South that once accepted and relished the roguish behavior of its political leaders.

Bibliography: Anita Schrodt, "Three Days in the Life of that 'Cajun Fella,'" *Biography News* 1 (April 1974): 398–99; Biographical information courtesy of governor's office; *The New York Times:* 5–16–79; 2–11–80; 2–14–80; 2–15–80; 2–17–80; 11–2–80; 10–23–83; 10–24–83; 11–7–83; 11–13–83; 3–3–85; 3–10–85; 9–15–85; 12–19–85; 3–23–86; 10–14–86; 10–17–86; 2–28–87; 3–31–87; 6–27–87; 10–22–87; 10–26–87; *Newsweek:* 3–11–85; 11–25–85; 10–26–87; *The Chronicle of Higher Education,* 9–23–87.

Charles "Buddy" Roemer (Courtesy of governor's office)

ROEMER, Charles "Buddy," 1988–

Born in Shreveport, Louisiana on October 4, 1943; the son of Charles Elson II and Adeline McDade Roemer Elson. In 1974 he married the former Patti Crocker. The couple have three children, Caroline, Charles, and Dakota.

Roemer graduated from Harvard University with an A.B. in 1964 and an M.B.A. in 1967. A former member of the Urban League's Board of Directors, he was a delegate to the Louisiana Constitutional Convention of 1972. From 1981 to 1988, he was a U.S. Representative from Louisiana's First District, a member of the Banking, Finance, Urban Affairs, and Small Business Committees.

Roemer entered a crowded field in the 1987 Louisiana governor's race, seeking to block incumbent Edwin Edwards' quest for an unprecedented fourth term. The flashy and flamboyant Edwards had been a popular governor and effective administrator during his years in office, but had fallen on hard times recently due to his own personal legal troubles and the state's plummeting economic fortunes. Louisiana had been hurt badly by the decline in oil revenues and falling prices for oil and natural gas upon which its economy depends. Seen as vulnerable, Edwards was challenged by four major candidates: Secretary of State Jim Brown; Representative W.J. (Billy) Tauzin; Congressman Bob Livingston; and Roemer. Under its unique open primary system, Louisiana chooses its state officials in an unusual manner at an unusual time. Every candidate, regardless of party, runs in a single primary in October. If someone gets 50 percent of the primary vote, he is automatically the winner of the governorship; if not, a runoff is held between the two top vote getters.

As the October 24, 1987 primary approached, Roemer was given little chance of victory. He had placed last in the polls all summer. Other candidates, including Republican Bob Livingston, seemed far more promising contenders. But in the final two weeks of the race, Roemer launched an aggressive TV ad campaign and vaulted past everyone to win. A Democrat with appeal to conservatives, he cast himself as the champion of those who wanted to take on the state's entrenched political power structure. Denouncing the Edwards administration as corrupt, he ran as a reform candidate who disdained contributions from political action committees and disclosed all financial sources. Roemer's slogan "A Revolution for Louisiana" obviously attracted large numbers of voters who were convinced the state needed a change. Although Edwards denounced his opponents as enemies of the weak, needy, elderly, and black, most of the state's leading newspapers endorsed Roemer. The fact that Roemer carried a substantial number of parishes in southern Louisiana—Edwards' home base—indicated that the sentiment for change was pervasive. According to political analysts, although voters outside Roemer's home district knew little about him, they were "swept up in sea of change and voted for the candidate they perceived as being the greatest change for the political system." The election also changed enough seats to turn the state senate in a more conservative direction.

Roemer polled 33.1 percent of the vote to Edwards' 28.1 percent. Other results were: Livingston, 18.5 percent; Tauzin, 9.9 percent; Brown, 8.8 percent. Minor candidates shared the remaining 1.6 percent of all votes cast.

Roemer won by drawing on a coalition of college-educated, affluent, under-55 voters, tied into his congressional district base in northern Louisiana. His victory was an historic one, winning as he did without any of the traditional courthouse gang, black or white. Practically no public officials supported him, and he made no deals with other candidates to pull out the victory over Edwards.

What was even more surprising about Roemer's primary victory was the dramatic fashion in which he came into the governor's office. According to Edward Renwick, the director of the Institute of Politics at Loyola University, the campaign was the "most unusual" in the state's recent history. Although Roemer and Edwards, as the primary's two top finishers, were scheduled to compete in a runoff election on November 21, 1987, Edwards astounded friends and enemies alike when he conceded the race to Roemer a few days after the primary bid. When two other major candidates endorsed Roemer, Edwards withdrew from the race rather than face a humiliating result in the runoff.

Roemer's victory was seen as a turning point in state politics. Dr. Joseph Logsdon, a historian at the University of New Orleans, compared Roemer to Huey Long, the populist from northern Louisiana, whose slogan, "Every man a king," swept him into the governorship in 1928. Long, like Roemer, won with just a plurality, and his opponent pulled out, just like Edwards. According to Logsdon, Long and Roemer were similar kinds of candidates. Long, too, was youthful, used the local media well, and was a master of radio. Like him, Roemer's pithy slogans calling for a Louisiana "revolution" played well on television.

With more than four months between his victory in the primary and his inauguration, Roemer sought a role in solving the state's budget crisis. In an unprecedented move, he tried to get some control over state policy and spending in this waiting period. He felt he had no choice: if cuts were not made immediately, they would have to be much larger after his March inauguration. In an unusual move, he asked departing Governor Edwards to appoint either him or one of his associates as a commissioner of the administration, with responsibility for the day-to-day operations of government. The move was necessary, Roemer insisted, because Edwards had not moved to avoid a budget crisis.

By the time of Roemer's March 14, 1988 inauguration, state budget projections forecast a $170 million gap between revenue and expenditures. With the decline in oil and gas revenue that enriched Louisiana earlier in the decade, the state also had an estimated $600 million in short term debt, which began to come due in April.

In his inaugural address, Roemer promised "a new Louisiana," with a new image "as a place where investors, businessmen and women invest and create jobs." He explained that the foundations of his administration would be fiscal responsibility, excellence in education, a drive for economic development, protecting the environment, and ethics in government. He promised to end cronyism in state politics, revamp the budget and tax structure to eliminate $1.2 billion in cumulative deficits, and to improve the state's educational system.

Roemer's first order of business was a special legislative session to deal with budget reductions and government reorganization. In late March 1988, the legislature approved giving Roemer extraordinary power to deal with the state fiscal crisis by slashing government spending. The legislature gave the governor authority to cut as much as 20 percent from department budgets, to eliminate entire programs, and to close institutions if necessary to keep the state from running out of cash.

Roemer's long term goals include restructuring the state's tax system so that local government has more taxing power to pay for services, and diversifying the state's economy to make it less reliant on oil and gas. In May 1988, he signed a wide-ranging agreement with the governors of Arkansas and Mississippi to coordinate efforts to improve conditions in the Delta area, one of the nation's poorest regions. The agreement called for cooperation ranging from the search for foreign investment in highway construction to improvements in schools and health facilities.

In the area of education, Roemer has called for major reforms of Louisiana's public colleges and universities. He has called for changes in the governance and admissions standards of the state's colleges and universities and wants the state colleges to establish more distinct missions and programs.

Bibliography: Michael Baron *et al., The Almanac of American Politics 1986* (New York and Washington, D.C., 1985); Jaques Cattell Press, *Who's Who in American Politics, 1985–1986* (New York, 1985); *The Chronicle of Higher Education:* 9–23–87; 11–4–87; 4–27–88; *USA Today,* 3–14–88; *The New York Times:* 2–28–87; 3–31–87; 6–27–87; 10–22–87; 10–26–87; 11–3–87; 11–20–87; 3–15–88; 3–27–88; 5–14–88.

Joseph Edward Brennan (Courtesy of governor's office)

MAINE

Born on November 2, 1934 in Portland, Maine, the son of John J. Brennan and Katherine (Mulkerin) Brennan. A Roman Catholic, Brennan is divorced. He has two children, Joseph and Tara.

Brennan served in the United States Army from 1953 to 1955. He received a B.S. degree from Boston College in 1958, and an LL.B. from the University of Maine in 1963. Admitted to the Maine bar in that year, he began a private law practice in Portland. A Democrat, Brennan was elected to the Maine House of Representatives in 1965, and in 1967 he served as assistant minority leader. He became attorney for Cumberland County in 1971. In 1973 he served in the Maine Senate, acting as minority leader.

In 1974 he made an unsuccessful race for the governorship, losing in the primary to George J. Mitchell, a man he would later appoint to fill Edmund S. Muskie's seat in the U.S. Senate. Mitchell subsequently lost the general election to Independent James B. Longley.

Brennan's defeat did not dampen his political ambitions. In 1975 he was appointed attorney general of Maine, chosen by the state legislature to serve terms beginning both in 1975 and in 1977. In that office, he became nationally prominent when he took a hard line in opposing the damage claims of the Penobscot and Passamaquoddy Indian tribes, who asserted that Maine had taken 12.5 million acres of land from them without the approval of the United States Congress. Brennan sought to make the federal government pay the claims.

His persistence in the case is credited by many for his victory in the 1978 gubernatorial race. In the 1978 Democratic gubernatorial primary, he defeated Phillip L. Merrill by almost 12,000 votes. Richard S. Carey placed third in the race. During the campaign, United States Attorney General Griffin Bell threatened to sue the state unless a settlement was reached with the Indians. Brennan won the general election with more than 50 percent of the vote, defeating two opponents: Republican Linwood Palmer and Independent Herman C. Frankland. The major issues of the campaign were the Indian claims and Palmer's call for a mandatory limit on state spending.

During his first term Brennan vetoed a bill banning smoking in all public places. He also sought an injunction to force striking state employees to return to work, and appointed George Mitchell to succeed Edmund Muskie as United States Senator when Muskie resigned to become United States Secretary of State. Although Brennan had toyed with the idea of appointing himself to the position, he ultimately decided against it. In 1979, an energy assistance bill for Maine was enacted at the governor's request. Brennan finally reached an out-of-court settlement in 1980 with the Indian tribes for $81.5 million, a settlement which the federal government quickly approved. Maine later received some federal compensation.

Although political observers felt Brennan to be "less than dynamic" during his first four years in office, he stuck with his pledge not to increase the state's broad based taxes. Despite some problems from a Republican-controlled senate and some close numbers in the house, he was able to make some quiet progress in a number of areas.

In 1982 he handily beat back a primary challenge from Representative Georgette B. Berube of Lewiston, and easily defeated Charles L. Cragin in the general election by a margin of 281,066 votes to 172,949. Proud of his record of no income tax increases, he was the first Democrat since the Civil War to win every county in a gubernatorial election.

As governor, Brennan served three terms on the Executive Committee of the National Governors' Association. He also served in 1982 as chairman of the New England Governor's Conference, and co-chairman in 1982 of the New England Governors-Eastern Canadian Premiers. In 1984, he resisted pressure from party leaders to challenge incumbent Republican William S. Cohen for his U.S. Senate seat.

Constitutionally barred from seeking a third term in 1986, he ran for and won the house seat of Congressman John McKernan, a moderate Republican, who was himself running for governor. With his election, Brennan became the first Democrat to hold the First District Congressional seat in more than a decade. Generally seen as a liberal Democrat— he was the only sitting governor to endorse Senator Ted Kennedy's presidential bid in 1980—he was inclined to favor more generous government spending on social welfare issues. In Congress, Brennan holds seats on the Armed Services and Merchant Marine and Fisheries Committees.

Bibliography: The New York Times: 3–24–78; 10–30–85; *The Boston Globe,* 11–5–78; *USA Today,* 3–30–83; *Maine House and Senate Register,* 1985; *The Portland Press Herald,* 12–22–86; Michael Barone *et al., The Almanac of American Politics, 1984, 1988* (New York and Washington, D.C., 1983, 1987).

John R. McKernan, Jr. (Courtesy of governor's office)

McKERNAN, John R. Jr., 1987–

Born in Bangor, Maine on May 20, 1948; the son of John R. McKernan and Barbara Guild McKernan; a Protestant, McKernan is the divorced father of a son, Peter.

As a teenager, McKernan helped manage his family's Bangor newspaper when his father died. He graduated from Bangor High School in 1966, where he was a standout athlete. After graduation from Dartmouth in 1970, McKernan joined the Army National Guard, serving from 1970–1973. In 1971 he enrolled at the University of Maine School of Law, from which he graduated in 1974.

While still in law school, McKernan, a Republican, won election to the state legislature from an at-large Bangor district. He served two terms, 1972 to 1976, the last as the Republicans' assistant floor leader. As a state legislator, he is remembered for his authorship of Maine's returnable bottle law.

During his second term in the legislature, McKernan practiced law in Bangor. Leaving the legislature in 1976, he joined the Portland law firm of Verrill and Dana.

Deciding to return to public service in 1982, he ran for Maine's first congressional district seat when the incumbent challenged Senator George Mitchell for re-election. Victorious in his congressional bid, McKernan served on the House Education and Labor Committee, the Merchant Marine and Fisheries Committee, the Government Operations Committee, and the Select Committee on Children, Youth, and Families.

In 1986, McKernan ran for governor upon the constitutional ineligibility of incumbent Joseph Brennan to seek re-election. It was a unique political swap, with Brennan seeking McKernan's congressional seat while McKernan chose to succeed Brennan in the statehouse. As an environmentalist with strong business support, McKernan was seen as the Republicans' strongest contender since they last won the governorship in 1962. McKernan won the race, but with only 40 percent of the vote. The rest was split among three contenders: Attorney General James Tierney, a Democrat with consumerist and environmentalist credentials, who gained 30 percent; independent Sherry Huber, a critic of nuclear power who had lost the 1982 Republican gubernatorial primary race, who polled 15 percent; and independent John Menario, a former Portland city manager, who drew 15 percent. McKernan based his campaign on leading Maine into a prosperous high tech future without abandoning environmental concerns. In the opinion of political observers, his views on taxes and services appeared only mildly different from those of retiring Governor Brennan.

In office, McKernan pledged to expand the state's vocational education system and to improve communication between state government and the university system. He has been a strong supporter of Maine's only nuclear power plant, the Maine Yankee, one of the nation's most reliable and economical reactors.

Bibliography: Biographical information, courtesy of governor's office; Jaques Cattell Press, *Who's Who in American Politics, 1985–1986* (New York, 1985); Michael Barone *et al., The Almanac of American Politics, 1984, 1988* (New York and Washington, D.C., 1983, 1987); *The Chronicle of Higher Education:* 10–22–86; 11–12–86; *The New York Times,* 10–4–87.

Harry Roe Hughes (Courtesy of Governor Hughes)

MARYLAND

HUGHES, Harry Roe, 1979–1987

Born on November 13, 1926 in Easton, Maryland, the son of Jonathan Longfellow and Helen (Roe) Hughes. An Episcopalian, Hughes married Patricia Ann Donoho on June 30, 1951, by whom he is the father of Ann Donoho and Elizabeth Roe.

Hughes grew up in Denton, Maryland, and was educated in Caroline County public schools. He served in the United States Navy Air Corps in 1944 and 1945, attended Mercersburg Academy in Mercersburg, Pennsylvania, and studied for a time at Mount Saint Mary's College in Emmitsburg, Maryland before receiving a B.S. from the University of Maryland in 1949. Hughes played briefly with the New York Yankees' Easton farm club. In 1952 he received an LL.B. degree from George Washington University School of Law. Admitted to the Maryland bar that year, he practiced law in Denton.

In 1954 Hughes was elected as a Democrat to represent Caroline County in the Maryland House of Delegates. He was elected to the Maryland Senate in 1958, where he served as majority floor leader in 1965. His years in the legislature were stamped by his courage in supporting civil rights measures in the 1950s and 1960s. Hughes chaired the Maryland Democratic party in 1969 and 1970, and in the latter year served as chairman of a commission to study the state's role in financing public education. That commission's report led to the assumption by Maryland's state government of most public school construction costs. In 1971 Hughes left both his law practice and the Maryland Senate when Governor Marvin Mandel named him to head the state's new Department of Transportation. While with the agency, he oversaw construction of the Baltimore, Maryland and Washington, D.C. subways, and the redevelopment of Baltimore's waterfront. Hughes resigned as secretary in May 1977, over what he alleged was improper influence with state procedures in awarding contracts for the Baltimore subway. The move was fortuitous, for he left the Mandel administration politically unscathed by the scandals that were later to destroy it. He then returned to the practice of law, this time with a firm in Baltimore, but afterwards entered the 1978 Democratic gubernatorial primary.

The incumbent governor that year was Blair Lee, a Democrat who had become chief executive when Marvin Mandel was convicted on numerous charges stemming from an alleged improper attempt to influence legislation concerning a racetrack in Upper Marlboro, Maryland. Although experts predicted that Lee would win the election, his connections with Mandel were damaging enough to cause voters to choose Hughes from among three candidates challenging the incumbent. Hughes was opposed in the general election by J. Glenn Beall, Jr., a former United States Senator and the offspring of an old and distinguished Maryland political family. Hughes received little support until the *Sun* newspapers of Baltimore decided to endorse his candidacy. He went on to defeat Beall by the largest popular vote margin in a century—718,328 votes to 293,635. In the election Beall took only rural Alleghany and Garrett counties in the western part of Maryland.

On January 11, 1979, three judges of the United States Fourth Circuit Court of Appeals ordered a re-trial in the Mandel case, and the former governor was briefly reinstated as the lame-duck chief executive of the state. Hughes thus assumed office from Mandel, not Lee, when he was sworn in on January 17, 1979. The full Fourth Circuit Court confirmed Mandel's conviction about six months later, and he was imprisoned on charges of racketeering and mail fraud. At the same time, Spiro Agnew, Mandel's immediate predecessor as governor, was defending himself from civil charges stemming from his conviction on federal bribery charges. It was Hughes' mild mannered, clean image that helped him secure the governorship in the face of voter disgust with such scandals. He was seen as an "outsider" who would set things right.

In 1982 Hughes overcame light opposition in the primary from the veteran state legislator Harry McGuirk and faced Robert Pascal, also a state legislator, in the general election. Pascal charged the governor with being weak on crime, while others perceived Hughes as lacking in leadership. However, after Hughes called a special session of the legislature to consider the state's response to federal cuts in unemployment benefits, this show of strength, coupled with Pascal's difficulty in raising campaign funds, enabled the incumbent to win easily. The final count was 705,910 votes for Hughes and 432,826 for his opponent, with Pascal showing real strength only in the Baltimore suburbs.

Hughes was a popular governor, known for his steady, although passive and bland, leadership style. Although he had been one of the nation's most experienced politicians, he came to office in most voters' eyes as a new face, retaining a non-political image that worked to his advantage. He is credited with restoring dignity to state government after the scandals of the Mandel administration. His years in office were seen as non-controversial, although he did have some rocky moments over budget and prison issues in his first few years. Achievements of his first term included: approval of a $144 million tax relief program; reform of educational funding formulae; the passage of a condominium conversion law; a raise in the state's legal drinking age; a heralded visit to mainland China; and re-allocation of the state's environmental regulations to the Department of Health and Mental Hygiene.

During his second term, he had two impressive achievements: cleaning up Chesapeake Bay and banishing political scandals and tinges of corruption from the state capital. Unfortunately, he was hurt politically by a 1985 crisis in the state's savings and loan industry. Disclosures of mismanagement at some large institutions led to runs by depositors, prompting Hughes to freeze assets at many institutions. Disgruntled depositors then led rallies against him, blaming the governor for not handling the predicament aggressively enough.

Barred by law from seeking a third term as governor in 1986, he was an early favorite to win the U.S. Senate seat opened up by the retirement of Republican incumbent Charles Mathias. The savings and loan crisis, however, which jeopardized the deposits of 200,000 people, badly reversed Hughes' fortunes. In the September 1986 Democratic senatorial primary, he lost his party's nomination to five-term Congresswoman Barbara Mikulski, who eventually went on to win the Senate seat. The campaign drew national attention from politically active women, many of whom viewed Mikulski as a leading contender to become the first Democratic woman elected to the Senate since Maurine Neuberger of Oregon in 1960. Hughes drew only 13 percent of the primary vote to Mikulski's 53 percent. Also in the race was Representative Michael D. Barnes, a Democrat from Montgomery County, who polled 30 percent. In the opinion of political observers, Hughes' decline in popularity was directly attributable to the savings and loan crisis, which in the words of one, had become "an unshakeable albatross around the governor's neck."

Bibliography: Washington Post: 11–8–78; 7–1–81; 7–1–82; 11–3–82; *The New York Times:* 12–22–85; 7–13–86; 8–31–86; 9–8–86; 9–10–86; 11–5–86.

William Donald Schaefer (Courtesy of governor's office)

SCHAEFER, William Donald, 1987–

Born in West Baltimore on November 2, 1921; the son of William Henry Schaefer and Tululu (Skiffer) Schaefer. An Episcopalian, Schaefer is a bachelor.

Educated in Baltimore's public schools, he graduated from Baltimore City College in 1939 and from the University of Baltimore Law School in 1942. His legal career put on hold by U.S. entry into World War II, Schaefer joined the Army, achieved officer rank, and took charge of administering military hospitals both in England and on the continent. After his tour of duty, he remained in the U.S. Army Reserves, ultimately retiring with the rank of colonel.

After the war, Schaefer resumed his legal career, practicing real estate law. He went on to earn a Master of Laws degree from the University of Baltimore in 1952 and later formed a general practice law firm with two colleagues. His keen concern for city planning and housing in Baltimore motivated his entrance into the public arena, and prompted him to take a leadership role in citizen associations. His community involvement propelled him to a seat on the Baltimore City Council in 1955, where he served until 1967. In 1967 he was elected council president, and in 1971 mayor of the city. Inaugurated as mayor on December 7, 1971, he served four consecutive terms until he was elected governor.

As mayor, Schaefer initiated a highly innovative urban rejuvenation program, which drew upon the resources of federal, state, and local government as well as those of the private sector. These initiatives led to a widespread revitalization of the city's neighborhoods and to its emergence as a major tourist center. Schaefer's restoration of the Baltimore Inner Harbor area with its showpiece "Harborplace" drew national acclaim. He also strengthened the city's diversified local economy, insisted on the delivery of services to neighborhoods, and bridged the gap between black and white. His programs attracted $1.2 billion in new investments that tripled the city's tax base and retained 39,500 industrial jobs.

Schaefer's work as mayor earned him acclaim as one of the nation's most effective urban executives. He was the recipient of eight honorary doctorates, and the U.S. Conference of Mayors bestowed upon him the highest accolades. He was the fifth person in the nation to receive the "Distinguished Public Service Award" from Brandeis University.

In 1986 Schaefer sought the Democratic gubernatorial nomination to succeed Harry Hughes, constitutionally ineligible to seek a third term. His opponent in the September 9 primary was Attorney General Stephen H. Sachs, an aggressive prosecutor whose oratory and message were reminiscent of John F. Kennedy. Seeking to embrace the traditional Democratic coalition of labor, minorities, and women, Sachs made public education the centerpiece of his campaign. He also argued that the election of

Schaefer, a longtime friend of disgraced former Governor Marvin Mandel, would mark a return to political cronyism—a charge hotly denied by Schaefer, who was untouched by the scandals of the Mandel administration. Sachs also tried to spark interest in his candidacy with the selection of a popular black politician as his running mate, Representative Parren J. Mitchell, a civil rights activist who was dean of the state's congressional delegation. Nevertheless, Schaefer won the primary in a landslide.

His opponent in the general election was State Representative Thomas J. Mooney, who had run unopposed for the Republican nomination. Mooney, however, lacked support even from his own party and the results of the election were never in doubt. Schaefer won by the greatest margin of victory in state gubernatorial history, sweeping Maryland's 23 counties and the city of Baltimore with an unprecedented 82 percent of the vote.

Schaefer began making public policy even before he took office. In December 1986 he learned of the proposed closing of a major corporation in western Maryland. In an attempt to save jobs and to help displaced workers and their families, he immediately marshalled state forces and headed for Allegheny county. Together with his top advisors and the Maryland Congressional delegation, he devised a plan of state and federal action to meet the needs of the company and its employees. As a result, the corporation decided to keep its headquarters in Cumberland, saving 600 jobs. The incident is indicative of Schaefer's oft-cited "Do It Now!" approach that is the hallmark of his leadership style.

Major achievements of Schaefer's administration thus far include a plan to hold onto the state's windfall from federal tax reform; an increased gas tax; and changes in workers' compensation and medical malpractice policies. He has launched a drive for a $200 million complex of two new professional sports stadiums in downtown Baltimore, one for football, one for baseball. In the area of education, he has proposed that the state give a financial bonus to parents who save to pay for their children's college education. He has also argued for more clearly defined missions for public colleges and universities, and expanded research programs in the University of Maryland system. In 1988 he signed into law a bill that makes the state the first to ban the sale of some cheap pistols. In a highly controversial move, he threatened to withhold state funds from poverty lawyers unless they promise not to sue the state. Although the governor has repeatedly emphasized that he is a strong supporter of the rights of indigent and disabled people to legal representation in civil lawsuits, he wants to eliminate an inappropriate use of state funds, saying that the state does not have any responsibility to finance long expensive lawsuits against itself.

Although political observers feel that Schaefer looks like the opposite of an ideal politician—he is not photogenic, squirms when interviewed, dislikes confrontation—all agree that he has been the dominant figure in state politics since 1986.

Bibliography: Biographical information courtesy of governor's office; *The Chronicle of Higher Education:* 11–12–86; 2–17–88; Michael Barone et al., *The Almanac of American Politics 1988* (New York and Washington, D.C., 1987); Jaques Cattell Press, *Who's Who in American Politics, 1985–1986* (New York, 1985); *The New York Times:* 12–22–85; 7–13–86; 9–8–86; 9–10–86; 11–5–86; 1–22–87; 7–1–87; 7–8–87; 5–24–88.

Michael S. Dukakis (Courtesy of governor's office; Credit: Richard Sobol)

MASSACHUSETTS

DUKAKIS, Michael S., 1975–1979, 1983–

Born on November 3, 1933 in Brookline, Massachusetts, the son of Panos and Euterpe (Boukis) Dukakis, who were Greek immigrants. Dukakis is married to Katharine Dickson; he is the father of three children—John, Andrea, and Kara.

Dukakis attended Brookline High School, graduating in 1951. He received his B.A. degree in 1955 from Swarthmore College, where he earned highest honors in political science. He served in the United States Army from 1956 to 1958, including duty in Korea. Dukakis received an LL.B. from Harvard in 1960, graduating with honors. After being admitted to the Massachusetts bar, he practiced law. In 1962 Dukakis was elected to the Massachusetts House of Representatives, serving until 1970. There he sponsored legislation for housing, conservation, and consumer protection. He was the first legislator in America to introduce a no-fault automobile insurance bill, which was passed by the state in 1971. In 1970 Dukakis lost in an attempt to become lieutenant governor. He then returned to his private law practice, but remained active in public affairs. He served as moderator of "The Advocates," a public television debate program, and helped to monitor state agencies to ensure efficient government.

In 1974 Dukakis ran against incumbent Republican Governor Francis W. Sargent, after winning the Democratic gubernatorial nomination with 58 percent of the vote over Robert H. Quinn. Promising the most open campaign in Massachusetts history, he pledged to reduce the size of the governor's staff, balance the state budget, and reduce spending. Dukakis declared that the first thing he would do upon becoming governor was "to begin to introduce the idea of productivity and efficiency goals and standards into state government." Helped by an anti-Republican year in an anti-Republican state, Dukakis took 56 percent of the vote.

As chief executive, Dukakis spent much of his time trying to correct the fiscal problems of Massachusetts. He reduced the number of public employees and made other cuts in state spending, which restored Massachusetts to fiscal responsibility. He worked to regulate state agencies, continued to support consumer protection, and was involved in efforts to alleviate the state's energy shortage.

Christened "Jerry Brown East" by the press, Dukakis impressed many voters by eliminating many of the trappings of the governor's office. He continued to live in his own modest home, grew vegetables in his garden, and got rid of his state limousine in favor of the Boston subway. Still, though citizens were impressed by his unquestioned honesty and competence, many were turned off by his lack of warmth. Dukakis was hurt most of all by the way he handled taxes. Elected as a liberal reformer intent on stopping the state's spiraling taxes and public spending, he did slash the budget and turn around the nearly bankrupt state. In the process, however, he was forced to approve the largest tax increase in Massachusetts history, after having given the voters a "lead pipe guarantee of no new taxes." In office Dukakis disappointed many of the liberals who had supported him by cutting state services and programs. He made enemies and antagonized allies in the legislature, with whom he wrestled over the budget for almost his entire first year in office. He also earned the reputation of being a cold intellectual, who could not compromise with legislative interests. In retrospect, his governorship during his first term "cannot be said to have been a success," in the words of one political observer.

Nonetheless, Dukakis' defeat in the 1978 Democratic gubernatorial primary jolted liberals across the nation. His opponent was Edward J. King, the former director of the Massachusetts Port Authority and head of a business promotional group called the New England Council. King campaigned on a pledge to cut property taxes by $500 million, slash social spending, and create a pro-business atmosphere. Outspending Dukakis on advertising by a margin of two to one, he used sophisticated polling techniques to identify voter grievances against Dukakis. Dukakis, on the other hand, did little campaigning, relying on polls that showed him with a wide lead. In a stunning upset, he was defeated by King, 51 percent to 42 percent (with a third candidate garnering seven percent of the vote). King went on to defeat the Republican Francis Hatch, a moderate state representative, in the general election.

Dukakis' behavior after his defeat served to alienate him from an increasingly divided state Democratic party. He was criticized especially for his failure to support King, a conservative, in the general election. Vulnerable becasue of his rigid stance against cronyism and his refusal to wheel and deal politically, Dukakis was even rebuffed by the Massachusetts Executive Council, which voted to ask President Jimmy Carter to keep him out of his cabinet.

After leaving office, Dukakis assumed the position of lecturer and director of Intergovernmental Studies at Harvard's John F. Kennedy School of Government, where he taught courses in management at the state and local level and joined a group of faculty members developing studies in the new field of public management.

By 1982, however, Dukakis was ready to make a surprising comeback and reclaim the governorship. In a rerun of their bitter 1978 contest, Dukakis challenged the incumbent King for the Democratic nomination in a primary billed as an early referendum on "Reaganomics." A conservative Democrat often referred to as "Ronald Reagan's favorite governor," King presented himself as an advocate of the common man, and took conservative positions on capital punishment, mandatory sentencing, and drunk driving. King's openly pro-business attitude, with its emphasis on tax-cutting, reduction in state regulation, and crackdown on welfare abuse, had pleased many businessmen, but voters were increasingly displeased with what they perceived as his inept handling of the budget and legislature and his scandal-ridden administration. Not only did Dukakis attack King as a "cheerleader for Reagonomics," but he made effective use of the issue of corruption in state government. One of King's cabinet secretaries was convicted and sent to prison for taking money; another old friend, a deputy commissioner in the Revenue Department, hanged himself after disclosure of a scandal over payoffs to revenue officials.

Dukakis hired professionals from Washington, D.C. to help project a campaign that highlighted integrity and competence. Running on the theme of "honest and effective leadership," he put together one of the largest field organizations ever assembled for a statewide race. In expanding the organization of the liberal coalition that elected him in 1974, he raised $2 million from a broader base of small contributors than did King, and with it was able to overpower King's advantages of incumbency and his own substantial war chest. Dukakis was greatly aided by a resounding endorsement from the *Boston Globe,* which described the King administration as "one of the weakest in the modern history of the Commonwealth."

In May 1982 68 percent of the delegates to the state's first Democratic convention in eight years passed a non-binding resolution supporting Dukakis for the nomination. In the September 1982 primary, the most expensive in the state's history and one that received extensive national coverage, Dukakis defeated King, receiving 53 percent of the vote to the incumbent's 47 percent. The bitter grudge match drew the largest number of voters in the history of a Massachusetts primary. Dukakis' support had come from liberals, suburban residents, and the state's relatively large number of intellectuals, while King drew upon blue-collar workers in the old industrial cities and in Roman Catholic, Irish, and Italian communities.

In the general election, Dukakis faced Republican John Winthrop Sears, a well-to-do Boston city councilman. The race was billed as a classic contest between a liberal and a conservative, one that pitted an ethnic Democrat against a Brahmin Republican. Dukakis tried hard in his campaign to shed the reputation for humorlessness and arrogance which he had acquired as governor. Properly chastened after his previous defeat, he presented himself as a bridge builder and a seeker of consensus. He stressed his opposition to the death penalty, his support for gun control, and his concern about problems such as mass transit and human services. In a state where there are three Democrats for every Republican, Dukakis won handily, gaining 59 percent of the vote.

In his inaugural address, Dukakis pledged to "fight Reaganomics and its philosophy of indifference with all the energy I can summon." Serving with Lieutenant Governor John Kerry, he again faced difficult economic circumstances. Achievements of his second term included the development of programs to aid the estimated hundreds of homeless Massachusetts citizens and to create jobs for the thousands of the state's unemployed.

Dukakis won a third term in November 1986, with the biggest victory margin of any Massachusetts governor in this century. He defeated his Republican opponent George S. Kariotis with 69 percent of the vote, garnering 1,157,786 votes to his opponent's 525,364.

Since returning to office in 1983, Dukakis has made economic development the keynote of his administration. Presenting himself as a new breed of competent, technocratic, managerial governor, he takes credit for the state's booming, high-tech economy. In all, more than 300,000 new jobs have been created, and 54,000 new businesses started in the state since 1983. He has also worked to bring strong economic development initiatives to regions of the state suffering from declining industries and the competition of foreign imports. He has also signed into law an education reform program for Massachusetts public schools; initiated open-space acquisition programs to save valuable areas across the state from over-development; signed into law a workers' compensation reform bill; and led the fight against drunk driving on state highways. Perceived as a classical Northern liberal, he signed the nation's first law to guarantee health insurance to all state residents, and also enacted the first program in the country to allow AIDS victims to remain at home to die rather than in hospitals. His efforts to win passage of model plant closing and right-to-know legislation have helped protect Massachusetts workers.

In New England, Dukakis has served as chiarman of the New England Governors' Conference and as chairman of the Committee on Economic Development for the Coalition of Northeast Governors. Nationally, he has been chairman of the Committee on Economic Development and Technological Innovation of the National Governors' Association and chairman of the Committee on Industrial and Entrepreneurial Economy for the Policy Commission of the Democratic National Committee. In 1984, he presented the platform to the National Democratic Convention in San Francisco, and in August 1986 was elected chairman of the Democratic Governors Association.

In March 1987, Dukakis entered the race for the 1988 Democratic presidential nomination, saying he had the "experience to manage" and "the values to lead." Surprising even political pundits with his fund-raising ability and organizational talent, he emerged from a field of seven contenders to win the party's presidential nomination, garnering enough delegates by the end of the spring primaries to ensure his coronation by the National Democratic Convention meeting in Atlanta in July 1988.

Selecting Senator Lloyd Bentsen of Texas as his running mate, Dukakis faced a tough election against Republican nominee George Bush. As a candidate, he offered his accomplishments as governor of Massachusetts as models to be followed on the national level, and presented himself as a "CEO" who knows how to make government work. Voicing the impassioned concern that is so much a part of traditional Democratic appeal, he stressed the problems of adult illiteracy, the misery of the homeless, the need for changes in the welfare system, and the responsibility of society toward older Americans.

Despite a last minute rally in the polls, Dukakis suffered a decisive defeat, with Bush winning a solid 6–5 victory in the popular vote and a commanding majority in the electoral college. With his political future in doubt, Dukakis returned to the Massachusetts Statehouse to deal with a deteriorating economic climate.

In a surprise announcement several weeks after the election, he stunned supporters with his decision not to seek another term as governor when his term ends in 1990. There is further speculation that Dukakis is planning to seek the Democratic Presidential nomination in 1992.

Bibliography: Biographical information courtesy of governor's office; *The New York Times:* 7–27–86; 9–19–86; 9–21–86; 12–28–86; 1–6–87; 3–1–87; 3–17–87; 4–30–87; 6–3–87; 6–14–87; 11–26–87; 1–10–88; 1–20–88; 4–22–88; 6–2–88; Charles Kenney and Robert L Turner, *Dukakis: An American Odyssey* (Boston, 1988); *The Chronicle of Higher Education,* 11–12–86; Fox Butterfield, "Dukakis," *New York Times Magazine* (May 8, 1988); Michael S. Dukakis and Rosabeth Moss Kanter, *Creating the Future: The Massachusetts Comeback and Its Promise for America* (Summit Books, 1988); "Is Dukakis Another Carter?" *Newsweek* (April 18, 1988); "A Hard Look at Dukakis' 'Massachusetts Miracle,' " *Newsweek* (Feb. 22, 1988); *USA Today,* 4–29–88.

James Johnston Blanchard (Courtesy of governor's office)

MICHIGAN

BLANCHARD, James Johnston, 1983–

Born in Detroit, Michigan on August 8, 1942; the son of James Robert Blanchard and Rosalie Johnston Webb Blanchard. A Unitarian, Blanchard married Paula Parker in 1966. In 1987, the pair announced their divorce because of longstanding irreconcilable differences. They have one son, Jay.

Blanchard earned his B.A. and M.B.A. in business administration from Michigan State University. He holds a law degree from the University of Minnesota.

He began his public service career in 1968 as a legal advisor in the Michigan Secretary of State's office. In 1969 he became a Michigan Assistant Attorney General and served in that capacity for five years. He was also a lawyer in private practice with the Bloomfield Hills firm of Beer and Boltz before being elected to Congress in 1974 as a representative from Michigan's 18th Congressional District.

A Democrat, Blanchard served four terms in Congress. From 1976 to 1982, he served as assistant Democratic whip. In Congress, he was a member of the Banking, Finance and Urban Affairs Committee, Science and Technology Committee, and chairman of the House Subcommittee on Economic Stabilization. As chairman, he conducted an extensive series of hearings on the revitalization of the U.S. economy with a focus on the problems facing the industrial sectors of the country. As the author of the Chrysler Loan Guarantee Act, he was best known for getting the Chrysler bailout passed in the House. Besides economic revitalization, his legislative interests included budgeting and government spending, energy, preserving the Great Lakes, cities, housing, and foreign policy. He also served on the President's Commission on the Holocaust.

Blanchard was elected to the governorship in 1982, defeating Republican conservative R. H. Headlee with 51.4 percent of the vote. Political analysts believe that his role in engineering the Chrysler bailout was central to his victory.

When Blanchard was inaugurated as the state's 45th governor on January 1, 1983, Michigan faced a $1.7 billion deficit, record high unemployment, and the worst credit rating in the nation. Working with his cabinet, members of the legislature, and leaders of the state's business, labor, education and local government communities, he tackled the state's finances, upgrading the state's credit rating and launching an aggressive small business and economic development program. Among his first acts in office was to call for a tax increase. Although he understood that higher taxes might make the state less attractive to business, he felt that with the state's huge deficit, he had no choice. Although rather unpopular during his first year in office, he rebounded as the state's economic health improved. In less than three years Blanchard was able to declare solvency day (November 8, 1985), marking Michigan's return to fiscal health and the end of a decade of deficit. During his first term he helped Michigan outpace the nation in creating new jobs, restored education as a top state priority, and undertook the most aggressive prison construction program in the state's history. He also wooed and won an assembly plant that Mazda decided to build in the United States, and encouraged Japanese auto parts suppliers to open operations in Michigan. Putting the state on the road to developing a more diversified private sector economy, he developed strategy to use Michigan's manufacturing expertise to specialize in high-skill, capital intensive, flexible manufacturing areas.

For all these accomplishments, *Newsweek* magazine credited Blanchard with leading "one of the most dramatic economic turnabouts in the recent history of state government." As the state's economy picked up, Blanchard was able to get rid of the temporary tax hike passed during his first year in office, thus depriving the Republicans of a major campaign issue in his drive for re-election. Identifying himself with the burgeoning pride in the state's economic revival, he and his party reaped benefits from the recovery and growth of Michigan's economy.

His 1986 campaign for re-election drew national attention because of his Republican opponent, William Lucas, who would have made history by becoming the nation's first black governor. Lucas, a former FBI agent, Wayne County Sheriff, and Wayne County Executive, became the center of nationwide Republican efforts to portray the party as open to minorities. In a highly publicized switch, he himself had abandoned the Democrats to join the GOP in 1985. Lucas campaigned on a platform of toughness on crime, efficiency in government, and control of government spending. As executive of Wayne County, which includes Detroit and surrounding suburbs, he had eliminated the county budget deficit of $140 million a year by cutting payrolls, slimming the bureaucracy, and bringing in a private company to manage a debt-ridden county-owned hospital. The health of the state economy, however, deprived Lucas of the economic issue. Although he won the support of anti-abortion groups with his outright opposition to abortion, he made little headway with voters in his calls for lower taxes and a tougher stance on crime.

Blanchard, on the other hand, with his economic development theme "Working Together for Michigan," attracted voters who might normally have voted Republican. According to political analysts, race was not a factor in the campaign: Lucas lost few votes because of race, but neither did his candidacy capture the imagination of many black voters. Blanchard's 68 percent to 31 percent victory was the highest margin in a gubernatorial election since 1928 and the best Democratic percentage since 1835.

During his second term, Blanchard proposed a unique program to assist parents with financing the costs of their children's college education; worked to encourage universities to work more closely with businesses to stimulate economic development; vetoed a bill that would have raised the state speed limit to 65 m.p.h. on rural stretches of Michigan's interstate highways; and signed into law the nation's first bill making surrogate parenting contracts for profit a crime. He was chairman of the Democratic Platform Committee for the 1988 Democratic National Convention.

According to political observers, state voters are confident that Michigan is on the way to a sounder economy and pleased with the leadership of Blanchard and his party. He appears to be the commanding figure in state politics, with no competitors of equal stature on the scene.

Bibliography: Biographical information courtesy of governor's office; *The Chronicle of Higher Education:* 10–22–86; 11–12–86; Jaques Cattell Press, *Who's Who in American Politics, 1985–1986* (New York, 1985); Michael Barone *et al., The Almanac of American Politics, 1984, 1986, 1988* (New York and Washington, D.C., 1983, 1985, 1987); *The New York Times:* 5–5–85; 9–26–85; 10–29–86; 11–5–86; 6–17–87; 7–2–87; 7–12–87; 6–27–88; 6–28–88.

Rudy Perpich (Courtesy of governor's office)

MINNESOTA

PERPICH, Rudy, 1976–1979, 1983–

Born in Carson Lake, Minnesota on June 27, 1928, the son of Anton and Mary (Vukelich) Perpich. A Roman Catholic, Perpich is the brother of Tony, Joseph, and George. He married Lola Simic of Keewatin, Minnesota on September 4, 1954, and is the father of Rudy Jr. and Mary Susan.

Perpich attended Hibbing High School and Hibbing Junior College in Minnesota, and received his A.A. degree in 1950; he was graduated from Marquette University with a D.D.S. in 1954. Perpich served in the United States Army as a sergeant from 1946 to 1947. A member of Minnesota's Democratic-Farmer-Labor party, he was on the Hibbing Board of Education from 1952 to 1962, served in the Minnesota Senate from 1963 to 1970, and was lieutenant governor of Minnesota from 1971 to 1976. On December 30, 1976, Governor Wendell Anderson resigned and Perpich was elevated to the office, as provided by Minnesota's constitution. Perpich then appointed former Governor Anderson to fill the seat of Walter Mondale, the vice president-elect, in the United States Senate.

Perpich served as the 34th governor of Minnesota from 1976 until January 1979. The son of immigrants from Eastern Europe, he became the state's first governor of that ethnic background, the first to come from the Iron Range region of Minnesota, and the first Roman Catholic. His success as a dentist and later as a politician was a classic American success story that endeared him to Minnesota's large Slavic population. Perpich's father Anton had moved to the state from Yugoslavia when he was 20 to work in the ore mines of the Iron Range, and Governor Perpich was later to claim that this background shaped him, leading him to champion the rights of the poor and minorities. His unorthodox personal style also proved to be exceptionally popular. A believer in the work ethic, he vowed to make government more productive, and to crack down on waste and inefficiency. Perpich ordered phones removed from state cars, cut down on travel and the use of state vehicles, and even banned coffee from his office in protest over its high price. Committed to providing citizens access to their chief executive, he maintained an open door policy and attracted attention by showing up unheralded and unexpectedly in public places. At one point, he even allowed reporters to rummage through his office drawers when they asked permission.

Nevertheless, the friendly and easygoing Perpich also had his critics. Some said he acted without thinking and often without heeding the advice of his staff; others claimed that he had no clear-cut program or vision for Minnesota. His biggest problem, however, was his link to the Democratic-Farmer-Labor party that was drawing increasing criticism in the state. By early 1978 the Republicans had begun to make the point that all of Minnesota's top statewide positions were filled by people who had not been elected to them—a view which the voters apparently shared, judging by the results of the 1978 elections. The DFL suffered some shattering defeats that year. Seeking election to his own term, Perpich was vulnerable on account of his role in the controversy which had ensued over Senator Anderson's appointment. He also faced a strong challenger in Republican Albert H. Quie, a 20-year veteran congressman from Minnesota's First District.

Seizing on the popularity of "Proposition 13" sentiment in a high tax state, Quie advocated a 10 percent across-the-board tax cut and a constitutional amendment limiting state spending to growth in personal income. The voters responded positively, apparently reassured that Quie's reputation as a political moderate would keep him from slashing spending to ridiculous extremes. He defeated Perpich by a margin of 54 to 46 percent, in an election in which Perpich failed to carry some normally Democratic counties. Perpich attributed his upset defeat to poor campaign organization, and to a split between the conservative and liberal wings of his party. Quie's triumph was also widely interpreted as a victory for right-to-life groups in Minnesota. Although both men had taken anti-abortion stands, right-to-life groups felt that Quie had done more for them.

Perpich lived in Vienna after he left office in 1979. Working for Control Data Corporation overseas, he became vice president and executive consultant to Control Data Worldtech, an international trade division of the Minneapolis-based computer concern. Perpich saw his new career as "an opportunity for me to promote Minnesota in international trade, breaking down barriers."

With Quie's retirement from office in 1983 after a single term and huge budget deficits, Perpich staged a comeback attempt in which he was widely perceived as the underdog. Still, he scored an upset victory in the Democratic primary that year, defeating popular State Attorney General Warren M. Spannaus and airline mechanic Ellsworth Peterson. Perpich earned 51 percent of the vote, winning huge majorities in his home base, the economically hard hit Iron Range.

Perpich was a strong favorite in the general election against Republican Wheelock Whitney, a wealthy businessman. The central focus of the 1982 campaign was on the financial health of Minnesota. Perpich, who contrasted the prosperous condition of the treasury when he left office to its depleted state four years later, won an overwhelming victory, gaining 59 percent of the vote to Whitney's 40 percent.

With his victory, Perpich became the only person in Minnesota history to hold the gubernatorial post for two non-consecutive terms. He was sworn in as the state's 36th governor on January 3, 1983.

Seeking re-election in 1986, he faced a tough primary challenger in George Latimer, mayor of St. Paul for an unprecedented six terms. In the campaign, Perpich emphasized his role in creating jobs and cutting taxes, while Latimer focused on leadership issues. Perpich won the nomination of the Democratic-Farmer-Labor party, with 57 percent of the vote to his opponent's 41 percent.

In the general election, Perpich faced former state representative Cal Ludeman, the candidate of the Independent-Republican party. Perpich promised tax reform and to make Minnesota "the manpower state" so it would be more attractive to business. His policies of wooing business and disciplining but not dismantling Minnesota's welfare state attracted voters, and he won the election, 56 percent to 43 percent. Although this was a solid victory, it was less than he won by in 1982, and suggested to political observers that the DFL no longer commanded an automatic majority in state elections.

During his years in office, Perpich has sought to be called the "jobs governor." Campaigning on the need for job creation in the state, he joined labor, business, agriculture, education, and the private sector in efforts that put 100,000 more Minnesotans to work than ever before in state history, and created a total of 200,000 new jobs. A 1984 survey in *USA Today* identified Minnesota as having the best workforce in the nation for high-tech development, and credited Perpich with being one of the nation's best governors for promoting growth within that area.

Another priority of the Perpich administration has been education reform. Upon taking office, he championed a 26 percent increase in the state's investment in elementary, secondary, and post-secondary education. He also initiated a 70 percent increase in grants and scholarships, three new engineering schools, a natural resources research center, new buildings and a new focus for the University of Minnesota, and an investment in up to 100 new endowed university chairs. He also supported a controversial program allowing high school students to take courses at public and private colleges, using school aid to pay tuition.

In fiscal areas, Perpich spearheaded the drive for a $1 billion income tax cut in 1985. He also delivered a simplified tax form, demanded a strong tax compliance program to find and prosecute cheaters, and proposed the creation of a budget reserve, or "rainy day fund." In 1987 Minnesota imposed the highest cigarette tax in the nation, intended not only to raise revenue and to finance health care programs, but to make smoking so expensive that it becomes prohibitive. Perpich has said he wants to make Minnesota smoke free by the year 2000.

During his years as governor, Perpich has served as chairman of the National Governor's Association Committee on International Trade and Foreign Relations. In 1987, he decided not to seek the Democratic nomination for president in 1988, a move that had been encouraged by some advisers and family members. He promised to focus on the continued economic expansion of the state for the remainder of his term, one that he has already announced will be his last.

Bibliography: Biographical information courtesy of governor's office; "From the 'Dumps' to Governor," *New York Times Biographical Service* 7 (December 1976): 1775–76; *The New York Times:* 12–31–76; 4–10–77; 11–2–78; 1–10–79; 11–1–80; 2–16–82; 9–15–82; 11–1–82; 1–5–84; 9–9–86; 9–11–86; 9–14–87; *The Dallas Morning News,* 8–1–87; *The Chronicle of Higher Education:* 11–12–86; 2–18–87; 1–13–88; Michael Barone *et al., The Almanac of American Politics, 1986, 1988* (New York and Washington, D.C., 1985, 1987).

William Forrest Winter (Courtesy of governor's office)

MISSISSIPPI

WINTER, William Forrest, 1980–1984

Born in Granada, Mississippi on February 21, 1923, the son of William Aylmer Winter and Inez (Parker) Winter. A Presbyterian, Winter married Elise Varner on October 10, 1950; they are the parents of Anne, Elise, and Eleanor.

Winter received a B.A. from the University of Mississippi in 1943. Immediately after graduating, he entered the United States Army and served with the infantry in the Philippines. In 1946, after three years of military service, he returned to the University of Mississippi, receiving an LL.B. in 1949 and graduating first in his class. Winter was admitted to the Mississippi bar that year, and established a law practice in Granada. The previous year he had begun his political career, becoming a Democratic member of the Mississippi House of Representatives. Except for a brief stint in the United States Army during the Korean conflict in 1951, he served in the Mississippi legislature until 1956, when he became state tax collector. In 1964 he became state treasurer.

Winter was defeated in the Democratic gubernatorial primary in 1967 by John Bell Williams, who had split with the national party to support Barry Goldwater's 1964 presidential campaign. Winter, characterized by Williams as "too liberal for Mississippi" during the campaign, eventually returned to private legal practice. He joined the firm of Ludlum, Winter, and Stennis (the last partner being the son of United States Senator John Stennis). In 1971 Winter was elected lieutenant governor, and the following year he received the Margaret Dixon Freedom of Information Award from the Associated Press. Winter's second try for the governorship failed in 1975, when he lost in the primary to Charles C. Finch. Political observers attributed his loss of both races to his reputation for racial moderation. He then returned to the full-time practice of law before mounting a successful bid for the governorship on his third attempt in 1979. In 1979 Winter defeated Lieutenant Governor Evelyn Gandy in the Democratic primary runoff for governor, and went on to win the general election over Republican Gil Carmichael, a Meridian, Mississippi businessman making his second attempt at the governorship, by a vote of 413,620 to 263,702. Winter took every county except Jackson, which he lost narrowly. His victory was interpreted as an historic one for Mississippi. Although the state had not elected an outspokenly segregationist governor since 1967, it had never elected an explicit supporter of integration until Winter's victory in 1979. As governor, he changed the face of state politics by bringing blacks into the Democratic party and by increasing black voter registration.

The keynote of Winter's term as governor was the strong belief that state government can affect the future course of citizens' lives. Soon after his election he tried to improve the state's cultural image by inviting such celebrities as Turner Catledge, Eudora Welty, Dean Rusk, Willie Morris, and William Styron for dinner and conversation at the governor's mansion. During his term a uniform state tax assessment was discussed by the legislature, and a bill was introduced requiring that both the theory of evolution and Biblical explanations of the origin of man be taught in Mississippi schools. Winter sought to stimulate small business in the state, which had the lowest *per capita* income in the nation. He described Mississippi as being "picked on" when the federal government attempted, through the United States Supreme Court, to claim waters near a chain of islands located off the state's Gulf Coast. Winter also opposed the dumping of nuclear waste in salt domes situated along the coast. Despite a frustrating battle with the legislature, Winter and his staff successfully achieved passage of the landmark Education Reform Act, the first in the nation. He also obtained a one-half cent sales tax increase to fund educational programs. Political observers believe this package of educational reform to have been the major achievement of Winter's administration. Under his tenure, Mississippi began to move from a state whose low taxes were its greatest attraction to one which began to concentrate on raising the skills and abilities of its workforce.

Constitutionally barred from seeking a second term, Winter was frequently mentioned as a top level executive appointee should Walter Mondale have won the presidency in 1984. As analysts had predicted, he chose to challenge Republican incumbent Thad Cochran for a U.S. Senate seat in 1984. A heavy favorite in the June Democratic senatorial primary, he overwhelmed three foes in a campaign that produced a light voter turnout.

His campaign, however, got off to a slow start earlier in the year when he first accepted and then rejected the chancellorship of the University of Mississippi in order to make the race. His challenge of Cochran was built largely around criticism of the Republican's support for Reagan administration cuts in such programs as Medicaid, AFDC, and Social Security. Cochran, however, used his image as a moderate and emphasis on service to his constituents in attempting to cut into Winter's support among black voters. That support, however, was problematic for Winter. In a state where blacks and whites haave traditionally been polarized, Winter's record as governor earned him the enmity of some whites, who felt his programs catered to blacks. Winter's 58 percent to 42 percent loss to Cochran was widely attributed to this polarization of racial attitudes, despite the fact that both candidates had pointedly sought the support of voters of both races. Although some observers feared that Winter's loss unmasked an undercurrent of racism in state politics—with the growing perception among voters that Democrats were becoming a party of blacks while Republicans were becoming a party of whites—others disagreed. In their opinion, problems for the Democrats stemmed largely from the problems Mississippians had with the top of the 1984 Democratic ticket.

With his defeat, Winter retired to his private law practice in Jackson. He is also a farmer, timber grower, and author of three books: *History of Mississippi; Mississippi 1990;* and *Mississippi Heroes.*

Bibliography: Meridian Star: 8–8–79; 8–29–79; 11–7–79; *New Orleans Times Picayune:* 1–20–80; 10–26–80; 5–16–81; 10–18–82; 12–22–82; *The New York Times:* 6–6–84; 11–7–84; 11–8–84; Biographical information courtesy of governor's office; Michael Barone *et al., The Almanac of American Politics, 1984, 1986, 1988* (New York and Washington, D.C., 1983, 1985, 1987); Peter J. Boyer, "The Yuppies of Mississippi: How They Took Over the Statehouse," *The New York Times Magazine* (February 28, 1988).

William A. Allain (Courtesy of governor's office)

ALLAIN, William A. ("Bill"), 1984–1988

Born on February 14, 1928 in Washington, Mississippi, a small rural community in Adams County. A Catholic, Allain was married for six years to Doris J. Rush. The couple divorced in 1970.

Educated in public schools and a graduate of Natchez High, Allain completed pre-law studies at the University of Notre Dame and received his law degree from the University of Mississippi. He served in the U.S. Army Infantry for three years during the Korean conflict, with much of his service taking place in combat zones. Receiving an honorable discharge in 1953, he practiced law in Natchez until 1962 when he accepted a position as assistant attorney general for the state. Holding the post from 1962 to 1975, he often defended the state against civil rights lawsuits during the turbulent years of the movement.

In 1979 Allain was elected attorney general of Mississippi in his first statewide race. During four years in that office, he earned a reputation as one of the leading consumer advocates in the state by giving Mississippi its first Office of Consumer Affairs. He became a popular figure in the state by using the office to fight telephone company and utility rate increases, to battle rigged games at the annual state fair, and to take on powerful state legislators by filing a suit to bar them from serving on executive boards and commissions. He also won a refund for many power company customers.

In 1983 Allain sought the Democratic nomination for governor upon the constitutional ineligibility of incumbent William Winter. He faced four other contenders in the August 2 primary: former Lieutenant Governor Evelyn Gandy, a lawyer and long-time public servant; Mike Sturdivant, a farmer with extensive motel holdings; state representative Lonnie Johnson; and Billy Marvin Davis, a farmer. Allain (with 35.4 percent) and Gandy (with 38.2 percent), the two top vote getters, squared off against each other in the August 23 runoff. Gandy, who had won the field of five, was the favorite. Making her second bid for the state's highest office, she was trying to become Mississippi's first woman governor. A veteran of 35 years in state government, she had been a state representative, state treasurer, state insurance commissioner in addition to her current position as lieutenant governor.

The two candidates agreed on substantive issues—the need to improve education, employment, health care, and criminal justice, and to hire more blacks in state government positions. Both candidates made special efforts to attract black voters, and each had the backing of some prominent black leaders. They tangled, however, on the issue of how best to deal with rising utility rates. Allain, who strongly opposed rate increases for utilities, campaigned for utility regulation and the removal of legislators from state boards and commissions. Portraying himself as a fighter against the utilities who would look out for the underprivileged, he linked Gandy to the "old guard" responsible for Mississippi's ranking last among states in such categories as education, economic development, and per capita income.

Gandy, in turn, branded Allain a one-issue candidate who had alienated the legislature during his own tenure in state government. Heeding the analyses of political pundits who claimed that her previous defeat in the 1979 gubernatorial primary had turned on her perceived "softness," she emphasized her "toughness" and depicted herself as an experienced leader whose time had come. Neither candidate made gender an issue in the race.

Allain won the primary with 52.3 percent of the vote to Gandy's 47.7 percent, running strongly among black voters across the state. In the general election, he faced Leon Bramlett, a farmer and businessman, who was seeking to become the state's first Republican governor since Reconstruction. The little-known Bramlett had been a high school football hero and all American end at the U.S. Naval Academy. Both candidates agreed that their poor state needed better education, less crime, and more jobs.

Unfortunately, however, the campaign degenerated into a mud-slinging contest, as the state reverberated with charges of homosexuality leveled at Allain by four of Bramlett's strongest supporters. Late in the campaign, three of Bramlett's largest contributors and an advisor to his campaign charged that Allain frequently paid for sexual relations with black male prostitutes over several years. Around the state, some newspapers called for Allain's resignation, others called for a postponement of the November 8 election, and still others condemned Bramlett and the Republicans for engaging in gutter politics.

Allain, who vigorously denied the allegations, easily swept to victory. The favorite all along, he was also the beneficiary of voter backlash against the vicious smear. He drew 55 percent of the vote to Bramlett's 39 percent. Independent candidate Charles Evers, the former mayor of Fayette and brother of the slain civil rights leader Medgar Evers, trailed far behind with 4 percent, while two other minor candidates polled 1 percent each.

Political observers believed that, despite his solid victory, Allain remained crippled by Bramlett's allegations. According to one observer, he became "almost a hermit as governor, and the state lost much of the momentum it had built up during the Winter years." His powers as governor were constitutionally limited. Many long-time legislative leaders had more say over the budget than he did. In 1985, Allain faced a teachers' strike over poor salaries, a state court order to correct prison overcrowding, and a feisty legislature that was challenging him on his attempt to hold the line on spending. One important accomplishment was his appointment of a 350-member biracial commission to study the state's 1890 constitution, which had been designed primarily to keep blacks out of the state political process. Allain said he assembled the commission because many sections of the constitution were "not designed for Mississippi's needs in the 20th century, much less the 21st." Allain also managed to get a constitutional amendment passed allowing state governors to run for a second consecutive term, but he himself chose not to make the race for re-election.

Upon his retirement from office, Allain returned to the private practice of law. An attorney for more than 25 years, he has gained recognition among his fellow attorneys as one of Mississippi's foremost constitutional lawyers and one of its most effective trial advocates.

Bibliography: Biographical information, courtesy of governor's office; Jaques Cattell Press, *Who's Who in American Politics, 1985–1986* (New York, 1985); Michael Barone *et al., The Almanac of American Politics, 1986, 1988* (New York and Washington, D.C., 1985, 1987); *The New York Times:* 8–3–83; 8–4–83; 8–23–83; 8–24–83; 10–28–83; 11–2–83; 11–9–83; 11–10–83; 12–12–85.

Ray Mabus (Courtesy of governor's office)

MABUS, Ray, 1988–

Ray Mabus was born on October 11, 1948 in Ackerman, Choctaw County, Mississippi, the overachieving only child of a prosperous timber farmer. His father was an inveterate traveler who showed his son the world beyond Mississippi. By the time Mabus was 19, he had lived in Mexico, seen Teheran, and journeyed on the Trans-Siberian Railroad. He graduated from the University of Mississippi after three years, then studied political science at Johns Hopkins on a Woodrow Wilson fellowship. After receiving an M.A. from Johns Hopkins, he graduated with honors from Harvard Law School. He later joined the high-powered Washington, D.C. firm of Fried, Frank, Harris, Shriver, and Kampelman.

Mabus served in the U.S. Navy on a guided missile cruiser, was counsel to a subcommittee of the Agricultural Committee of the U.S. House of Representatives and, like his father and uncle, has also been a tree farmer in Choctaw County.

From 1980 to 1983 he was legal counsel to Governor William Winter. In that role, he was instrumental in securing passage of the landmark Education Reform Act of 1982, a strengthened law against drunk drivers, Mississippi's first open records act, and legislation to give low-interest home loans to Mississippians.

In 1983, in his first bid for elective office, he ran successfully as a reform candidate for state auditor. Although the post for generations had been seen as a backwater in state politics, Mabus used it as a potential springboard to prominence. He took on the most powerful and entrenched politicians in the state—county supervisors and other local power barons who could dispense county labor and equipment contracts in exchange for political loyalty. Auditing the state's 82 counties, he pressed court action, and won $1.7 million in reimbursements for the state. His actions prompted an FBI investigation that led to more than 40 indictments of public officials. Mabus' crusade brought him national attention. His role in restoring a favorable credit rating to five counties impressed Wall Street bond brokers, and he gained a statewide reputation as a reformer which would become his platform in his race for governor.

In 1987 incumbent Governor Bill Allain chose not to seek a second term, although voters, with his backing, had approved a constitutional amendment permitting consecutive terms for governors for the first time since the 19th century. The Democratic race was therefore wide open. In the August 4, 1987 primary, Mabus drew 37 percent of the vote in a multi-candidate field that included former Governor Bill Walter (1972–1976). He faced second-place finisher Mike Sturdivant, a Glendora businessman, in the August 25 runoff. The race was an expensive, acrimonious one. Sturdivant, who spent more than $1.6 million on the campaign, was an aggressive opponent, accusing Mabus of accepting contributions from Wall

Street bond brokers. Mabus countered with ads criticizing Sturdivant for being a plantation owner, for taping commercials in Texas, and for wrongly implying that all the jobs he had helped to create were in Mississippi. Campaigning against what he called "the old time politics and old-time politicians," Mabus won the nomination in an overwhelming victory.

In the general election he faced Republican Jack Reed, a 63-year-old businessman and former chairman of the State Board of Education who had won his party's nomination by a 7–2 margin. Reed, a formidable campaigner, was hoping to become the state's first Republican governor since General Adelbert Ames left office in 1876. Political observers believed he was his party's best hope in several elections to claim the office for the GOP. Reed, who stumped as an advocate of change, sought to portray Mabus as a man who would raise taxes if he got into office. He criticized Mabus for his pledge to increase teachers' salaries to the average of other southeastern states. While Reed said that he too favored raising salaries—currently among the lowest in the nation—he believed that this would have to be done slowly. He charged that Mabus' plan would lead to increased taxes, sharp cuts in other state services, or both. Republican strategists said the issue was effective in part because it raised the question of whether Mabus was experienced enough to be governor. National Republican party leaders such as Vice President George Bush and Congressman Jack Kemp, stumped the state in Reed's behalf.

Mabus, however, fresh from his impressive primary victory, went into the campaign with broad support. He battled back, arguing that his election would offer the state its best chance for change, and for improving its image around the nation. Campaigning on the theme "A New Day for Mississippi," Mabus promised "basic drastic change," and he dramatically vowed that Mississippi would "never be last again." His campaign was heavy on image. Through two primaries and the general election, he spent a record $2.9 million.

The result was an historic victory for Mabus, who hailed his win as a triumph for "a new generation of leadership." His 53 percent to 47 percent win over Reed was seen as a signal that the South was changing, and political analysts nationwide were quick to publicize the significance of the win. A cover story in the Sunday New York Times Magazine called the victory of the 39-year-old Mabus (who became the nation's youngest governor) a sign that the "yuppies had taken over Mississippi."

Mabus was seen to be as much a product of change in Mississippi as he was its author. He came back to the state and entered politics when Mississippi was, for the first time, ready to vote for a politician who talked about pocketbook issues and not race. He won significant support from affluent young professionals in urban areas who had been drifting toward the Republicans, as well as winning the black vote by nearly a 9 to 1 margin. Mabus was viewed as a prototype of a new sort of Southern politician, one adept at building black-white coalitions. Emphasizing innovation, he and the new breed of which he is representative are socially progressive yet fiscally conservative, because of the relative lack of resources with which to fund programs. The race also indicated that the power of local politicians (the classical courthouse crowd) to deliver votes was at an all-time low. Alongside Mabus, voters swept into office a group of progressive, reform-minded politicians in their 30s who pledged to help the new Governor "unravel the status quo."

Upon his inauguration, Mabus and his supporters immediately began working on replacing the state constitution, written in 1890 by the state's powerful planter class in reaction to Reconstruction. He also planned an immediate pay raise for state teachers, the consolidation of many of the state's agencies, commissions, and boards, and the active advancement of blacks. While claiming he has a mandate for change, Mabus faces powerful resistance. His plans to be an activist governor and to expand the power of his office make a showdown with the legislature—long used to dominating state politics—inevitable. He faces the enmity of the political establishment he campaigned against as well as the distinct reservations of many Mississippians who are firmly resistant to change. There are also fears that his programs will carry a bigger price tag than the impoverished state can afford, especially given his promise not to raise taxes.

Within three months after taking office, Mabus faced a simmering dispute over the leadership of the state's Democratic party that threatened to tarnish his progressive and reformist image. At issue was his attempt to oust the party's acting state chairman, Ed Cole, who had hoped to become the first black Democrat to lead a state party. The governor and his supporters pointed out that Cole was not among the early supporters of the Mabus campaign, and that he should be replaced by a person more supportive and attuned to Mabus' philosophy. The dispute was an important one for Mabus, since he has vowed to rebuild the state party.

Another important accomplishment of Mabus' early months in office was his participation in a wide-ranging agreement with the governors of Arkansas and Louisiana to coordinate their efforts to improve conditions in the Mississippi Delta area, one of the nation's poorest regions.

Bibliography: Biographical information courtesy of governor's office; *The Chronicle of Higher Education:* 9–23–87; 11–11–87; Peter J. Boyer, "The Yuppies of Mississippi: How They Took Over the Statehouse," *New York Times Magazine* (Feb. 28, 1988); *The New York Times:* 8–26–87; 11–3–87; 11–4–87; 11–5–87; 3–20–88; 5–14–88.

Christopher Samuel Bond (Courtesy of Senator Bond)

MISSOURI

BOND, Christopher Samuel ("Kit"), 1973–1977, 1981–1985

Born in St. Louis, Missouri on March 6, 1939, the second son of Arthur Doerr and Elizabeth (Green) Bond. Bond is the grandson of A. P. Green, who funded the refractories company of that name in Mexico, Missouri, A sixth-generation Missourian, he attended school from grades one through four in Tucson, Arizona. He attended public school in Mexico, Missouri from the fifth through the tenth grades, and completed his secondary education at Deerfield Academy, Deefield, Massachusetts, graduating in 1956. Bond received his college education at Princeton University, where he graduated *cum laude* from the Woodrow Wilson School of Public and International Affairs in 1960. He received his law degree in 1963 from the University of Virginia, graduating first in his class. On July 1, 1963, Bond accepted a clerkship with the United States Court of Appeals for the Fifth Circuit in Atlanta, Georgia, and served Chief Judge Elbert P. Tuttle, He held that position until June 30, 1964. In November 1964 he was employed by Covington and Burling, a law firm in Washington, D.C., where he remained until October 1967. Bond then returned to Mexico to practice law. He was married on May 13, 1967 to Carolyn Reid, in Lexington, Kentucky. They met in Atlanta, where she was employed as a speech therapist in the public schools. Mrs. Bond, who is from Owensboro, Kentucky, holds a master's degree in guidance and counseling from the University of Kentucky, where she was a member of Phi Beta Kappa. She also holds a bachelor's degree in speech and hearing therapy. The Bonds have one son, Samuel Reid Bond, born on Janaury 26, 1981.

In 1968 Christopher Bond made an unsuccessful bid for the ninth district seat in the United States House of Representatives. In January 1969 he became an assistant attorney general under Attorney General John C. Danforth, and served as chief counsel of the Consumer Protection Division; he resigned that position in June 1970 to run for state auditor. Bond was elected state auditor on November 4, 1970, and took office on January 12, 1971. The 28th state auditor of Missouri, he was, at 31 years of age, the youngest person to hold the office up to that time. He won by more than 200,000 votes, the largest margin by which a Republican ever had been elected to a statewide office in the history of Missouri. He was state auditor when he ran for chief executive in 1972 and defeated Democrat Edward L. Dowd by a vote of 1,029,451 to 832,751.

Bond was inaugurated as the 47th governor of the state of Missouri on Janaury 8, 1973, when he was 33 years of age. At the time he was the youngest governor in the nation and the youngest chief executive in the history of Missouri. Bond was the ninth Republican chosen governor, and his victory marked the first election of a Republican to that office in 32 years. During his first term Bond established a merit system of hiring, led a petition drive for a strict campaign contribution law, and secured passage of a strong open meetings law. Other accomplishments included the "circuit-breaker bill" (which provided property relief for low income senior citizens), increased funding for education, passage of a law requiring mandatory sentences for persons convicted of committing a crime with a gun, reinstatement of capital punishment for premeditated murder, establishment of the Department of Consumer Affairs, Regulation and Licensing to protect Missouri consumers, creation of the Office of Public Counsel to represent consumer interests before the Public Service Commission, and passage of a nationally recognized child abuse reporting law. Bond's economic development programs also brought many new jobs to the state. During his first term he served as chairman of the Economic and Community Development Committee of the National Governors' Association, chairman of the Midwest Governors' Association, and chairman of the Republican Governors' Association. Bond was selected as one of the Jaycees' Ten Outstanding Young Men of America in 1974. He served as a trustee of the School of the Ozarks, Point Lookout, Missouri, from 1970 to 1975. In 1973 he received an honorary doctor of laws degree from Westminster College, Fulton, Missouri, and William Jewell College, Liberty, Missouri.

In November 1976 Bond was narrowly defeated for re-election by Joseph P. Teasdale. From 1977 to 1979 he worked in Kansas City as president of the Great Plains Legal Foundation, a not-for-profit, public-interest law firm representing individual citizens and groups who could not otherwise afford an attorney in significant public policy battles before federal agencies and in the courts. The primary focus of the Great Plains Legal Foundation is to pursue cases where governmental regulatory barriers operate against the consumer. Bond resigned his position as president of the foundation in the spring of 1980 to run again for the office of governor. During his campaign for a second term, he established the following as his priorities: bringing 200,000 jobs to Missourians, providing job training and preparation, providing better education for Missouri children, improving care for the elderly, meeting the needs of children, and improving crime prevention methods.

In November 1980 Bond was elected to a second term as governor of Missouri, defeating Joseph Teasdale by a vote of 1,098,950 to 981,884.

When he took the oath of office on Janaury 12, 1981, he faced a serious fiscal crisis. Immediately upon taking office, he was forced to cut the operating budgets of state departments by $63 million to balance the budget. By the end of his term, he had reduced spending and left the state with a surplus. Despite tight budgetary constraints, he was able to launch new programs for economic development, crime control, and job training, as well as establishing a nationally acclaimed early childhood education program. Bond's administration brought about a crackdown on welfare fraud, an aggressive plan to collect child support payments from absent parents, the establishment of the Governor's Commission on Crime, the establishment of the Silver Citizens Discount Card Program, increased efforts to collect delinquent state taxes, approval by the voters of a $600 million bond issue for capital improvements, and the signing of commercial agreements between both the Republic of China and Japan and the state of Missouri. Bond also served as chairman of the National Governors' Association Committee on Community and Economic Development.

Constitutionally barred from seeking a third term, Bond made a successful run for the U.S. Senate in 1986. His opponent was Democratic Lieutenant Governor Harriet Woods, a former state senator who narrowly lost a hard fought race for the U.S. Senate against incumbent John C. Danforth in 1982. Her election as lieutenant governor in 1984 averted a Republican sweep of statewide offices.

The two were battling for the seat being relinquished by retiring Democrat Thomas Eagleton. The race was one of the most closely watched in the nation, one of a few key contests that experts predicted would determine whether the Republicans kept their majority in the Senate. The campaign was a bitter and costly one: Bond raised $4.4 million; Woods, $3.7 million. Both candidates were skillful and tireless, but contrasting campaigners.

Woods was a charismatic speaker who captivated audiences. Her political positions were seen by voters as reflecting compassion for people. Trying to run on farm belt discontent, she made the demand for a moratorium on farm foreclosures the centerpiece of her campaign. Her negative television advertising backfired, however. In what became known as the "crying farmer commercial," Woods tried to picture Bond as uncaring. The spot showed a farmer breaking into tears as he told of losing his farm. Bond countered with the charge that her message was distorted and misleading.

Bond, long considered a moderate in state politics, adopted a conservative stance for the campaign, welcoming three visits by President Reagan and identifying with the administration on most issues. He pictured Woods as a liberal, using the term almost as if it were an epithet. On most issues, their differences were clearly defined. Bond supported the president's Star Wars Initiative; Woods opposed it. She called for a moratorium on the debts of troubled farmers; he said a moratorium would just make matters worse. Bond favored conservative issues: aid to the Nicaraguan rebels, and an amendment giving authority on the issue of abortion to the states.

Having a popular record as governor and being the best known public figure in the state, Bond won handily, with 53 percent of the vote, the only Republican candidate nationally to win a seat previously held by a Democrat. Bond's victory gave the Republicans both Senate seats for Missouri, a predominantly Democratic state. In the Senate he serves on three committees: Agriculture, Nutrition, and Forestry; Banking, Housing, and Urban Affairs; and Small Business.

Bibliography: Biographical information courtesy of Senator Bond; Michael Barone *et al., The Almanac of American Politics 1988* (New York and Washington, D.C., 1987); *The New York Times:* 11–5–80; 3–5–83; 11–8–84; 10–1–86; 11–5–86; 11–6–86.

John David Ashcroft (Courtesy of governor's office)

ASHCROFT, John David, 1985–

Born in Chicago, Illinois on May 9, 1942; the son of fundamentalist minister James Robert Ashcroft and Grace Pauline Larson Ashcroft. A member of the Assemblies of God Church, he married Janet Elise Roede, an attorney, in 1967. The couple have three children: Martha, Jay, and Andrew.

Ashcroft graduated with honors from Yale University in 1964, and from the University of Chicago Law School in 1967. Returning to Missouri, he joined the business faculty of Southwest Missouri State University as an associate professor. He and his wife also practiced law together in Springfield and later co-authored two textbooks, *College Law for Business* (1971) and *It's the Law* (1979). Ashcroft also authored numerous articles published in law reviews and other professional journals. In addition to his legal career, Ashcroft developed his musical talents in gospel singing and song writing. He was well known as a gospel singer throughout churches in Missouri.

Ashcroft moved to Jefferson City from Springfield in 1972, when Governor Christopher S. Bond appointed him to fill an unexpired term as state auditor. As the state's 29th auditor, Ashcroft assumed the responsibilities of reviewing the financial records and operational efficiency of all state agencies and most of Missouri's counties. As auditor, Ashcroft recommended new procedures to save millions of dollars for state taxpayers. He was credited with making improvements in the office and with reducing the time span between audits.

Although Ashcroft lost a congressional primary in 1972 and the state auditor's race in 1974, he retained a loyal following among conservatives in the largely rural southwestern part of the state.

In January 1975 Ashcroft was appointed assistant attorney general under John C. Danforth. He served until April 1976 when he resigned to run for attorney general. Successful in his bid, he won re-election in 1980 by more than 580,000 votes. His 64.5 percent vote total was the largest margin and highest percentage by which a Republican had ever been elected to statewide office in the history of Missouri.

As attorney general, Ashcroft was most visible as an opponent of a settlement of a federal school desegregation lawsuit in St. Louis, a settlement that would have cost the state more than $100 million. In 1980 he established the Attorney General's Council on Crime Prevention, a forerunner of the Governor's Crime Commission, which Ashcroft directed as chairman. Under his leadership, the Crime Commission pushed legislation through the general assembly and worked to strengthen local law enforcement. Also during his tenure, Ashcroft served as president of the National Association of Attorneys General, and was also appointed chairman of its Budget Committee. For four years he represented the 50 state attorneys general in the American Bar Association House of Delegates. In June 1983, the National Association of Attorneys General presented Ashcroft with the prestigious Wyman Award, given annually to the state attorney general who has done the most to advance the objectives of the association and who demonstrated exemplary service in office that year.

Ashcroft sought the governorship in 1984, when incumbent Governor Christopher Bond was constitutionally barred from seeking a third term. He won the Republican gubernatorial nomination by defeating Gene McNary, St. Louis County Executive, in the August 1984 primary. Ashcroft polled 244,536 votes (67 percent) to McNary's 115,519 votes (32 percent). The race was Missouri's most expensive gubernatorial primary, with McNary spending $1.4 million to Ashcroft's $1.3 million.

In the general election Ashcroft faced Democratic Lieutenant Governor Kenneth J. Rothman, a veteran legislator from the St. Louis area. Unlike many other races, the campaign paired two ideological opponents: Ashcroft, a conservative Republican and Rothman, a moderate-to-liberal Democrat. Ashcroft had built his political career upon being religious, conservative, and family oriented. His positions on issues—against new taxes and for higher educational achievement—were both conservative and popular, and he won a solid victory in the race. Receiving 57 percent of the vote, he won by more than 280,800 votes and carried 107 of Missouri's 114 counties in one of the largest Republican gubernatorial victories in the state's history. Ashcroft was also the first Republican governor since 1928 to succeed another Republican governor.

Ashcroft became the 48th governor of Missouri on January 14, 1985. A central focus of his administration has been to provide Missourians with an environment of opportunity, development, and growth. He has made excellence in education and economic development his top priorities as governor.

In the area of education, he has promoted a plan to allow families to set up "Family Savings Accounts" in banks and other financial institutions. Appointed chairman of the National Governors' Association Task Force on College Quality, he and his team issued a national report in 1985 emphasizing that assessment can improve academic programs and that funding formula incentives can be used to improve undergraduate learning. He has also served as chairman of the National Governors' Association Task Force on Adult Literacy, leading the governors' national effort to promote action on the problem of adult illiteracy. In 1987 he succeeded Governor Bill Clinton of Arkansas as chairman of the Education Commission of the States, an interstate compact to help state political and educational leaders improve the quality of education nationwide.

Another focus of the Ashcroft administration has been welfare reform. In 1987, he proposed a plan to require every applicant for welfare to fill out a job application form. If no job were available, or if the applicant needed more education, the person would be required to enroll in free adult education classes and to work toward a high school diploma. If additional education was not required, a system of welfare-to-work provided job training and help in learning how to search and interview for jobs. The program also provided stipends for incidental expenses, day care assistance, and other support services.

In his 1988 campaign for re-election, Ashcroft easily defeated State Representative Betty Cooper Hearnes, wife of the former Democratic governor.

Bibliography: Biographical information, courtesy of governor's office; Michael Barone *et al., The Almanac of American Politics 1988* (New York and Washington, D.C., 1987); Jaques Cattell Press, *Who's Who in American Politics, 1985–1986* (New York, 1985); *The Chronicle of Higher Education,* 7–15–87; *The New York Times:* 8–7–84; 11–6–84; 11–8–84; 1–14–85; 2–22–87; 7–12–87.

Ted Schwinden (Courtesy of governor's office)

MONTANA

Born on August 31, 1925 in Wolf Point, Montana, the son of Michael James and Mary (Preble) Schwinden. A Lutheran, Schwinden married the former Jean Christianson, a registered nurse, in 1946. They have three children—Mike, Chrys, and Dore—and two grandchildren—Jordan and Erin.

Ted Schwinden began his formal education in a rural one-room schoolhouse. After graduating from Wolf Point High School in 1943, he enlisted in the United States Army, serving in both Europe and Asia during World War II. He was honorably discharged as a staff sergeant in 1946. Schwinden then attended the Montana School of Mines in Butte for one year before transferring to the University of Montana in Missoula. There he received a B.A. in 1949 and an M.A. in 1950, both degrees in history and political science. From 1950 to 1954 he did postgraduate work at the University of Minnesota. Schwinden has owned and operated a grain farm in Roosevelt County, Montana since 1954.

A Democrat, Schwinden began his political career in 1958, when he was elected to the Montana House of Representatives from Roosevelt County. Named to the Legislative Council from 1959 to 1961, he served as house minority whip during the 1961 session. Over the course of the next decade, he held a variety of prestigious administrative positions and appointments. In 1965 he was elected president of the Montana Grain Growers Association, a position he held for two years. In 1968 he was selected by United States Secretary of Agriculture Orville Freeman to represent the United States on a wheat trade mission to Asia. Schwinden was named by Montana Governor Forrest Anderson to be Commissioner of State Lands in 1969. Reappointed by Governor Thomas Judge in 1973, he served until 1976. During this same period, from 1973 to 1976, he also served as chairman of Montana's Bicentennial Advisory Committee.

In 1976 Schwinden was elected lieutenant governor of Montana, and he served from 1977 until 1981. In that capacity he was responsible for overseeing the state's role in natural resources, agriculture, and energy issues.

Characterized by political observers as a "folksy rancher with few enemies," Schwinden defeated incumbent Democratic Governor Thomas

Judge to gain the Democratic gubernatorial nomination in 1980, gaining 51 percent of the vote to Judge's 42 percent. Two minor candidates shared the remaining seven percent. Although Judge, as the incumbent, had been expected to win re-election, or at the very least renomination, his liberal reputation may have worked against him. So too, some said, did his personal style and manner. After two four-year terms, his personality "did not wear well," wrote one political observer. In the general election Schwinden easily defeated Jack Ramirez, a Republican state legislator, by attracting 55 percent of the vote. Although Ramirez had won some popularity by pushing a tax cut through the legislature, the fact that he was a corporate lawyer from Billings caused him to be viewed by some as a "city slicker and protector of monied interests." Schwinden carried all but a few scattered counties in the state, a testimony to the strength of the Democratic party in Montana. It is still difficult for a Republican to win statewide office, and the Democrats have now been in continuous control of the governorship since 1968.

Philosophically, Schwinden believes that Democrats have won governorships in the West by responding, in his words, to a popular desire for progress "coupled with protection." He feels that measured economic development and environmental protection can go hand in hand. Schwinden has achieved a certain amount of national publicity as part of a group of western governors anxious to ensure that the states, rather than Washington bureaucrats, have a greater voice in determining the nation's energy and water policies. "We know we have a responsibility to share our resources and be part of the energy solution," he told a reporter for *Newsweek* magazine. "What we don't want to do is turn over control to outsiders—and that means OPEC, Washington, and the East Coast." In 1982 Schwinden received extensive press coverage because of a dispute with Reagan administration Interior Secretary James Watt over mineral development and coal leases in the Powder River Basin of Montana and Wyoming. Schwinden also involved himself in a growing controversy among western states over interstate water sales and transfers. The lack of water is a crucial issue in the arid Rocky Mountain states, yet Schwinden gave his backing to a proposal that would clear the way for Montana to sell some of its own surface water to developers in other states. This, he said, would not only enable the state to earn money, but would also help to expand markets for Montana's huge coal reserves. (Presumably, the water would be used in coal slurry lines to move coal across the country.) Some members of Schwinden's own party attacked the plan, however, which they said could touch off a water war in the West.

During his first term in office, Schwinden also vetoed controversial legislation designed to eliminate the United States Supreme Court's exclusionary rule in Montana. Despite strong objections from the insurance industry, he signed a bill that made Montana the first state in the nation to prohibit discrimination based on sex or marital status in all types of insurance and pension plans.

Governor Schwinden won a second term as chief executive in November 1984 by easily defeating Republican State Senator Pat Goodover. Schwinden captured 70 percent of the vote in that election, compared with Goodover's 26 percent, the largest victory margin in Montana history.

Like a number of other Rocky Mountain governors, Schwinden has retained his popularity with voters despite years in the spotlight. During his years in office, tourism has gone from being a minor industry to the state's second largest employer, just behind agriculture. While he has drawn praise for his "Build Montana" programs, it has been his unique personalized approach to government and his pleasant low key style that has most endeared him to voters. He has won plaudits for his accessibility and for such gestures as listing his home telephone number in the Helena directory. Some Democratic critics, however, have faulted him for relaxing the state severance tax on coal and for not backing unions more strongly.

In August 1987 he disappointed supporters with his announcement that he would not be seeking a third term in 1988. After 27 years in public office, he and his wife planned "to put our family first."

In the race to succeed him, two candidates emerged from the June 1988 primaries: former Democratic Governor Thomas L. Judge (1973–1981) and former State Senator Stan Stephens, a Republican. The primary race was marred by tragedy when the early favorite among the Democrats, Secretary of State Jim Waltermire, was killed in an airplane crash in April 1988. In the November 1988 general election, Stephens went on to defeat Judge for the governorship, gaining 53 percent of the vote to the former governor's 47 percent.

Bibliography: Biographical information, courtesy of governor's office; Michael Barone *et al., The Almanac of American Politics, 1982, 1986, 1988* (New York and Washington, D.C., 1981, 1985, 1987); *The New York Times:* 11–5–80; 4–23–81; 4–26–82; 11–22–82; 2–18–83; 4–23–83; 6–6–84; 11–8–84; 8–31–87; 6–9–88.

Joseph Robert Kerrey (Courtesy of Governor Kerrey)

NEBRASKA

Born in Lincoln, Nebraska on August 27, 1943. His father, James, was a builder and businessman; his mother, Elinor, an instructor at the University of Nebraska. A Congregational Christian, Kerrey is the divorced father of two children, Benjamin and Lindsey.

Kerrey graduated in 1961 from Lincoln Northeast High School where he participated and lettered in football, swimming, and golf. He earned a degree in pharmacy from the University of Nebraska, graduating in 1965.

In 1966 Kerrey enlisted in the Navy, graduating as an ensign from Officers Candidate School in 1967. In the course of training he attended Army Airborne and Ranger Schools and completed underwater demolition training. He was selected for the U.S. Navy SEAL team and in January 1969 deployed to Vietnam as the platoon officer of a 14-man SEAL team. Kerrey won a Medal of Honor for Vietnam Combat action in which his foot was blown off. He was also awarded the Bronze Star, the Purple Heart, and Vietnamese Campaign Ribbons. The SEAL team's West Coast Training Camp was named Camp Robert Kerrey in his honor.

Kerrey returned to the Midwest in 1970 to pursue a career in pharmacy. In 1972, he and brother-in-law Dean Rasmussen built and organized the first Grandmother's Skillet Restaurant in Omaha. When the restaurant was destroyed by a tornado in 1975, Kerrey and Rasmussen rebuilt and expanded it, developing outlets in Omaha and Lincoln and establishing related sports and fitness enterprises.

A virtual unknown in political circles, Kerrey declared his candidacy for governor on February 15, 1982. His race with incumbent Charles Thone was referred to by the *New York Times* as "one of the more interesting battlegrounds in the 1983 election." As a young and colorful Kennedyesque Democrat, Kerrey was an unusual political commodity in Nebraska, a conservative state that had given Ronald Reagan his third largest majority (72 percent) in 1980. An editorial in the *North Platte Telegraph* entitled "Strangely, a Nebraskan," described Kerrey as political kin to Jerry Brown of California, and the conservative Thone organization attempted to portray him as an ultraliberal who had participated in anti-war activities and who, as a member of Lincoln's Human Rights Commission, had led an unsuccessful effort to enforce an equal rights ordinance for homosexuals. Although voters viewed Kerrey as a novice in agricultural matters, they held Thone responsible for a Nebraska farm economy described by some as the bleakest since the 1930s. In a state plagued by sagging farm prices and high interest rates, Thone had also had to seek a tax increase since the recession of the early 1980s had forced the state budget into deficit. Kerrey promised to attract jobs with more aggressive economic development and took advantage of the fact that Thone had made enemies, notably the state's education lobby, through his support of unaccredited fundamentalist schools. Charging that Thone had concealed deficits and mismanaged the state, he tried to make the contest a battle between excellence and mediocrity.

Most important was the difference in style between the two men. Thone liked to tell audiences that he was "what Nebraska is all about," an honest, hard-working fellow who came off the farm and thought of himself as more of a "workhorse than a showhorse"—all in contrast to the polished and city-bred Kerrey. Voters, however, were swayed by what the Nebraska Democratic chairman called Kerrey's "extraordinary political organization and his charismatic ability to move people." Considered to have run one of the most effective campaigns in state history, Kerrey won the election narrowly, 51 percent to 49 percent.

The Democratic Kerrey was a popular governor in this predominantly Republican state, winning approval ratings as high as 74 percent. Handsome and energetic, he lent glamour to the farm state by his much publicized liaison with actress Debra Winger, who met Kerrey in 1983 while filming the movie *Terms of Endearment*. His fling with the actress, which included overnight visits to the Governor's Mansion, was breathlessly reported in the gossip magazines. Rather than damaging his reputation with voters, however, the affair seemed to delight his constituency. Bringing a refreshing brand of agrarian populism and liberalism to Nebraska, Kerrey was a rising star among the elite corps of electable Western Democrats, spurring talk of higher office and comparisons with John F. Kennedy. In the words of Lynn Cutler, vice chairman of the Democratic National Committee, he was a man of "star quality" who was increasingly attracting national attention from the press. His stature as an administrator was enhanced by leading his farm state through a time of economic crisis and emerging with his popularity intact.

With his rising reputation, Kerrey's October 1985 announcement that he would not seek a second term in 1986 understandably sent waves of shock and dismay through the Democratic party. His surprise statement disappointed both state and national Democrats. Kerrey said his decision was based on the feeling "that it is time for me to move on to a future different from being an elected politician." While Nebraskans speculated that he was feeling tired of publicity surrounding his relationship with Winger, he, on the contrary, simply explained that he had never viewed himself as a career politician and had never wanted to be one. By leaving politics behind and insisting on his own agenda Kerrey—in the opinion of political analysts—was emblematic of a generation of national leaders more influenced by Vietnam than by World War II, a generation affected more by campus protest than by the Depression. Others predicted that a return to the national stage was inevitable.

With the completion of his term in January 1987, Kerrey joined the investment banking firm of Printon, Kane and Co., opening its Lincoln, Nebraska office. A millionaire, he was chairman of the Board of Grandmother's Skillet Restaurants, and general managing partner in Kerrey Holdings which includes Prairie Life Center, the Cottonwood Club fitness and recreational centers, Sun Valley Lanes, and other business and real estate investments. Kerrey Holdings is also a partner in Bates Video Productions.

Political analysts who predicted Kerrey's return to political life proved correct. He expressed an interest in running for president in 1988, explaining that many Democrats encouraged him to make the race after Senator Gary Hart's withdrawal in May 1987. Kerrey's support had helped Hart win the 1984 Democratic presidential primary in Nebraska. Instead, however, Kerrey chose to seek election to the U.S. Senate in 1988. Holding a big lead in the polls ever since it was known he would enter the race, he overwhelmed Ken Michaelis, a little known perennial candidate, in the May 1988 primary, winning 91.6 percent of the Democratic vote. His opponent in the November 1988 general election will be incumbent David K. Karnes, an attorney whom Governor Kay Orr appointed to the seat in March 1987 upon the death of Senator Edward Zorinsky. In the first election of his career, Karnes survived an aggressive primary challenge from four-term Congressman Harold J. Daub, bitter that he had been passed over by Orr for the seat he had long regarded as a future target. According to political observers, Kerrey's own popularity, as well as the promising aspect of a competitive presidential race, made the former governor the clear favorite in the fall campaign. In a race that turned largely on questions of personality, Kerrey won handily, even in a predominantly Republican state. Political observers have already targeted him as one of the faces to watch in the 101st Congress.

Bibliography: Biographical information courtesy of Governor Kerrey; "Fresh Faces in the Mansions," *Newsweek* (Nov. 15, 1982); *Nebraska Blue Book, 1984–1985;* Jaques Cattell Press, *Who's Who in American Politics, 1985–1986* (New York, 1985); Michael Barone *et al., The Almanac of American Politics 1986* (New York and Washington, D.C., 1985); *The New York Times:* 1–21–82; 9–23–82; 10–22–82; 11–4–82; 11–21–85; 5–13–87; 11–21–87; 2–9–88; 5–8–88; 5–10–88; 5–12–88.

Kay Stark Orr (Courtesy of governor's office)

ORR, Kay Stark, 1987–

Born Kay Stark in Burlington, Iowa on January 2, 1939; the daughter of Ralph Robert Stark and Sadie Stark. A Presbyterian, she married William D. Orr in 1957. Mr. Orr is senior vice president and director of agencies for Woodmen Accident and Life Insurance Company. The couple have two children, John and Suzanne.

Orr received her public schooling in Iowa and California, and then attended the University of Iowa, where she met her husband. In the early 1960s the family moved to Lincoln, Nebraska, where she began her career in politics working on the 1964 presidential campaign of Senator Barry Goldwater. Beginning with her election as co-chair of the Lancaster County Young Republicans in 1967, she has since been honored with many party positions, including election as delegate to the National Republican Conventions of 1976, 1980, and 1984. She led Ronald Reagan's Nebraska campaign during his ill-fated presidential bid of 1976, and co-chaired former Governor Charles Thone's successful 1978 campaign. She then served as the governor's executive assistant until June of 1981, when she was appointed Nebraska State Treasurer. She was then elected to that office by a wide margin in 1982, the first woman ever elected by Nebraska voters to a statewide constitutional office. She completed her four-year term as state treasurer on the day she took the oath of office as Nebraska's governor.

In 1984 she became the first person, male or female, other than a member of Congress or a state's governor, to serve as co-chair of the Republican National Convention's Platform Committee. She has also served as a member of the Executive Committee of the National Association of State Treasurers. In 1985 she was appointed to the U.S. Department of Agriculture's National Agricultural Research and Extension Users Advisory Board, and to the President's Advisory Committee on the Arts for the John F. Kennedy Center for the Performing Arts.

Orr became governor of Nebraska in a race historic for several reasons. In 1986 this conservative but populist farm state became the first ever to nominate women as the gubernatorial candidates of both major political parties. After defeating 1984 senatorial candidate Nancy Hoch to win the Republican gubernatorial nomination, Orr faced Democrat Helen Boosalis, the former mayor of Lincoln. Both Orr and Boosalis were well-known figures in state politics. Boosalis, a former League of Women Voters activist, launched her political career on the Lincoln City Council in the late 1950s. She served 16 years on the council, then two terms as the mayor of Lincoln, from 1975 to 1983. In that period she became president of the U.S. Conference of Mayors. Her most recent position was director of the Nebraska Department of Aging.

Although the Nebraska campaign became a symbol of women's political progress, neither candidate came out of a feminist tradition. On the contrary, both were party regulars who first entered politics as volunteers and then worked their way up the political ladder. While the race made feminist history, it did not become a feminist crusade. The National Organization for Women, the National Women's Political Caucus, and the Women's Campaign Fund stayed out of the contest because both women opposed abortion. Although Boosalis supported the Equal Rights Amendment, she was personally opposed to abortion except in cases of rape or incest, or to save the mother's life. Orr, on the other hand, was opposed both to the Equal Rights Amendment and to legalized abortion in all instances. She did, however, credit the feminist movement for awakening her and other women to new roles and new possibilities.

In the contest between the two women, what are frequently called women's issues stayed in the background. Most of the political debate concerned problems endemic in the Midwest, chiefly the troubled farming sector and the need for jobs and economic development. The race was seen as a referendum on President Reagan's policies and their effect on the state's beleaguered farmers. While Boosalis ran as a harsh critic of federal farm policy, Orr—unlike other farm state Republicans—made no attempt to distance herself from the president. Rather, her campaign focused on Boosalis' fiscal policies. She portrayed her opponent as a Democrat committed to increased taxing and spending, charges that Boosalis angrily denied. The campaign became a referendum on taxes, with Orr, an opponent of sales tax increases, defeating Boosalis, who said they might be necessary. There was little evidence that state Republicans suffered from the farm revolt apparent elsewhere, in Iowa or the Dakotas, for example. Orr won handily, with 53 percent of the vote, all the while proclaiming her support for Ronald Reagan. All three Republican House members were also easily re-elected.

With her election, Orr became the first woman to be elected governor of Nebraska, and the first Republican woman governor in the United States. She was also one of the few Republicans elected governor of Nebraska in recent history: Democrats had held the office for 20 of the 28 years preceding her election.

As governor, Orr faced serious challenges. She had to deal with a state whose agriculture-based economy was in trouble, one that faced both a shrinking population and declining state revenues. Serious budget difficulties were brought on in part by the Tax Reform Act of 1986. Because the state's tax system is tied directly to the amount of federal tax paid by citizens, state revenues dropped by $24 million in 1987 and $36 million in 1988. While the legislature was pressed to adjust the state individual income tax to accommodate the drastic changes enacted by Congress, Orr, unlike other Western governors, refused to consider a tax increase.

Saying her administration would be "marked by optimism and tempered with realism," Orr outlined her agenda: creating jobs, reforming the state tax system, and improving education. Her program got off to a rough start, however. Early in her administration, she pushed an economic development plan of tax benefits to businesses that moved to Nebraska or expanded there, a plan linked by critics to a threat by one of Omaha's largest employers, Con Agra Inc., to leave the state because of its tax structure. A companion bill cut income taxes at the top and bottom of the scale, but left many lower-to-middle income taxpayers paying more. Opponents charged that these economic initiatives represented a surrender to corporate blackmail, and some, such as the Center for Rural Affairs, a group of farm advocates, said both measures were too pro-business. One month after the economic measures passed, a poll by the *Omaha World Herald* indicated that only 53 percent of Nebraskans approved of Orr's job performance, while 33 percent disapproved—the worst rating for a Nebraska governor in 17 years. Orr countered that her motives were misunderstood. Within six months after the bill passed, more than 100 Nebraska companies had in fact expanded. Critics continued to charge, however, that the law merely cut state revenue because there were all homegrown businesses that would have expanded anyway.

In the area of education, however, Orr's proposals for increased spending for higher education brought wide expressions of support. She planned to increase university research to bolster economic development, and to seek more private contributions for public colleges. Yet even in this predominantly Republican state, her popularity still lags behind that of her Democratic predecessor, Bob Kerrey.

Early in her term, Orr made a controversial appointment that divided her own party. After the death of Democratic Senator Edward Zorinsky in March 1987, she named little-known businessman David K. Karnes to the post, alienating party stalwarts. Defending her appointment of Karnes, who had been her second congressional district chairman in the 1986 campaign, Orr claimed the right to put her own stamp on party structure.

Nationwide, Orr has drawn much attention in Republican party circles. She headed the platform committee for the 1988 Republican National Convention, the first woman ever to hold that position. Her name was also included on a long list of possible picks as George Bush's vice presidential running mate. Within the National Governors' Association, her committee assignments have been Agriculture, Economic Development and Technological Innovation, as well as Transportation, Commerce and Communications. She also serves on the NGA's Adult Literacy Task Force.

Bibliography: Biographical information courtesy of governor's office; *The Chronicle of Higher Education,* 11–12–86; *USA Today,* 6–7–88; Jaques Cattell Press, *Who's Who in American Politics, 1985–1986* (New York, 1985); Michael Barone *et al., The Almanac of American Politics 1988* (New York and Washington, D.C., 1987); *The New York Times:* 5–18–86; 9–16–86; 10–30–86; 1–9–87; 3–21–87; 2–9–88.

Richard H. Bryan (Courtesy of governor's office)

NEVADA

BRYAN, Richard H., 1983–

Born on July 16, 1937 in Washington, D.C.; the son of Oscar W. Bryan and Lillie Pleasants Bryan; An Episcopalian, Bryan married Bonnie Fairchild in 1962. The couple have three children: Richard, Leslie, and Blair.

A second generation Nevadan, Bryan displayed his interest in government early, when he served as president of his sophomore and senior classes at Las Vegas High School. He is a 1959 graduate of the University of Nevada-Reno, where he served as student body president during his senior year. After graduation he entered the U.S. Army as a second lieutenant and became a captain in the Army Reserve. He continued his education at the University of California Hastings College of Law where he earned his law degree with honors.

Bryan served as deputy district attorney in Clark County from 1964 to 1966. In 1966 he was appointed as the first public defender in Nevada, the youngest person in the nation to hold that position. He served in that capacity from 1966 to 1968, when he was elected to the Nevada State Assembly. There he was named outstanding freshman assemblyman. After serving two terms in the assembly, he was elected to the Nevada State Senate, where he chaired the Taxation and Education Committees. State senator from 1972 to 1978, he then served as Nevada Attorney General from 1978 to 1982.

The attorney general's post became Bryan's springboard to the governorship. In 1982 he mounted a successful challenge to incumbent Republican Robert List, who was blamed for the state's economic difficulties. The recession of 1981–1982 had punctured the prevailing myth that gambling was recession-proof. List also had to deal with two other problems that severely affected the state's number one industry—New Jersey's entrance into competition for legalized gambling dollars, as well as an increase in air fares due to higher jet fuel prices. List was also harmed by his fiscal policies. His reliance on the sales tax as a source of needed revenue did not bring in the projected income he had expected. Bryan, making economic diversification the theme of his campaign, won with 54 percent of the vote. Bryan won re-election easily in 1986. Winning nearly 80 percent of the Democratic primary vote against businessman Herb Tobman, he faced State Treasurer Patty Cafferata in the general election.

He won the race "almost by acclamation," with 72 percent of the vote, becoming a kind of consensus choice as state revenues increased and growth continued.

During his two terms in office, Bryan has strongly supported economic diversification, the promotion of tourism, and an improved educational system. Hoping to raise taxes on casino revenues to pay for various programs, he wants to increase the salaries of faculty in the state university system and expand engineering programs at the University of Nevada's Las Vegas and Reno campuses. He has proposed allocating $195,000 to scholarship funding in order to encourage top high school graduates to enter teaching.

Bryan is a member of the National Governors' Association, serving on the Committee on Economic Development and Technological Innovation, the Committee on International Trade and Foreign Relations, the Task Force on Adult Literacy, the Task Force on Jobs, Growth, and Competitiveness, and chairing the Subcommittee on Tourism. He is also president of the Council of State Governments.

In 1986 there was some speculation that Bryan would run for the U.S. Senate seat of retiring incumbent Paul Laxalt. Foregoing that race, he announced instead that he would challenge Senator Chic Hecht in November 1988. Polls taken in the year preceding the contest showed Bryan with a large lead over the Republican incumbent. Although he suffered a bit from voter displeasure with the national Democratic ticket, the highly popular Bryan went on to defeat Hecht, winning 51 percent of the vote to the incumbent's 47 percent.

Bibliography: Biographical information courtesy of governor's office; Jaques Cattell Press, *Who's Who in American Politics, 1985, 1986* (New York, 1985); Michael Barone *et al., The Almanac of American Politics, 1986, 1988* (New York and Washington, D.C., 1985, 1987); *The Chronicle of Higher Education:* 11–12–86; 2–18–87; *The New York Times:* 12–1–85; 3–29–88; *U.S. News and World Report,* 10–4–82.

John H. Sununu (Courtesy of governor's office)

NEW HAMPSHIRE

SUNUNU, John H., 1983–

Born in Havana, Cuba on July 2, 1939; a Roman Catholic, Sununu married the former Nancy Hayes in 1958. His wife is a former chairman of the New Hampshire Republican State Committee, and currently serves as first vice president of the New Hampshire Federated Republican Women. The couple has eight children.

Sununu did his undergraduate and graduate work at the Massachusetts Institute of Technology, where he earned his Ph.D. in the field of mechanical engineering in 1966. From 1965 until his election as governor, he served as president of JHS Engineering Company and Thermal Research, Inc., in addition to helping found and serving as chief engineer for Astro Dynamics from 1960 to 1965. From 1968 to 1973 he was associate dean of the College of Engineering at Tufts University, where he had been an associate professor of medical engineering since 1966. He was invited to join the Advisory Board of Technology and Policy Programs at MIT in August 1984.

Assuming the governorship with a background of nearly 20 years experience as an educator, engineer, and small businessman, he was first elected in 1982, winning re-election in 1984 and again in 1986. A Republican, he defeated incumbent Hugh Gallen in 1982 when Gallen, faced with fiscal difficulties, refused to promise that he would veto any state sales or income taxes. Taking this no tax "pledge" has long been seen as critical to victory in New Hampshire. Because of Gallen's reluctance to do so, the newcomer Sununu won the election, gaining 52 percent of the vote to Gallen's 46 percent. In 1984 he won an overwhelming victory against Chris Spirou, the minority leader in the State House of Representatives, who accused Sununu of being a "cheerleader" for the controversial Seabrook nuclear power plant. Winning 67 percent of the vote to his opponent's 33 percent, Sununu made no secret of his staunch defense of nuclear power. Campaign issues were similar in 1986, when an accident at the Chernobyl plant in the Soviet Union again pushed the issue of nuclear power to center stage. Sununu's opponent, Democratic attorney Paul McEachern, assailed Sununu as "the world's champion proponent of nuclear power." He also challenged Sununu's position on a federal proposal to put a nuclear waste dump in central New Hampshire. Sununu, however, focused his campaign on the economy. Under his leadership, New Hampshire moved from a $40 million budget deficit to a surplus of more than $21 million. It also boasted the nation's lowest unemployment rate and strong growth in personal income. Sununu again won handily, 54 percent to 46 percent.

Sununu has earned both regional and national recognition since taking office. That recognition gained him the chairmanship of the Coalition of Northeastern Governors; the chairmanship of the Republican Governors' Association; the chairmanship of the New England Governors' Association; and the vice chairmanship of the Advisory Commission on Intergovernmental Relations. Vice chairman of the National Governors' Association in 1986, he assumed the chairmanship in 1987. Claiming that there has been a "drastic overcentralization of power in Washington," he took the main task of his chairmanship to be a thorough examination of federal-state relations. Believing that the federal government has usurped too much of the states' authority and hobbled their ability to attack social and economic problems, he has even talked of the need for a constitutional amendment to address the problem.

Sununu has also served as chairman of the National Governors' Association Subcommittee on Energy; chairman of its Committee on International Trade and Foreign Relations; a member of the Committee on Transportation, Commerce and Communications; and chairman of the New Technology Education Task Force which issued the Governors Report on U.S. Education, 1991. Through his efforts the National Governors' Association and later the New Hampshire legislature endorsed model acid rain legislation. A supporter of aid to education, Sununu has requested continued increases in state spending for the University of New Hampshire system. In 1983, he became involved in a serious political debate over the uses of computer technology, the first of its kind in the nation. Asking the state legislature for money to computerize the system by which the state raises and spends more than one billion dollars per year, Sununu sparked a controversy with the legislature, which feared that it was creating a pool of information to which the executive branch would have access while it did not.

Sununu considers the major achievements of his administration to be turning around New Hampshire's financial situation while holding down government growth.

Sununu chaired George Bush's New Hampshire primary campaign in 1988, and served as Bush's representative to the Republican National Committee's platform panel at the Republican National Convention. He was also mentioned as a possible vice presidential running mate for Bush on the 1988 ticket.

Despite such national acclaim, Sununu unexpectedly announced that he had decided against seeking a fourth gubernatorial term in 1988. He said he would take a job in private business so that he could concentrate on personal matters, primarily to earn more money to help pay for his children's education. Sununu's surprise announcement threw open a gubernatorial race that was widely expected to be a sure win for him. One of George Bush's most loyal supporters and vocal surrogates in the 1988 presidential campaign, Sununu was named White House Chief of Staff in the new Bush administration.

Bibliography: Biographical information courtesy of governor's office; Jaques Cattell Press, *Who's Who in American Politics, 1985–1986* (New York, 1985); Michael Barone *et al., The Almanac of American Politics, 1984, 1988* (New York and Washington, D.C., 1983, 1987); *The Chronicle of Higher Education,* 11–12–86; *U.S.A. Today,* 6–7–88; *The New York Times:* 11–7–84; 5–6–85; 5–11–86; 9–11–86; 10–11–86; 7–6–87; 7–29–87; 5–17–88.

Thomas H. Kean (Courtesy of governor's office)

NEW JERSEY

Born in New York, New York on April 21, 1935, the son of Robert Winthrop and Elizabeth (Stuyvesant) Kean. Kean is married to Deborah Bye of Wilmington, Delaware; he is the father of Reed, Thomas, and Alexandra.

Kean's father served in the United States House of Representatives from 1939 to 1959. His ancestors include William Livingston, who was governor of New Jersey from 1776 to 1790. Kean attended St. Marks School, and was graduated from Princeton University. He earned an M.A. at Columbia University, but abandoned plans to go on for a Ph.D. after joining William Scranton's unsuccessful bid for the Republican presidential nomination in 1964. Kean taught American history and english in high schools for three years, directed a camp for disadvantaged children, and took part in the White House Conference on Youth in 1970 and 1971. He taught political science at Rutgers, New Jersey's state university, and worked as a commentator on the New Jersey Educational Network's evening news program. Kean also was president and chairman of the Realty Transfer Company of Elizabeth, New Jersey.

A member of the New Jersey General Assembly from 1967 to 1977, Kean was named speaker of that body in 1972, despite the fact that Republicans did not hold a majority of the seats. David Freidland, the Democratic minority leader of the previous assembly, had been passed over for the nomination as speaker in favor of a black pastor from Trenton. Freidland and two others retaliated by defecting to Kean, the Republican minority candidate. One disgruntled Democrat noted that "Jesus Christ has his Judas, the Democrats now have David Friedland."

Kean managed President Gerald Ford's successful New Jersey campaign in 1976, and in the following year lost the gubernatorial primary to State Senator Raymond H. Bateman. Four years later, however, Kean defeated seven other candidates to win the nomination. (Kean's principal opponent in that primary was Lawrence Kramer the mayor of Paterson, New Jersey.) Kean then met James Florio, a Democratic congressman from South Jersey, in the general election. Both men were rather moderate liberals—for instance, Kean had introduced New Jersey's first rent control bill—but Kean nevertheless spent much of his time disassociating himself from President Ronald Reagan. The final count was extremely close: 1,145,999 votes for Kean and 1,144,202 for Florio, with about 25,000 votes divided among 11 independent candidates. Although there were allegations that the national Republican party had tried to scare Democratic voters away from the polls by using a "ballot security" force, in the end Florio conceded the election without a court fight.

Despite the closeness of his election win, Kean went on to establish himself as one of the most popular governors in the state's history. In his campaign for re-election in 1985, he scored the biggest landslide victory in the state's history, defeating his Democratic opponent, Essex County Executive Peter Shapiro, with over 70 percent of the vote. The final vote total was 1,352,459 for Kean to 574,980 to Shapiro. The strength of Kean's victory also helped the Republicans win control of the state assembly for the first time in 12 years. In the campaign, Kean had received the endorsement of the AFL-CIO, the first time that the union had ever supported a Republican gubernatorial candidate. He also won 60 percent of the black vote, an achievement that made him a national celebrity and a rising star in national Republican party politics. After his win, Kean became a national spokesman for Republicans eager to widen party ranks to include more minority and blue-collar voters. He outlined his strategies and policies for opening up the party in his book, *The Politics of Inclusion* (Free Press, 1988).

During his first term in office, Kean signed increases in state income and sales taxes to close a budget deficit exacerbated by the recession of the early 1980s. Taking advantage of economic gains in the state caused by the national recovery, he created more than 350,000 new jobs during his first term, and the state's unemployment rate ran consistently below the national average. The gains of his first term continued during his second, with New Jersey undergoing a rapid transformation into a blossoming state with a thriving, diverse economy. Thousands of new jobs have been created, and the unemployment rate remains one of the lowest in the country.

During his years in office, Kean has also lowered business taxes, signed a death penalty law, persuaded the legislature to pass a law protecting freshwater wetlands, and overseen the divestment of state pension funds from companies doing business in South Africa. An adviser to President Reagan on welfare reform, he proposed a state "workfare" program that would require all able-bodied welfare recipients either to go to school or to seek employment.

His major achievements, however, have been in the area of education. Hailed as the "education governor" by the national press, he introduced major reforms in the state's teacher training programs as well as hiking the minimum starting salary for public school teachers. He has pushed for regular increases in state higher-education spending, launched a competitive grant program that provides money for institutions to carry out special initiatives, helped New Jersey state colleges lobby for a controversial plan to give them more control over financial matters, and pushed for a $90 million bond issue for higher education construction and equipment purchases. Frequently appearing as a panelist at higher education conferences, he has also been active in influencing national higher education policy. He has served as chairman of the Education Commission of the States, as co-chairman of the National Governors' Association panel on education, and as a member of a special teaching panel formed by the Carnegie Forum on Education and the Economy. He is also a member of Princeton University's Board of Trustees.

A moderate Republican, he supports the ERA as well as freedom of choice on abortions and gun control. Although he is known for his rather liberal stands on certain issues, including civil rights, aid to cities and the environment, he is a firm conservative on others. He vigorously supported President Reagan's large tax cuts, and also supports the President's plan to build a space-based missile defense system. Chairman of the Republican Governors' Association in 1987, he has relished using what he calls the "bully pulpits" available to him as he has traveled around the country promoting both his education reforms and his politics of inclusion. Frequently mentioned as a possible vice presidential running mate for George Bush in 1988, he was chosen instead to deliver the keynote address at the 1988 Republican National Convention in New Orleans.

Known as one of the nation's most innovative chief executives, Kean is widely expected to seek national office some day.

Bibliography: Biographical information courtesy of governor's office; *The New York Times:* 10–26–81; 9–17–85; 10–31–85; 11–1–85; 11–6–85; 11–7–85; 9–10–86; 10–9–86; 4–20–87; 12–27–87; 1–12–88; 1–13–88; 1–22–88; 1–31–88; *The (Newark) Star Ledger:* 10–24–86; 3–8–87; Michael Barone *et al., The Almanac of American Politics 1988* (New York and Washington, D.C., 1987); Thomas H. Kean, *The Politics of Inclusion* (New York, 1988); *The Chronicle of Higher Education:* "New Jersey's Education Governor," (Oct. 14, 1987); *U.S.A. Today,* 6–7–88; "The Statehouses: Action and Innovation," *Newsweek* (March 24, 1986).

Toney Anaya (Photo courtesy of Governor Anaya; Portrait by LeRoy N. Sanchez)

NEW MEXICO

Born in Moriarty, New Mexico on April 29, 1941, the son of Lauriano Anaya and Eufracia Martinez Anaya. Anaya married the former Elaine Marie Bolin of Hanover, Pennsylvania in 1963. The couple have three children: Kimberley, Toney, and Kristina.

Anaya graduated from the Georgetown University School of Foreign Service in 1963, where he majored in economics and political science. He received a law degree from Washington College of Law, American University, in 1967.

Anaya has held numerous positions in national and state government. Working for the U.S. Department of Labor from 1959 to 1966, he was executive assistant to the assistant secretary of state in the U.S. Department of State in 1966. In June 1966 he became chief legislative counsel to U.S. Senator Joseph Montoya (D-N.M.), a position he held from 1966 to 1969. In that post he researched, drafted, and provided staff support for the senator's legislative initiatives; monitored and advised the senator on all congressional legislation; assisted on legislative and appropriations committee hearings; initiated and monitored federally legislated and funded New Mexico projects; and assisted New Mexico municipalities, state agencies, and organizations seeking federal funding, technical assistance, and other support. From 1971 to 1972, he was chief of staff to New Mexico Governor Bruce King, serving as public ombudsman, aiding the enactment of legislative and budgetary requests, helping to establish and implement state policies, and assisting with the supervision and direction of state agencies. In 1975 he became attorney general of the state, serving in that capacity to 1978. His office focused on reducing government corruption, protecting consumer interests, and improving legal services to state government. He created units to scrutinize utility rate increases and to promote sound environmental and energy policies, and to combat narcotics trafficking, Medicaid fraud, and organized and white collar crime. He also coordinated legal services to improve the efficiency of state government efforts.

Anaya succeeded Bruce King as governor of New Mexico in January 1983. In the November 1982 election he had defeated Republican John Irick with 53 percent of the vote. Despite achievements in economic development, affirmative action, and the environment, his administration was a very troubled one, and he has been called "the most unpopular governor in state history." After riding a crest of national attention as the country's highest ranking elected official of Hispanic descent, he had an array of political problems.

One of the nation's most forthrightly liberal governors, he assembled a cabinet of liberal activists whose politics were out of touch with those of state voters. He was criticized for many of his political stands, like declaring New Mexico a sanctuary for Central American aliens, the only state to do so. Conservatives of both parties strongly opposed his efforts to revamp state government with the appointment of women, Hispanics, and blacks who shared his political views. Newspapers throughout New Mexico sharply criticized the appointment of his nephew to head the State Fair Board as well as his frequent excursions outside the state to stump for liberal candidates and to promote voter registration. He feuded constantly with the legislature, especially with a bipartisan conservative coalition that took control after 1984. He had to shelve his plan for major improvements in public education when the Democratic-controlled legislature defeated his proposal for a tax increase. A legislative commission killed his plan to invite out-of-state banks into New Mexico, a defeat reportedly attributable, at least in part, to indirect accusations from the governor that local banks had threatened to call in the personal loans of legislators who voted for the plan. And he faced still other problems: public outrage over his commutation of death sentences; the conviction of three of his appointees for felonies; a high turnover in his staff and cabinet; and an investigation by U.S. Attorney William Lutz into his personal finances.

By 1985 Anaya was conceding openly that New Mexico wasn't ready for his brand of progressive government, and that he looked forward to a career in real estate development at the end of his term. As he became the focus of various FBI investigations including allegations of payoffs from contractors and questionable real estate transactions, there was even some speculation that he might be forced to resign before his term ended in December 1986. Anaya was constitutionally ineligible to seek a second term, but no political observer felt he could have won one. His approval rating had dipped to 22 percent in the polls, and Democrats desperately struggled to separate themselves from his troubled administration. Controversial right to the end, he was the subject of an unflattering psychological portrait in *Albuquerque Living Magazine* the month before he left office. The article and accompanying interview portrayed the governor as a lonely man who had lost touch with his family and did not have friends in whom to confide.

Controversy followed Anaya even after his retirement from office. In January 1987 he was appointed president and general counsel of the Mexican-American Legal Defense and Educational Fund, a Los

Angeles-based group founded in 1967 to fight discrimination against Hispanic-Americans. Less than two months later, however, he was abruptly dismissed by the group's Board of Directors in a bitter leadership struggle.

Anaya is currently owner and president of Toney Anaya and Associates, a Sante Fe law firm.

Bibliography: Biographical information courtesy of Governor Anaya; Jaques Cattell Press, *Who's Who in American Politics, 1985–1986* (New York, 1985); Michael Barone *et al., The Almanac of American Politics, 1986, 1988* (New York and Washington, D.C., 1985, 1987); *The New York Times:* 2–28–84; 9–12–86; 11–26–86; 1–20–87; 3–2–87; 11–21–87.

Garrey Carruthers (Courtesy of governor's office)

CARRUTHERS, Garrey, 1987–

Garrey Carruthers was born August 29, 1939 in Aztec, New Mexico. He and his wife Kathy have three children: Debi, Carol, and Steven.

He graduated from Aztec High School in 1957, and two years later served as state president of the Future Farmers of America. He earned a bachelor's degree in agriculture from New Mexico State University in Las Cruces in 1964 and a master's degree in agricultural economics from New Mexico State University in 1965. Earning a Ph.D. in economics from Iowa State University in 1968, he returned to Las Cruces to teach agricultural economics and agricultural business at New Mexico State. His association with the university continued until 1985, when he resigned to run for governor.

In 1974, Carruthers became a White House Fellow under President Gerald Ford. Returning to Las Cruces after the fellowship, he served as acting director of the New Mexico Water Resources Research Institute from 1976 to 1978. He also accepted a 1976 appointment from President Ford to serve on the commission that screens White House Fellows.

In 1977, he was elected chairman of the New Mexico Republican party, a post he held until 1979. In 1981, President Reagan appointed him assistant secretary of the Interior Department, where he served under controversial secretary James Watt. He served in two key administration positions until 1984, when he returned to New Mexico.

State Republicans were optimistic about their prospects in the 1986 gubernatorial race, thanks to the political troubles of outgoing Democratic incumbent Toney Anaya. The oil and gas crisis had also hurt the economy. Carruthers, as the Republican nominee for the state's top post, was favored over his Democratic opponent Ray Powell, a retired engineer and businessman. The selection of non-political technocrats by both parties was no accident, attributable at least in part to voter displeasure with Anaya and state government. In an ironic move, the Democrats tried to portray Carruthers as a conservative version of the mercurial Anaya, a man as likely to anger voters with his conservative ideology as Anaya did on the opposite side of the spectrum. His office under Interior Secretary James Watt had also been plagued by allegations of irregularities, and Democrats warned of his tendency toward brash, simplistic approaches. Thus they tried to convince voters that Powell's calm approach was the only real alternative to the current administration. They also hoped to capitalize on widespread voter dissatisfaction with the state's Republican-controlled house, which they believed could temper the Anaya fallout. In the opinion of pollsters, however, the low-key Powell was not the ideal candidate to wage the dramatic uphill race.

Carruthers promised to streamline government and to promote economic development. His campaign stressed such issues as educational and managerial competence. Making much of the fact that he was a political outsider and not a member of the legislature, he won with 53 percent of the vote.

Carruthers was sworn in as the state's 24th chief executive on January 1, 1987, the state's first Republican governor in 16 years. Since taking office he has disappointed some conservatives with his generally moderate approach to issues, but others have hailed the benefits of his go-slow start. One political observer defended his actions: "He's following perhaps the most unpopular governor in the state's history. The state probably would have reacted negatively to a more forceful role." Despite lingering economic problems in one of the nation's poorest states, Carruthers has drawn good grades for his political skills and aggressive travels around the state. He asked for a tax increase during his first year in office, saying he had no alternative, since the state had been chronically short of funds for the last four years. Although the Democrats who control the legislature reacted coolly to his proposal to revamp the state's welfare system, one of his legislative priorities, he has received generally positive marks in a state where Democrats outnumber Republicans almost 2–1.

Carruthers is also stressing an economic development program and is formulating plans for the improvement of higher education. The legislation seeks to increase the quality of students who are entering and graduating from college in the state by raising high school graduation requirements, starting a competitive grant program to improve academic departments at the state's colleges and universities, and moving all remedial courses from the state's four-year institutions to community colleges. He is seeking major increases in faculty salaries, and wants to change state formulas for financing colleges so they won't depend as heavily on enrollment. Other plans include starting a telecommunications program so that professors can teach courses on more than one campus, and developing a program so that researchers at the two national laboratories located in New Mexico could be paid to teach courses on a part-time basis at public colleges and universities.

In 1987 President Reagan appointed Carruthers to a commission to study the ways that government functions might be turned over to private business. The twelve-member "Commission on Privatization" has been asked to "probe the entire dimension of government operations."

Bibliography: Biographical information courtesy of governor's office; Jaques Cattell Press, *Who's Who in American Politics, 1985–1986* (New York, 1985); Michael Barone *et al., The Almanac of American Politics 1988* (New York and Washington, D.C., 1987); *The Chronicle of Higher Education,* 11–12–86; *The New York Times:* 8–31–86; 9–12–86; 11–21–87.

Mario Matthew Cuomo (Courtesy of governor's office)

NEW YORK

CUOMO, Mario Matthew, 1983—

Born in Queens, New York on June 15, 1932; the son of immigrant parents, Andrea Cuomo and Immaculata Giordano Cuomo. A Roman Catholic, Cuomo has been married since 1954 to the former Matilda Raffa. They are the parents of five children: Margaret, Andrew, Maria, Madeleine, and Christopher.

An alumnus of Queens public schools and St. John's Prep, Cuomo graduated *summa cum laude* from St. John's University in 1953, and tied for top of class honors at St. John's University School of Law in 1956. For a brief time, he played professional baseball with the Pittsburgh Pirates organization, before an injury cut short his career. After a stint as a confidential legal assistant to Judge Adrian P. Burke of the New York State Court of Appeals in 1956, he entered private law practice with the firm of Corner, Weisbrod, Froeb, and Charles. He also taught as a part-time law professor at St. John's Law School for 17 years.

Cuomo first came to public attention in 1972 when he settled the Forest Hills housing controversy at the request of New York Mayor John Lindsay. Having earlier resolved a similar crisis in Corona, Queens, in Forest Hills he worked to preserve a low-income housing project in a middle class neighborhood. He later wrote a highly acclaimed book, *Forest Hills Diary: The Crisis of Low-Income Housing* (Random House, 1974), which contained his reflections on the dispute. In 1975 he was called upon again to be a factfinder in a nursing home controversy. His actions here led to the creation of the Moreland Act Commission and the appointment of a Special Nursing Home Prosecutor.

These activities started Cuomo on the path to a public service career. In 1975 he was appointed secretary of state by Governor Hugh Carey. At the governor's request, he acted as a roving negotiator in statewide crises; he settled the Co-op City rent strike controversy, and mediated the Mohawk Indian lands claim dispute. In addition, he was responsible for the first revision in more than 70 years of the state's lobbying law, convened the first statewide arson conference, and fought for new rules for real estate brokers and against blockbusting. In 1978 he was elected lieutenant governor. In his new position he assumed additional responsibilities as chairman of the State's Urban and Rural Affairs Cabinets as well as head of the State Advisory Council on the Disabled. He also assumed leadership as the state's first Ombudsman, helping thousands of New Yorkers through the maze of state agencies and regulations.

Entering the 1982 race for governor of New York, he waged a come-from-behind fight to defeat New York City Mayor Ed Koch to win the Democratic gubernatorial nomination. In the September 23, 1982 Democratic primary, he defeated the outspoken mayor by 60,544 votes. His opponent in the general election was Republican Lewis Lehrman, a political unknown who had made millions by building the Rite-Aid drugstore chain. The campaign provided a vivid contrast between two ideological opponents: the conservative Lehrman advocated tax cuts and a stern approach to crime, while the liberal Cuomo, an inspiring orator, defended in uplifting language the classic positions of the welfare state. Cuomo was elected with 51 percent of the vote, capturing the statehouse by a 180,386 vote margin. His day-by-day accounting of his campaign was published in the spring of 1984 by Random House as *The Diaries of Mario M. Cuomo: The Campaign for Governor.* In 1986 he won re-election with a record 64.6 percent of the vote. His opponent was Westchester County Executive Andrew P. O'Rourke.

Throughout his years in office Cuomo established himself as a caring, committed, hard-working and thoughtful leader. His first-term accomplishments included a tax cut, balanced budgets, an increase in aid to education, and job creation. He has also initiated programs to reform the criminal justice system, to improve state budget practices, to ease the burden on counties through state assumption of the local share of many Medicaid costs, and to provide permanent shelter for the homeless. His tenure in office includes a long list of other accomplishments, including billion-dollar bond issues to rehabilitate roads and to improve the environment; the allocation of $8.6 billion to rebuild New York City's transit system; and the establishment of a new program to subsidize the purchase of prescription drugs among the elderly. He has also supported state spending increases for higher education and efforts to give public universities more authority over their state allocations. In 1988 he proposed a pioneering new program of grants called "Liberty Scholarships" that would provide an extraordinary incentive to low-income students to continue their education. The first such effort on a statewide level, the program guaranteed that any poor seventh grade student who eventually graduated from high school would receive enough money from the state to attend one of its public colleges.

Cuomo is widely regarded to be one of the most charismatic governors New York State has ever had. In the opinion of political observers, one area in which his governorship has been a great success has been in his ability not just to articulate the liberal agenda, but to educate the public, raising its consciousness, compassion, and awareness. A 1984 address at the University of Notre Dame on "Religious Belief and Public Morality" was highly acclaimed, outlining as it did a philosophy on church-state relations from the perspective of a Catholic governor. Regarded as the best speaker American politics has produced in at least the last half century, he made a ringing keynote address to the 1984 Democratic National Convention that immediately raised his prospects as a likely presidential nominee. His surprise decision in February 1987 not to seek the presidency in 1988 shocked friends and opponents alike, and threw the campaign for the 1988 Democratic presidential nomination wide open.

Bibliography: Biographical information courtesy of governor's office; Robert S. McElvaine, *Mario Cuomo: A Biography* (Scribner's, 1988); Jaques Cattell Press, *Who's Who in American Politics, 1985–1986* (New York, 1985); Michael Barone *et al., The Almanac of American Politics, 1984, 1988* (New York and Washington, D.C., 1983, 1987); *The Chronicle of Higher Education:* 11–12–86; 1–13–88; *The New York Times:* 11–2–86; 11–5–86; 11–6–86; 12–16–86; 2–17–87; 2–21–87; 1–6–88.

James Baxter Hunt (Courtesy of North Carolina Museum of History)

NORTH CAROLINA

HUNT, James Baxter, 1977–1985

Born on May 16, 1937 in Greensboro, North Carolina, the son of James B. Hunt, a farmer and soil conservationist, and Elsie (Brame) Hunt, a teacher. A Presbyterian, Governor Hunt is the brother of Robert Brame Hunt. He married Carolyn Joyce Leonard on August 20, 1958, by whom he is the father of Rebecca, Baxter, Rachel, and Elizabeth.

Hunt was graduated from Rock Ridge High School and attended North Carolina State University, receiving a B.S. degree in agricultural education in 1959 and an M.S. in agricultural economics in 1962. He received a J.D. from the University of North Carolina Law School in 1964, eventually establishing a law practice in Wilson. Hunt served as chairman of "Young Voters for Terry Sanford" in 1960, and as national college director for the Democratic National Committee in 1962–63. In 1964 he went to Nepal for two years under the sponsorship of the Ford Foundation, where he became an economic advisor to the government. Elected president of the State Young Democratic National Convention, Hunt was appointed assistant state party chairman in 1969.

In the Democratic primary for lieutenant governor on May 6, 1972, Hunt defeated Roy Sowers, Margaret Harper, Allen Barbee, and Reginald Grazier. Reversing a Republican trend in the state, he was elected lieutenant governor in the November election, defeating John Walker, the Republican candidate, by over 200,000 votes. Four years later Hunt sought the Democratic nomination for governor, and in the August 1976 primary he received 52.3 percent of the vote, defeating Edward M. O'Herron, Jr., George M. Wood, Thomas E. Strickland, and Jetter Braker. In the general election he attracted 1,081,293 votes, compared to 564,102 for the Republican candidate, David T. Flaherty. Hunt was inaugurated on January 6, 1977.

In his inaugural address, Hunt called for a "new beginning" which would "eliminate the last vestiges of discrimination." He advocated a renewed emphasis on the teaching of reading in the public schools, and supported a new utilities regulation structure that would reflect consumer interests. Hunt named a black and a woman to high level posts, and actively promoted the appointment of blacks to judicial positions. In 1978 he was urged by a number of organizations, including Amnesty International, to free the "Wilmington 10"—a group of nine black men and one white woman accused of firebombing a Wilmington, North Carolina grocery store. The Soviet Union contended that the imprisonment of this group was a human rights violation, and critics of the trials maintained that the defendants had been convicted in a politically charged atmosphere which included tampering with evidence by state officials. Hunt declared that there had indeed been a fair trial, although he decided that the sentences were too long and reduced the terms for the prisoners. All 10 were on parole within a year.

In 1980 Hunt, who could succeed himself after the passage of a 1977 constitutional amendment, engaged in a primary struggle with former Governor Robert Scott. Scott asserted that Hunt had failed to deal adequately with mill workers' claims that they had contracted brown lung disease while on the job, but Hunt still managed to win the primary. Later in 1980 Hunt was the focus of a brief assassination scare while attending the Democratic National Convention. In November of that year he easily defeated Beverly Lake, the Republican candidate, by 1,847,432 votes to 691,449. Those counties which Hunt lost in the election were located predominantly in the mountainous western region of the state. With his victory, Hunt became the first person to serve two terms as governor of North Carolina since the Civil War.

Hunt's eight-year administration was widely regarded as highly successful. During his years in office, the state achieved sustained economic growth with higher wage levels and one of the nation's lowest unemployment rates. Industries invested $15.5 billion in new and expanded plants in North Carolina, producing 250,000 additional jobs. The state's work force grew by 15 percent from 1975 to 1985, and by the time Hunt left office the state was well on its way to recovering fully from the 1981 national recession.

Hunt also pumped money into education, and insisted on competency tests for students and teachers alike. In the opinion of political observers, he did a great deal to change the tone of public life in the state, to abandon old southern traditions of racial segregation, and to create a mood of tolerance and open-mindedness toward different cultural attitudes.

Hunt also worked to build a strong Democratic party in North Carolina, and had important involvement in party affairs at the national level. In 1981 he chaired the Hunt Commission, concerned with the Democratic party process for presidential delegate selection.

In 1984 Hunt waged an especially acrimonious campaign for the U.S. Senate against conservative Republican incumbent Jesse Helms, who was running for his third term as one of the Senate's most outspoken conservatives. The race attracted national attention, for it was seen as a nationwide ideological clash between conservatives and moderates, the old versus the new South. Liberals and conservatives alike poured millions of dollars in campaign contributions into the state, in a contest christened by Helms as a referendum "on the conservative cause." It also became the most costly senate campaign in U.S. history.

Hunt, as a moderate Democrat, became the candidate of all those, both inside and outside North Carolina, who sought to end Helms' senate career. He based his campaign on his support for economic and educational reforms designed to make the state more attractive to high-tech industries. Yet he drew criticism even from supporters for some of his political positions. Instead of making Helms defend his record, Hunt adopted positions on military and foreign policy similar to the incumbent's. Experts believed that Hunt, knowing the power of the conservative vote, sought to minimize his differences with Helms by supporting organized school prayer, the B-1 bomber, the MX missile, and the Stealth bomber, and by opposing the nuclear freeze. He also favored a gradual increase in military spending. Nonetheless, Helms won an easy victory, attributed by political analysts to the Reagan landslide of that year.

After his defeat, Hunt returned to private law practice in Raleigh, North Carolina. Despite the prodding of state and national Democratic leaders, he declined to make another race for the senate in 1986. Hunt had been widely regarded as the Democrats' strongest candidate to win the seat being vacated by retiring incumbent John P. East. Hunt explained that he was reluctant to put his family through the grueling ordeal of another campaign.

In May 1987 Hunt was named chairman of the National Board for Professional Teaching Standards, newly created by the Carnegie Foundation.

Bibliography: Biographical information courtesy of governor's office; *North Carolina Legislative Manual, 1983–1984;* Michael Barone *et al., The Almanac of American Politics, 1984, 1986, 1988* (New York and Washington, D.C., 1983, 1985, 1987); *The New York Times:* 12–15–79; 12–8–81; 2–5–84; 4–22–84; 4–29–84; 5–7–84; 5–9–84; 5–27–84; 8–12–84; 11–4–84; 11–8–84; 1–6–85; 9–13–85; 5–16–87; 10–15–87.

James G. Martin (Courtesy of governor's office)

MARTIN, James G., 1985–

Born in Savannah, Georgia on December 11, 1935, the son of Arthur M. Martin, a Presbyterian minister, and Mary Grubbs Martin. A Presbyterian, Martin married Dorothy McAulay in 1957. The couple have three children: James, Emily, and Benson.

Martin graduated from Davidson College in 1957 and received a doctorate in chemistry from Princeton University in 1960. Returning to Davidson as a professor of chemistry, he remained in that post until 1972 when he left for Washington as a congressman. Prior to his election to Congress, he had served three terms as a Mecklenburg County Commissioner. During those terms in office, he was elected commission chairman and served as president of the North Carolina Association of County Commissioners.

First elected to Congress in 1972, he served six terms on Capitol Hill, becoming a senior member of the powerful Ways and Means Committee and rising to a position of Republican party leadership as chairman of the House Republican Research Committee. Due to his technical education and background, he became an expert on issues relating to food additives, the environment, and toxic wastes. He successfully led the fight against banning saccharin, the artificial sweetener. As a chemist, he argued that the sweetener was not dangerous and helped more people than it harmed. For his work in this and other areas, Martin was honored with the Charles Lathrop Parsons Award, given by the American Chemical Society for outstanding public service by an American chemist. He was the first elected official ever to receive the award. As a conservative Republican, he received an 86 percent approval rating from the U.S. Chamber of Commerce for his 12 years of service in Washington.

Martin gave up what was considered to be a safe Republican seat to make the run for governor of North Carolina in 1984. An ardent advocate of supply-side economics, Martin argued that President Reagan needed loyal fiscal conservatives like himself at the state level. Never having campaigned statewide before, he began at 30 points behind in public opinion polls. He also had to overcome the higher name recognition of his Democratic opponent, State Attorney General Rufus Edmisten, a one-time assistant to former U.S. Senator Sam Ervin. To combat these obstacles, he visited all 100 of the state's counties on a series of "Jim Martin Listens" tours. He campaigned on a pro-business platform, with special emphasis on economic development. Promising to carry on in the tradition of the state's pro-education governors, he proposed a $300 million pay increase for public school teachers. Noting the economic and political progress made by blacks and women in the state, he departed from the path of other Republican aspirants for state office by refraining from appealing to racism. In that sense, his campaign was viewed by political observers as one more indication of the growing sophistication of voters in both North Carolina and in the South generally in recent years.

Martin won the election with 54.3 percent of the vote, becoming only the second Republican elected governor of North Carolina in this century. His victory was due not only to his political talent and skill, but also to the Democrats' own troubles. Retiring Governor Jim Hunt had named no heir apparent, missing a chance to endorse House Speaker Carl Stewart in his 1980 primary bid against weak Lieutenant Governor Jimmy Green. The 1984 Democratic gubernatorial primary was therefore a bitter battle among 10 contenders. When Edmisten won, second place finisher Eddie Knox, the former mayor of Charlotte, reacted bitterly because he had not gotten the outgoing governor's support. Members of Knox's own family made a point of publicly endorsing Martin.

Because Martin's candidacy had such broad appeal to middle-income voters, political analysts are predicting that he should be able to build a strong Republican party in the state. With young middle-class whites brought into the GOP, Democrats stand in danger of losing their base. His election marked a real turning point in North Carolina politics. For the first time, the state's governor and both U.S. Senators were Republicans.

According to political observers, Martin has a chance to distinguish himself in office. He inherited a state economy rapidly on the upswing, but at the same time in need of upgrading. To sustain economic growth, he has proposed tax cuts designed primarily to attract more business to North Carolina, and to undercut its reliance on the troubled tobacco industry. Encountering heavy opposition from Democratic leaders who argued that the state cannot afford the loss of revenue, he clashed bitterly with the Democratic legislature and campaigned against them in 1986.

Nevertheless, governmental experts did not expect Martin to sharply change the course of government charted by his predecessor, moderate Democrat Jim Hunt. He has endorsed a road improvement program, more spending on schools, and an accelerated merit pay program for teachers.

Viewed as less doctrinaire than the state's other leading Republican, U.S. Senator Jesse Helms, Martin and Helms clashed in a bitter contest to determine control of North Carolina Republican machinery in the selection of the party's 1988 presidential nominee. Some observers feared that the dispute with Helms may have endangered Martin's 1988 re-election campaign, in which he faced a strong challenge from Lieutenant Governor Robert B. Jordan, a Democrat. Nevertheless, Martin defeated Jordan handily, winning 56 percent of the vote to the Democrat's 44 percent. With his victory, Martin became the first Republican governor of North Carolina ever to win re-election.

Bibliography: Biographical information courtesy of governor's office;

Jaques Cattell Press, *Who's Who in American Politics, 1985–1986* (New York, 1985); Michael Barone *et al.*, *The Almanac of American Politics, 1986, 1988* (New York and Washington, D.C., 1985, 1987); *The New York Times:* 2–13–84; 5–9–84; 6–6–84; 11–7–84; 11–8–84; 1–6–85; 3–1–87.

Allen Ingvar Olson (Courtesy of governor's office)

NORTH DAKOTA

OLSON, Allen Ingvar, 1981–1985

Born on November 5, 1938 in Rolla, North Dakota, the son of Elmer and Olga (Sundin) Olson. A Presbyterian, Olson is married to the former Barbara Benner of Grand Forks. They have three children—Kristin, Robin, and Craig.

Olson grew up on a farm near Sarles in northeastern North Dakota, a few miles from the Canadian border. He earned his B.A. in 1960 and his LL.B. in 1963, both from the University of North Dakota, where he was a member of Lambda Chi Alpha. He entered the United States Army in September 1963 as a lawyer in the Judge Advocate General Corps. Stationed at the Pentagon in Washington, D.C. and later in West Germany, Olson handled cases at both the trial and appellate levels. His last assignment was as chief of military justice for a major overseas command, and he received an army commendation medal for his services.

Returning to North Dakota in 1967, Olson became assistant director of the Legislative Council at the State Capitol in Bismarck, where he directed research on the state's first comprehensive study of strip mining, soil banks, and land reclamation. He was also involved in legislative studies on vocational education. From 1969 to 1972 Olson was in private practice with the Bismarck law firm of Conmy, Rosenberg, Lucas, and Olson. He first entered political life in 1972 when, running as a Republican, he was elected to the post of North Dakota Attorney General; he was re-elected to a second four-year term in 1976. That same year, he was a delegate to the Republican National Convention.

In 1980 Olson won 76 percent of the vote to defeat Labor Commissioner Orville W. Hagen and gain the Republican gubernatorial nomination. Although North Dakota is historically a Republican state, the Democrats had been in control of the statehouse for 20 years. By 1980, however, incumbent Democrat Arthur A. Link, seeking his third term as chief executive, was politically vulnerable. Olson charged that Link favored too high a severance tax on mineral exploitation, an issue of great importance in a state with rich deposits of lignite coal. By contrast, Olson ran on a platform that called for more development. His position, which was closer to the Reagan administration's policy of exploiting America's mineral and energy resources more extensively, enabled Olson to win the general election with 54 percent of the vote to Link's 46 percent. On January 6, 1981, he was sworn in as the 28th chief executive of North Dakota.

Governor Olson received national publicity as one of the governors from five western coal-producing states who pushed the Reagan administration for a stronger state role in determining the pace of coal development. Weakening oil prices and subsequently reduced state royalties, coupled with low farm prices, also forced Olson to devote attention to the problem of falling state revenues. Faced with the necessity of budget cuts midway through his first term, Olson chose to cut building funds, state raises, and grants to localities.

Olson was a member of North Dakota's Emergency Commission, Industrial Commission, Board of University and School Lands, Water Commission, Indian Affairs Commission, and Board of Pardons. By statute, he also served on a number of other boards and commissions, but delegated much of this authority to Lieutenant Governor Ernest M. Sands, who was the first occupant of that office to serve as a direct member of a gubernatorial administration.

In office, Olson served as chairman of the Western Governors' Policy Office. A member of the Executive Committee of the National Governors' Association, he was a member of the NGA's Agriculture Committee and Committee on Community and Economic Development. In addition, he chaired the NGA's Soil Conservation Task Force and its Legal Affairs Committee, as well as the Legal Committee of the Interstate Oil Compact Commission.

Olson was unexpectedly defeated in his 1984 campaign for re-election. Unopposed in the Republican primary, he faced Democratic state representative George A. Sinner in the general election. According to political observers, his loss was attributed to a series of political blunders on his part: he came under attack for redecorating his office and for buying a state airplane for his own use. Despite Ronald Reagan's landslide presidential victory in November 1984, the Republican Olson drew only 45 percent of the vote to his opponent's 55 percent.

The race was perhaps more interesting for the constitutional debate that followed it. In a colorful dispute, the state supreme court was asked to determine exactly when Olson was to relinquish his post to Sinner. Olson claimed he had the right to remain in office until January 6, four years after he took the job on January 6, 1981. He also argued that North Dakota governors have traditionally assumed office on the first day of the legislative session, which in 1985 was scheduled for January 8. Sinner, on the other hand, argued that he had signed his oath of office on December 31 and should assume the governorship the next day. Although Olson did not say publicly why he was refusing to step aside, at stake were two appointments to the state's highest court, the very court that was to decide the unprecedented dispute. The ruling was in Sinner's favor, and Olson left office on January 1, 1985. An attorney, he retired to private law practice.

Bibliography: Biographical information courtesy of governor's office; Jaques Cattell Press, *Who's Who in American Politics, 1985–1986* (New York, 1985); Michael Barone *et al., The Almanac of American Politics 1982, 1986* (New York and Washington, D.C. 1981, 1985); *The New York Times:* 9–3–80; 9–4–80; 11–22–82; 11–23–82; 3–5–83; 6–13–84; 11–8–84; 1–3–85; 1–5–85.

George A. Sinner (Courtesy of governor's office)

SINNER, George A., 1985–

George Sinner was born in Casselton, North Dakota on May 29, 1928. Married to the former Jane Baute, he and his wife are the parents of 10 children.

Sinner graduated from St. John's University in Minnesota with a B.A. in 1950. A prosperous sugar beet farmer, he was active with the Red River Valley Sugar Beet Growers Association, the Northern Crops Institute, and several other agricultural organizations. He is also a partner in Sinner Brothers and Bresnaton, a diversified farming operation in Casselton.

A Democrat, Sinner entered politics in 1962, serving in the state senate from 1962 to 1966 where he was a member of the Education Committee. An unsuccessful candidate for the U.S. House of Representatives in 1964, he was a delegate to the North Dakota Constitutional Convention in 1972. He also served as a member and former president of the State Board of Higher Education. Elected to the North Dakota House of Representatives in 1982, he served as chairman of the Finance and Taxation Committee.

In 1984, Sinner challenged incumbent Republican Allen Olson for the governorship. He won the Democratic nomination easily, defeating Anne Belle Bourgois, a supporter of political extremist Lyndon H. LaRouche, Jr., in his party's primary.

Political analysts believe that Sinner's unexpected victory over Olson was due as much to his opponent's gaffes and blunders as to his own political talents. Olson came under attack for frivolous spending like redecorating his office and buying a state airplane for his own use. Despite Ronald Reagan's landslide presidential victory in November 1984, Sinner managed to beat his Republican opponent by the convincing margin of 55 percent to 45 percent.

The days after the election provided some unexpected moments of colorful political drama, as both men continued to battle over exactly when one's term ended and the other's began. Olson maintained that his four-year term ran at least until January 6 (four years to the day after his 1981 inauguration), and that the new governor customarily has not taken office until even later, when the legislature convened. Sinner, on the other hand, maintained that he signed his oath of office on December 31 and was preparing to take office the next day. Although Olson did not admit this publicly, at stake in the historic dispute was the authority to fill two appointments to the state's highest court. In addition to the appointments question, Sinner said he wanted to take office on January 1 to consider the legality of bonuses totaling $20,000 awarded to 100 employees by various state agencies on December 31. He also planned to seek an immediate freeze on hiring. Asked to mediate in the constitutional tug of war, the state's highest court ruled in favor of Sinner, who took office on January 1, 1985.

In office, Sinner has been frustrated over his inability to convince voters that a tax increase is necessary. According to political analysts, however, he remains popular, and polls show him far ahead of possible challengers to his re-election bid.

Since taking office, Sinner has worked actively in North Dakota's behalf through the National Governors' Assocation. He is vice-chairman of the NGA Committee on Agriculture and chairs the U.S.-Canadian Task Force. He also chairs the Interstate Oil Compact Commission, which has a membership of 35 states. In 1988 he addressed the Western Governors' Association, calling for immediate plans to ease the drought difficulties of the area's farmers.

In his 1988 bid for re-election, Sinner easily defeated businessman and anti-tax crusader Leon Mallberg, winning 60 percent of the vote to his opponent's 40 percent.

Bibliography: Biographical information courtesy of governor's office; Jaques Cattell Press, *Who's Who in American Politics, 1985–1986* (New York, 1985); Michael Barone *et al., The Almanac of American Politics 1988* (New York and Washington, D.C., 1987); *U.S.A. Today,* 7–14–88; *The New York Times:* 6–13–84; 11–8–84; 1–3–85; 1–5–85.

Richard F. Celeste (Courtesy of governor's office)

OHIO

Born in Cleveland on November 11, 1937, the son of Frank P. Celeste and Margaret Lewis Celeste. A Methodist, Celeste married Dagmar Braun of Vienna, Austria on August 25, 1962. The couple has six children; Eric, Christopher, Gabriella, Noelle, Natalie, and Stephen.

Celeste graduated *magna cum laude* from Yale University in 1960, where he was selected as a Rhodes Scholar. He studied at Oxford University from 1960 to 1962. In 1963 he was appointed executive assistant to the U.S. Ambassador to India, Chester Bowles. During his four years in New Delhi, he traveled more than 60,000 miles throughout the sub-continent, taking a special interest in agricultural productivity and community development.

A Democrat, Celeste began his political career in 1970, when he was elected to the Ohio House of Representatives. Serving two terms in the legislature, he authored bills calling for voter registration reform, improved state employee retirement benefits, adoption reform, and revised pension systems.

Celeste served as lieutenant governor of Ohio from 1974 to 1978. Especially interested in social service programs for children and the elderly, he sponsored several programs aimed at increasing citizen participation in government.

In 1978 Celeste ran an unsuccessful race for the governorship, losing to incumbent Republican James Rhodes. Following his defeat, he was appointed director of the Peace Corps by President Jimmy Carter, a position he held from 1979 through January 1981.

Celeste was first elected governor of Ohio on November 4, 1982, defeating Congressman Bud Brown with 59 percent of the vote. It was an unprecedented victory for a Democrat in an Ohio gubernatorial race. During his first term, Celeste experienced ups and downs in his popularity. In his first year in office, he made permanent a "temporary" tax increase instituted by his predecessor James Rhodes, enraging voters who had misinterpreted his ambiguous campaign rhetoric on the issue. As his poll ratings plummeted, conservatives put a measure on the ballot to reverse the increase. Celeste fought back shrewdly, making the case for "positive" government that has become his trademark. Ads were run reminding voters that some Ohio communities closed their schools for lack of funds, and suggesting that this would happen again if the referendum passed. It failed by a solid margin, a result seen as a victory for Celeste.

Celeste won re-election in 1986, defeating former Governor James Rhodes in a contest seen as a replay of their earlier 1978 battle. The 77-year-old Rhodes, seeking a fifth term as governor, ran an old-fashioned campaign built around one issue—assertions of corruption and mismanagement in the Celeste administration. Celeste was badly damaged by a scandal affecting the Home State Savings and Loan Association in March 1985. While Celeste had received crucial financial support from the institution's owner, Democratic campaign contributor Marvin Warner, an investigation revealed that its affairs had not been properly regulated by the state. Celeste was also plagued by a series of felony indictments against several of his associates and campaign supporters. Rhodes also accused the Celeste administration of failures in economic development, of raising personal and business taxes, and of unethical conduct.

Celeste, however, stuck with his own positive economic themes, and capitalized on voter uneasiness with electing a 77-year-old candidate. He won easily, garnering 60 percent of the vote.

Among the achievements of Celeste's years in office are the following: restoring financial stability to the state; initiating a jobs program that put thousands of Ohioans to work; and bringing Ohio's schools and universities to national excellence. Establishing "Operation Jobs" to help create more than a half-million jobs for Ohioans, Celeste also began the "Buy Ohio" program which brought thousands of jobs and hundreds of thousands of dollars to Ohio companies. He also initiated a state travel and tourism campaign, "Ohio . . . The Heart of It All," which in two years brought 20,000 new full-time jobs to the state.

Dedicated to educational excellence, Celeste also started a series of programs to improve the quality of the state's colleges and universities. In the area of higher education, his major achievements have included keeping tuition costs down, improving academic programs, helping universities create new ties with business, and using his position to promote the state's colleges and universities. He also raised the amount of state funding received by educational institutions, spending 74 cents out of every dollar on schools from kindergarten through college.

Celeste also put a halt to rising utility rates, toughened the Certificate of Need Program to cut medical care costs, and reduced operating expenses for state government by eliminating 2,000 state employees. During his administration, the toughest missing children's law in the nation was signed; a health program was put into place creating a women's, children's, and infant's health clinic in every county in the state; and the Children's Trust Fund for abused and neglected children was established.

In August 1987, Celeste took himself out of consideration for the 1988

Democratic presidential nomination. Despite speculation that he would make the race, he explained that the run would be too expensive and take too much time from administering state affairs.

The recipient of several honorary degrees, Celeste is also the author of two books: *It's Not Just Politics, America* (Educational Forum, 1976), and *Pioneering a Hunger Free World* (Friendship Press, 1977).

Bibliography: Biographical information courtesy of governor's office; Jaques Cattell Press, *Who's Who in American Politics, 1985–1986* (New York, 1985); Michael Barone *et al., The Almanac of American Politics, 1984, 1986, 1988* (New York and Washington, D.C., 1983, 1985, 1987); *The Chronicle of Higher Education:* 10–1–86; 11–12–86; *Newsweek,* 6–15–87; *The New York Times:* 11–10–85; 9–21–86; 10–23–86; 6–5–87; 8–26–87; 6–6–88.

George Patterson Nigh (Credit: Photography Center, Inc.)

OKLAHOMA

NIGH, George Patterson, 1963, 1979–1987

First elected to the governorship in 1978 and re-elected in 1982, Democrat George Nigh will go down in Oklahoma history as the first chief executive to serve consecutive terms in office. Born in McAlester, Oklahoma on June 9, 1927, he is the son of Wilbur R. and Irene (Crockett) Nigh, who were grocery store owners. A Baptist, he and his wife Donna Skinner Mashburn have two children, Michael and Georgeann.

Nigh served a tour of duty aboard an aircraft carrier with the United States Navy from 1945 to 1946, after graduating from McAlester High School in 1945. He returned to Oklahoma to complete his education, received an associate degree from Eastern Oklahoma Agricultural and Mechanical College at Wilburton, and was graduated from East Central State Teachers College, Ada, with a B.A. degree in 1950. Before entering political life, Nigh taught history and government in McAlester High School, was a partner in a McAlester grocery, and owned and managed a public relations firm in Oklahoma City.

In 1950, at the age of 23, Nigh was elected to the Oklahoma House of Representatives, the youngest member ever to have been chosen to serve in that body at the time. Representing Pittsburgh County, he remained in the house for four terms before winning the post of lieutenant governor in 1958. At 31, he was the youngest person ever elected to that office in the history of Oklahoma. Nigh served four terms as lieutenant governor—1959–63, 1967–71, 1971–75, and 1975–79. In 1962 he waged an unsuccessful campaign for the Democratic gubernatorial nomination. Yet he did serve as chief executive for nine days in 1963 when, as lieutenant governor, he succeeded to the unexpired term of Governor J. Howard Edmondson, who had resigned. Nigh quickly appointed his predecessor to fill the United States Senate seat left vacant by the death of Robert S. Kerr on January 1, 1963.

In 1978, after Democratic Governor David L. Boren chose not to seek re-election but to run for the United States Senate instead, Lieutenant Governor Nigh faced a stern challenge to gain his party's nomination. The leading vote-getter in a three-man field, he was forced into a runoff against Attorney General Larry Derryberry, whom he eventually defeated with 58 percent of the vote. In the general election he travelled around the state in a "white hat brigade," an apparent attempt to imitate the housecleaning campaign that Boren had waged so successfully four years earlier, when he toured the state with a broom as his symbol. In the 1978 race Nigh narrowly defeated Republican candidate Ron Shotts, a 32-year-old former University of Oklahoma football star, who polled 47 percent of the vote to Nigh's 52 percent. After Governor Boren, also successful in his 1978 campaign, resigned to take his Senate seat, Lieutenant Governor Nigh became governor on January 3, 1979. The term to which he had been officially elected began five days later, with his inauguration on January 8, 1979. Nigh was the first lieutenant governor to be elected governor, and the only person to serve four times as the state's chief executive. In his 1982 campaign for re-election, he handily defeated Tom Daxon, Oklahoma's state auditor, 62 percent to 38 percent.

During his tenure as governor, Nigh served as chairman of the Southern Growth Policies Board and vice president of the Council of State Governments. Prohibited from seeking a third term as governor in 1986, Nigh left office on January 12, 1987. Unfortunately his administration took the blame for the hard times that had befallen the state thanks to declining oil revenues. Despite much speculation, he declined to run for the Senate in 1986. Nigh had been seen as a strong challenger to one-term incumbent Republican Don Nickles.

Bibliography: Wilbur Johnson, ed., *Directory of Oklahoma* (Oklahoma City, 1975); Oklahoma Department of Libraries, *Governors of Oklahoma: 1890–1979* (Oklahoma City, 1979); Michael Barone *et al., The Almanac of American Politics, 1982, 1984* (New York and Washington, D.C., 1981, 1983); *The New York Times:* 11–4–82; 9–13–85.

Henry Bellmon (Courtesy of governor's office)

BELLMON, Henry, 1963–1967, 1987–

Born September 3, 1921 on a farm near Tonkawa, Oklahoma, Bellmon is the son of George D. Bellmon and Edith Eleanor Caskey Bellmon. A Presbyterian, Bellmon married Shirley Osborn in 1947. The couple has three daughters, Patricia, Gail, and Ann.

Bellmon attended public schools in Noble County and graduated from Billings High School in 1938. He graduated from Oklahoma Agricultural and Mechanical College (now known as Oklahoma State University) in 1942 with a degree in agriculture. During World War II, Bellmon joined the U.S. Marines and served with a tank company for more than three years. He participated in four Pacific battles including Iwo Jima. Bellmon received the Legion of Merit and Silver Star for his military service.

A wheat farmer and cattle rancher, Bellmon began his political career at 25, when he was elected to the Oklahoma House of Representatives. He represented the people of Noble County from 1947 through 1949, when he returned to his Billings farm. Chairman of the Republican state committee from 1960 to 1962, he became the state's 16th governor in 1963, the first Republican to serve in that office. His first administration was well respected for its ability to reform and improve services to Oklahoma citizens. Limited by law to one term in office, he ran successfully for the U.S. Senate, serving two terms from 1969 to 1981. In the Senate he was a member of the budget committee. Announcing his retirement from the Senate in 1980, he explained that he had not enjoyed life in this "exclusive club," and did not like Washington.

Returning to his farm in 1981, Bellmon embarked on a series of public service roles. He was co-founder and served as co-chairman of the Committee for a Responsible Federal Budget. By appointment in 1983, he became director of the Department of Human Services, the state's largest agency. In 1985 he was appointed receiver of the financially troubled Cowboy Hall of Fame in Oklahoma City. He also joined the RAM Group, working to assist financially troubled farmers to avoid foreclosures. He served as a professor and lecturer at Oklahoma City University, Central State University, the University of Oklahoma, and Oklahoma State University, as well as working as a commentator for an Oklahoma City television station.

In 1986 when Oklahoma faced tough economic times brought on by a decline in oil prices, Bellmon sought to return to the governorship, claiming that the state was in a jam and couldn't afford to elect a "greenhorn." Widely respected by voters for his personal integrity, Bellmon presented himself as the safest bet for a state in trouble.

His Democratic opponent was David Walters, a 34-year-old businessman who campaigned as a newcomer and political outsider. He was the surprise winner of the Democratic primary, having survived a divisive six-way fight as well as a runoff race against Attorney General Mike Turpin. Walters hoped voters would see him as a fresh and youthful face against the veteran Bellmon. Although he had never held elective office before, he had worked in state government and was backed by some supporters of outgoing Governor George Nigh. Walters was harmed, however, both by his positions on issues and his campaign practices. In a curious role reversal, it was the Democratic Walters who stood firmly for a "right to work" law, hated by unions because it would ban the closed shop. His campaign was badly damaged by a mid-October court case in which he was accused of violating the campaign finance law by accepting $162,000 in loans from four supporters.

Bellmon's campaign focused on an aggressive program of economic development. He proposed a number of measures to encourage business expansion, including reducing the corporate income tax rate from 5 percent to 4 percent and lowering workers' compensation payments for businesses. While a fiscal conservative, Bellmon was not opposed to expanding spending on social services, such as providing medical care for poor pregnant women not on welfare. He hoped to attack the root causes of poverty through vocational education and expanded, accessible and affordable health care programs. One of these proposed the establishment of an indigent health care fund that would be distributed to hospitals all over Oklahoma. Bellmon was also unequivocal in his promises not to cut education budgets, and called for a referendum on the state's proposed "right to work" law—both proposals expected to gain him the backing of labor unions throughout the state.

State voters, obviously fearful of the austerity ahead, rejected both major party nominees. Bellmon won with only a plurality of the vote, 47 percent to Walters' 45 percent. Two minor party candidates split the difference.

With his inauguration on January 12, 1987, Bellmon became only the second governor in the state's history to serve more than one term. In his first months in office, he proposed a six-cent rise in the gas tax, across the board cuts in all spending except for education, and abolition of pension reserve funds. Citing the need for a smaller, more efficient state government, he proposed sweeping plans for the restructuring of many government agencies. In view of the drastic decline in the state's oil revenue, he also outlined a dramatic revamping of public higher education that would include closing some colleges, merging others, and establishing new governing boards for most remaining institutions. He also proposed a major study of the financial management of public higher education, as well as urging Oklahoma's public colleges and universities to start a variety of programs to assess student learning and to raise academic standards.

Bellmon has been described as an "old-fashioned Republican" who dislikes supply side deficits and new right cultural conservatives. He is a moderate conservative who has supported school busing and choice on abortion.

Bibliography: Biographical information courtesy of governor's office; Michael Barone *et al., The Almanac of American Politics 1988* (New York and Washington, D.C., 1987); Jaques Cattell Press, *Who's Who in American Politics, 1985–1986* (New York, 1985); *The Chronicle of Higher Education:* 11–12–86; 2–18–87; 9–23–87; *The New York Times:* 9–4–86; 9–17–86; 9–30–86; 2–22–87.

Victor G. Atiyeh (Courtesy of Governor Atiyeh)

OREGON

ATIYEH, Victor G., 1979–1987

First elected governor in 1978 following an unsuccessful campaign four years earlier, Republican Vic Atiyeh has had a long history of involvement in Oregon's political and civic affairs. Born in Portland, Oregon on February 20, 1923, he and his wife Dolores have two children. Atiyeh is an Episcopalian.

After attending the University of Oregon in Eugene for two years, Atiyeh joined Atiyeh Brothers, the Portland rug and carpet firm his father had established at the turn of the century. Widely known for his work with the Boy Scouts, where he holds the highest council and regional adult leadership awards, he served in the Oregon Legislature as a member of the Oregon House of Representatives from 1959 to 1964 and as a state senator from 1965 to 1978. Atiyeh was also senate Republican leader for three legislative sessions, and served as a delegate to the Republican National Convention in 1968, 1972, and 1976. As a legislator with a conservative reputation, he won the 1974 Republican gubernatorial primary in an upset, but lost to Robert Straub in the general election.

Atiyeh again won the Republican nomination for governor in 1978, only this time he was able to capitalize on Governor Straub's failure to provide strong leadership in the tradition of his predecessor Tom McCall, who had gained widespread publicity with his amusing suggestion that people visit Oregon for the scenery but then go back home rather than become a permanent drain on the state's resources. Projecting a forceful image, Atiyeh won a decisive victory against Straub, attracting 55 percent of the vote. As a conservative, he benefited from the post- "Proposition 13" climate, and his proposals to cut both taxation and government spending proved highly popular with Oregon's voters. Yet Atiyeh was also careful to campaign as a supporter of environmental measures in a state whose residents remained keenly aware of the importance of natural resources. His campaign literature heralded the fact that he had introduced major air and water quality bills into the Oregon Legislature more than a decade earlier, and he continued to insist that both conservation and the development of alternative energy sources were critical for the state's future.

Among the accomplishments of Atiyeh's first term were improvements in state management and productivity, reform in workers' compensation and welfare, and major new programs in energy and economic development. He also cut his own salary three times to help balance the budget. Although national news magazines reported that he was "running scared" in his 1982 campaign for re-election because of a depressed economy, especially in the critical lumber industry, Atiyeh continued to command widespread respect. He defeated his opponent, Democratic State Senator Ted Kulongowski, by winning 61.6 percent of the vote, Oregon's largest gubernatorial margin in 32 years. Atiyeh's record as a good administrator and his promise to broaden the state's economic base by bringing in new industries had particular appeal to Oregon voters in this election.

Atiyeh's priorities for his second term included property tax limitation, land use planning reform, renewed aid and commitment to higher education, continued emphasis on economic development, and establishment of special programs for public safety in Oregon's fishing and lumber industries. Committed to promoting responsible environmental policy, he led a successful campaign to put 12 miles along the Deschules River into public ownership. Under his leadership, the state legislature passed more environmental legislation in 1983 than at any time since the early 1970s. As governor, he was an active proponent of federal legislation to guarantee orderly growth of the Columbia River Gorge.

Moving to diversify and strengthen Oregon's timber-dependent economy without jeopardizing his concerns for environmental protection, Atiyeh took the following measures: dramatically reduced workers' compensation premiums that were the nation's highest; streamlined Oregon's innovative land-use laws; lobbied the White House for timber-contract relief; won legislative repeal of Oregon's controversial unitary-tax formula; launched a worldwide tourism initiative; led successful international and domestic trade missions; opened Oregon's first overseas trade office in Tokyo; and signed a sister-state agreement with China's Fujian and Taiwan Provinces.

As an administrator, he significantly reduced state government employment, won limits on state employment spending, cut paperwork and red tape, and reinstituted a state employee-suggestion program that saved Oregon taxpayers hundreds of thousands of dollars annually.

Demonstrating his concern for his constituents, he conducted frequent public open houses and maintained a citizens' representative program to assist Oregonians with questions and problems. When state residents began losing food stamp benefits in 1979, Atiyeh was instrumental in establishing Oregon Food Share, the nation's first statewide food bank. For his successful 1981 effort to enact laws against racial harassment, Atiyeh won the Distinguished Public Service Award of Oregon B'nai

B'rith and the highest honor for public service from the U.S. Department of Justice.

During his years in office, Atiyeh served as chairman of the Western Governors' Conference, vice chairman of the Republican Governors' Association, vice chairman of the National Governors' Association Committees on International Trade and Foreign Relations and Criminal Justice and Public Protection.

Barred from seeking a third term in 1986, Atiyeh left office in January 1987. He continues to serve on the Board of Directors of Atiyeh Brothers, the family-owned rug business started by his immigrant father and uncle at the turn of the century. He is presently a consultant in the area of international trade.

Bibliography: Biographical information courtesy of Governor Atiyeh; Jaques Cattell Press, *Who's Who in American Politics, 1985–1986* (New York, 1985); Michael Barone *et al.*, *The Almanac of American Politics 1986, 1988* (New York and Washington, D.C., 1985, 1987); "Where the GOP Will Hold Its Own," *U.S. News and World Report* (Oct. 4, 1982).

Neil Goldschmidt (Courtesy of governor's office; Credit: Photo Art Commercial Studios, Inc.)

GOLDSCHMIDT, Neil, 1987–

Born in Eugene, Oregon on June 16, 1940; the son of Lester H. Goldschmidt and Annette Levin Goldschmidt. Goldschmidt married Margaret Wood in 1965. The couple are the parents of two children, Rebecca and Joshua.

After graduating from South Eugene High School, Goldschmidt was student body president at the University of Oregon where he received his B.A. in political science in 1963. He earned a law degree from the University of California's Boalt School of Law in 1967 and was awarded an honorary doctorate from the University of Portland in 1980.

As a college student, Goldschmidt was a choke-setter and loading dock worker during the summers between 1960 and 1963. In 1964 he was an intern in the Washington D.C. office of former U.S. Senator Maurine Neuberger of Oregon. In Washington, he was recruited by Allard Lowenstein for voter registration work in the Freedom Summer civil rights campaign in Mississippi in 1964. A legal aid attorney in Portland from 1967 to 1969, he began his political career as a city commissioner there from 1971 to 1973. A Democrat, Goldschmidt was the youngest mayor of a major U.S. city when he became mayor of Portland in 1973 at the age of 32. He served as mayor until 1979 when he was named U.S. Secretary of Transportation by President Jimmy Carter. He served in that capacity through January 1981, upon the accession of the Reagan administration. As secretary of transportation, Goldschmidt authored "U.S. Automobile Industry, 1980," a report to the president.

At the close of the Carter years, Goldschmidt returned to Oregon where he joined Nike, the running shoe company based in Oregon. Working with Nike from 1981 through December 1985, he became head of its Canadian subsidiary, Nike Canada, in 1986. Goldschmidt has also served on the board of directors of Gelco Corp., Infocel Inc., Kaiser Foundation Health Plan, and National Semiconductor.

In 1986 Goldschmidt entered the Oregon governor's race, which saw him and Republican Norma Paulus locked in one of the state's closest gubernatorial contests in modern times. Elected two times by big margins as Oregon Secretary of State in 1976 and 1984, Paulus was striving to become the state's first woman governor.

The campaign was conducted against the backdrop of the state's continuing economic distress and high unemployment. Goldschmidt, campaigning under the cloud that Democrats had held the statehouse for only 10 of the previous 60 years, bluntly summarized that the race was "about jobs." He focused his campaign on a blueprint for Oregon's future, and stresed his role as an innovator while mayor of Portland in the 1970s. Hailed as a "public sector risk-taker in the entrepreneurial mold" by *The Portland Oregonian*, Goldschmidt was helped by his support from many businessmen and by his own business experience. He won the race over Paulus, 52 percent to 48 percent. Analysts attributed his victory to his economic program and to his record of cutting crime as mayor of Portland.

Goldschmidt is regarded as a liberal because of his attitudes on cultural issues, a position welcomed in a state usually regarded as a culturally liberal one. In office, he has called for "an activist state role in the economy." He has been willing to place more emphasis on economic growth and a little less on environmental protection, a reversal of state policies of a decade ago when many state residents feared growth as a foreboding of "incipient California-zation." He has supported an end to school closings mandated by excessive property tax levies, claiming that his efforts to promote the state as a good place to live and do business are harmed by such closings. In the area of higher education, he wants to increase faculty salaries and to improve relations between the academic and business communities.

Goldschmidt has received many awards and honors during his political career, including selection as one of the Ten Outstanding Young Men in the United States by the National Jaycees in 1972, and identification as one of the "200 Faces of the Future" by *Time* magazine in 1974. In 1980 he received the International B'nai B'rith Sam Beber Award for Outstanding Leadership.

Bibliography: Biographical information courtesy of governor's office; *The Chronicle of Higher Education,* 11–12–86; Jaques Cattell Press, *Who's Who in American Politics, 1985–1986* (New York, 1985); Michael Barone et al., *The Almanac of American Politics, 1988* (New York, 1987); *The New York Times:* 10–19–86; 5–19–87.

Richard Lewis Thornburgh (Courtesy of Governor Thornburgh)

PENNSYLVANIA

THORNBURGH, Richard Lewis, 1979–1987

Born in Pittsburgh, Pennsylvania on July 16, 1932, the son of Charles Garland and Alice (Sanborn) Thornburgh. An Episcopalian, Thornburgh married Virginia Hooton, a childhood sweetheart, who was later killed in a 1960 automobile accident. He is the father of John, David, and Peter by his first wife. On October 12, 1963, Thornburgh married Virginia Judson, a former New York schoolteacher, by whom he is the father of a son named William. As parents of a retarded son, the Thornburghs have taken a special interest in the needs of handicapped persons, and in 1985 were named "Family of the Year" by the Pennsylvania Association for Retarded Citizens.

Thornburgh received a bachelor of engineering degree from Yale University in 1954, and an LL.B. with high honors from the University of Pittsburgh in 1957. He has received honorary degrees from Washington and Jefferson College, Bucknell University, LaSalle College, Temple University, Lincoln University, Villanova University, St. Francis College, College Misericordia, Lehigh University, and Wheaton College in Massachusetts. Admitted to the Pennsylvania bar in 1958, Thornburgh was employed by the Aluminum Company of America for two years. He then joined the Pittsburgh law firm of Kirkpatrick, Lockhart, Johnson, and Hutchinson, where he worked until 1969. In that year the Nixon administration named him United States Attorney for the Western District of Pennsylvania. Thornburgh impanelled the first grand jury in the United States to investigate racketeering under the Organized Crime Control Act of 1970. He has personally never lost a legal case. In 1975 Thornburgh became deputy attorney general in charge of the Criminal Law Division of the Department of Justice, where he served until President Jimmy Carter took office. He then returned to his old Pittsburgh firm.

Running as a Republican, Thornburgh defeated Philadelphian Arlen Specter and five other candidates in the 1978 gubernatorial primary. He opposed Pete Flaherty, the former mayor of Pittsburgh, in the general election. Flaherty was expected to win easily, but instead he lost most of eastern Pennsylvania except Philadelphia, a development which cost him the election. The final vote was 1,966,042 for Thornburgh and 1,737,888 for Flaherty. During the campaign Thornburgh attacked Flaherty's record as

Pittsburgh's mayor, but he was careful to avoid raising that issue while in the Pittsburgh area. Traditional Democratic groups like the teachers' union were annoyed by Flaherty's fiscal conservatism and backed Thornburgh, who also did well with black voters.

Soon after being sworn in, Thornburgh faced the grave responsibility created by the Three Mile Island nuclear power plant accident. While there was no danger of a nuclear explosion, some radiation did escape as a result of the accident and a leakage of disastrous proportions was feared by responsible persons at the scene. Thornburgh's office was effective in avoiding panic and acting as a clearinghouse of reliable information, and the governor himself made a number of key decisions involving the public's safety. In the most crucial of these, Thornburgh proposed the evacuation of pre-school youngsters and pregnant women who were within five miles of the plant.

Pennsylvania's economy was severely disturbed during Thornburgh's first term, partly as a result of major cutbacks in federal aid to the state. In 1981 the economic situation was further complicated when a drought emergency was declared in the Delaware River basin.

Thornburgh received the 1982 Republican gubernatorial nomination without opposition. In the general election he defeated Allen Ertel, a congressman from the Harrisburg-Williamsport, Pennsylvania area. Ertel had tried to link the incumbent to the Reagan administration's economic policies, while Thornburgh emphasized property tax reform and his plan to end the policy of state-owned liquor stores. Ertel lost considerable ground when he failed to disclose his tax returns, after attempting to portray himself as the "poor man's candidate." The final vote was 1,872,784 for Thornburgh and 1,772,353 for Ertel, who won the Philadelphia vote handily but did not do well outside of the eastern part of the state.

During his second term, Thornburgh focused on resolving some persistent problems. In 1978 the state signed a consent order with the Environmental Protection Agency and a citizens' group, requiring mandatory vehicle emission tests in certain areas of the state. The Pennsylvania Legislature, however, overrode Thornburgh's veto and refused to appropriate funds to begin the tests. The United States Court of Appeals for the Third Circuit then blocked the use of $91 million in highway funds by the state. Eventually the legislature backed down and vehicle tests began. Yet another contentious issue concerned the reorganization of rail commuter lines in the Philadelphia area, as the Southeastern Pennsylvania Transit Authority took over commuter rail service from Conrail. Labor difficulties stemming from this change caused a brief shutdown of service, and a state judicial inquiry and review board later charged that Pennsylvania Supreme Court Justice Rolf Larsen had tried to organize opposition to the re-election of one of his fellow members of the court. He restored integrity and efficiency to Pennsylvania's state government and fostered expansion and diversification of the state's economy. He initiated innovative economic development policies, reduced taxes and indebtedness, and eliminated 15,000 unnecessary positions from the state bureaucracy. His programs for welfare and education reform, for upgrading the state's transportation system, and for reducing the state's crime rate were all nationally acclaimed. In a 1986 *Newsweek* poll Thornburgh was named by his fellow governors as one of the nation's most effective big state governors.

In 1986 Thornburgh considered running in the Republican primary against U.S. Senator Arlen Spector. Urged to make the race by conservatives who felt that Spector had not been sufficiently supportive of Reagan administration policies, Thornburgh declined to run when analysts predicted a divisive and costly primary battle that would have crippled the survivor in the general election.

Barred from serving a third term in the statehouse, Thornburgh left office in January 1987, becoming a partner in the Pittsburgh law firm of Kirkpatrick and Lockhart. He also taught at Harvard University, serving as Director of the Institute of Politics at the John F. Kennedy School of Government.

Even out of office, Thornburgh's reputation for honesty, integrity, and efficiency made him a rising star in national Republican political circles. Although he turned down a chance to become head of the FBI in 1987, his name continued to surface as a possible running mate for George Bush on the Republican presidential ticket of 1988. When in July 1988 the U.S. Justice Department was beset by recurring controversy due to allegations of impropriety lodged against Attorney General Edwin Meese, President Reagan tapped Thornburgh as Meese's successor. Confirmed unanimously by the U.S. Senate, he drew strength from two sources: his non-ideological approach to political and legal issues, and his strong reputation for integrity. Thornburgh will continue to hold the post of Attorney General in the new Bush administration.

Bibliography: Biographical information courtesy of Governor Thornburgh; Michael Barone *et al., The Almanac of American Politics, 1980, 1984, 1986* (New York and Washington, D.C., 1979, 1983, 1985); *The Philadelphia Inquirer:* 11–8–78; 11–3–82; *U.S.A. Today,* 6–7–88; *The New York Times:* 4–6–79; 12–14–80; 9–10–82; 1–3–85; 9–27–85; 12–13–85; 9–4–86; 9–8–86; 1–15–87; 5–1–87; 5–2–87; 7–13–88.

Robert P. Casey (Courtesy of governor's office)

CASEY, Robert P., 1987–

Born in Jackson Heights, New York on January 9, 1932; the son of Alphonsus and Marie Casey. A Roman Catholic, he is married to the former Ellen Theresa Harding. The couple has eight children.

Casey grew up in Scranton, Pennsylvania where he was senior class president and valedictorian of the class of 1949 at Scranton Prep. An accomplished athlete, he was named to the *Scranton Times'* 1949 All-Regional Basketball Team. Attending Holy Cross on an athletic scholarship, he played on nationally ranked Holy Cross basketball teams which included all-Americans Bob Cousey and Tom Heinsohn.

After graduating from Holy Cross with a B.A. in English, *cum laude,* in 1953, Casey attended the George Washington University Law School on a scholarship awarded by the University's trustees. A member of the Order of the Coif and research editor of the law review, he received his J.D. in 1956. After graduation he worked as an associate with the prestigious Washington, D.C. firm of Covington and Burlington. Two years later he returned to Scranton to begin his own law practice.

He began his political career in 1963, winning election as state senator from Lackawanna County. In office, he distinguished himself by authoring landmark environmental legislation which became a model for the Federal Clean Air and Water Act. In 1967 he was elected to serve as a delegate to the State Constitutional Convention. Serving as first vice president of the convention, he played a leading role in the writing and ratification of the state's current constitution.

In 1968 Casey was elected to the first of two consecutive terms as state auditor. From 1969 to 1977, he revolutionized the office of auditor general, turning it into a model of professionalism and efficiency. He won praise for putting the office on a professional basis, for fighting corruption, and for avoiding scandal at a time when Democrats in other state offices did not. In the words of one political commentator, Casey took a backwater agency long known as a haven for patronage and turned it into a "rushing current of reform."

In 1977 Casey returned to private law practice, although he continued to remain active in both Scranton civic affairs and national politics.

In 1986 he entered the Democratic gubernatorial primary to succeed retiring Governor Richard Thornburgh, a Republican, who was constitutionally ineligible to serve more than two consecutive terms. Despite losses in three previous Democratic gubernatorial primaries in 1966, 1970, and 1978, he won the nomination in a three-way race, defeating Edward G. Rendell and Steve Douglas. His opponent in the general election was Lieutenant Governor William Scranton 3rd, the son of a former state governor and presidential candidate. The race was seen as a "classic" contest between political generations. While Casey sought to portray the

39-year-old Scranton as a child of privilege and a product of the 1960s, Scranton countered by calling Casey a political relic, the product of a dead era of patronage politics and smokestack economics, and therefore ill-equipped to lead the state into the post-industrial age. The campaign was marred by negative political attacks, with Scranton's use of drugs as a student becoming a point of controversy. In TV ads, Casey painted Scranton as a laid-back, less than diligent lieutenant governor who missed most meetings of groups he was supposed to preside over, such as the state senate and Pardon Board.

Casey's victory over Scranton with 51 percent of the vote to the Republican's 48 percent was widely credited to his detailed and extensive blueprint for developing the state's economy. With his victory, he became the first Democrat to hold the governorship in eight years and only the second in the last quarter-century.

In office, Casey has focused on three key areas: the environment, education, and economic development. He has pumped new resources into long-delayed efforts to clean up toxic wastes, as well as proposing unprecedented increases in education funding. Pledging to forge an economically united state whose "inferiority complex shall end," he established the Pennsylvania Economic Development Partnership to create jobs for state workers and opportunity for state businesses. The council is empowered to direct development funds to people and places that need them most, and to industries whose future appears most promising. Casey has also pledged to continue efforts begun by the previous administration to rebuild the state's deteriorating infrastructure. He has also promised to upgrade water systems, sewers, and airports.

Bibliography: Biographical information courtesy of governor's office; Michael Barone *et al., The Almanac of American Politics 1988* (New York and Washington, D.C., 1987); *The Chronicle of Higher Education,* 11–12–86; *The New York Times;* 10–20–86; 10–22–86; 11–5–86; 11–6–86; 1–21–87; 6–30–87.

John Joseph Garrahy (Courtesy of Governor Garrahy)

RHODE ISLAND

GARRAHY, John Joseph, 1977–1985

Born on November 26, 1930 in Providence, Rhode Island, the son of John and Margaret (Neylon) Garrahy. A Roman Catholic, Garrahy married Margherite De Pietro in 1956; he is the father of Colleen, John, Maribeth, Sheila, and Seanna.

Garrahy attended the University of Buffalo in 1952 and the University of Rhode Island in 1953. A member of the United States Air Force from 1953 to 1955, he was elected to the Rhode Island Senate in 1962, where he served until 1968. He also acted as deputy majority leader of the Rhode Island Senate from 1963 to 1968. Garrahy has served on the Board of Directors of the National Council on Vocational Rehabilitation and the Governors' Council on Youth Opportunities. Running as a Democrat, he was elected lieutenant governor of Rhode Island in 1968. In 1976 Garrahy defeated James L. Taft in the general election by a vote of 218,561 to 178,254. Garrahy took the oath of office on January 4, 1977.

In 1978 Rhode Island endorsed the building of Interstate Highway 84. The state also agreed to return 1,800 acres which allegedly had been taken illegally from the Narragansett Indians. Unopposed in the 1978 Democratic primary, Garrahy defeated the Republican Lincoln C. Almond and Joseph A. Doorley, an Independent candidate, in a three-man race. Garrahy did little campaigning during the contest, but still managed to accumulate 197,386 votes compared to Almond's 96,596 and Doorley's 20,381.

Garrahy travelled to the Soviet Union in 1979 along with other governors to discuss strategic arms limitation with the Soviet Union's Vasily V. Kuznetsov. In 1980 he was unopposed in the Democratic gubernatorial primary and again was elected by defeating Vincent A. Cianci, the Republican mayor of Providence, by 299,174 votes to 106,729 in the general election. During his third term Garrahy tried to combat the state's image as "Poor Little Rhode Island"; he also allowed a ban on the sale of spray paint to minors to become law without his signature. In 1982 Garrahy again had no primary opposition. He proceeded to win a landslide victory over Vincent Marzullo by a vote of 246,566 to 79,602. In the wake of such victories—winning his last three terms by 3–1 margins—political observers speculated that Garrahy might very well have been the most popular governor in the nation.

During his four terms in office, he revitalized the state's economy, worked toward improving New England's energy position, modernized Rhode Island's human services departments and state institutions, and put into place numerous programs designed to maintain and protect the state's environment. He played an integral role in the state's acquisition of the vacant Quonset Point navy lands from the federal government; today the Quonset Point Industrial Park is a burgeoning center for economic development. During Garrahy's administration, 191 firms invested $340 million in new industrial space, creating or retaining 37,000 jobs. Under the governor's stewardship, Rhode Island's double digit unemployment dropped to its lowest level in 14 years, and for five years it was substantially below the national average.

Committed to improving human services, Garrahy did much to improve the quality of life not only in Rhode Island but throughout the New England region. As chairman of the National Governors' Association Subcommittee on Health Policy, he became spokesman for the nation's governors on health matters. He was also appointed to the chairmanship of the National Governors' Association Human Services Committee. He created the state Department of Elderly Affairs and the Department for Children and Their Families to address the needs of Rhode Island's elderly and young people. During his tenure as governor, the Department of Children and Their Families implemented one of the nation's most sophisticated credit tracking programs to prevent child abuse.

Garrahy's biggest political disappointment was voter rejection of his so-called "Greenhouse Compact" in a 1984 referendum. The $250 million, seven-year industrial development package included subsidies, tax changes, research facilities, and other incentives for business to relocate and expand in Rhode Island. Voters, perhaps concerned that the package would lead to higher taxes, perhaps skeptical of government's ability to produce economic growth, rejected the program overwhelmingly, by a margin of almost 80 percent of 20 percent.

Garrahy is currently a senior vice president with the merchant banking firm of G. William Miller and Co., Inc. of Washington, D.C. and Rhode Island. In addition, he serves as a Distinguished Visiting Professor at Providence College where he conducts a seminar on values in government.

Bibliography: Biographical information courtesy of Governor Garrahy; Michael Barone *et al., The Almanac of American Politics, 1984, 1988* (New York and Washington, D.C., 1983, 1987); Jaques Cattell Press, *Who's Who in American Politics, 1985–1986* (New York, 1985); *The Providence Journal:* 11–8–78; 11–9–78; 11–3–82; *The New York Times:* 1–5–77; 11–3–77; 6–14–84; 11–8–84.

Edward Daniel DiPrete (Courtesy of governor's office)

DIPRETE, Edward Daniel, 1985–

Born in Cranston, Rhode Island on July 8, 1934; the son of Frank A. DiPrete and Maria Grossi DiPrete. A Roman Catholic, DiPrete married the former Patricia Hines in 1956. The couple has seven children.

A graduate of Cranston public schools, LaSalle Academy, and the College of the Holy Cross, DiPrete is a veteran of the U.S. Navy, released as a lieutenant after serving in the western Pacific 1955–1959. After this Navy stint, he worked in a small real estate business started by his father before entering public service. He was first elected to the Cranston School Committee in 1970. Re-elected in 1972, he served as chairman through 1974. In 1974, he was elected as an "at-large" member of the Cranston City Council, and re-elected in 1976. He was elected mayor of Cranston on November 7, 1978, and re-elected on November 2, 1982 by the largest majority in the city's history, 83 percent. As mayor, he developed a reputation for getting things done without stirring up controversy.

In 1984 DiPrete sought the governorship upon the retirement of four-term incumbent Joseph Garrahy. He waged an aggressive campaign against State Treasurer Anthony J. Solomon, who suffered from a divided Democratic organizaiton. Solomon had won his party's nomination in one of the most expensive and bitter primaries in state history. His opponent had been Joseph Walsh of Warwick, whose allies had seized control of the party from retiring Governor Garrahy. Many political analysts believed that the battle between Solomon and Walsh, who traded charges of lying and fiscal irresponsibility, made it possible for the Republicans to win the governor's office for the first time in 16 years. DiPrete's victory over Solomon, by an impressive margin of 60 percent to 40 percent, was seen as an historic one for the Republican party. Republicans also won five out of nine statewide offices, the first time in 40 years that the party held a majority of statewide posts. Analysts attributed the sweep to a perception by state voters that the old Democratic leadership was tainted by corruption and incompetence.

DiPrete easily won re-election in 1986, defeating political newcomer Bruce Sundlun, a rich businessman who spent liberally on his campaign. DiPrete won 64.7 percent of the vote to his opponent's 32.4 percent.

An avowedly pro-business politician, DiPrete has worked for the revival of the state after several decades of decline. Rhode Island has suffered from the decay of its textile and jewelry industry, and from the consequent loss of population, especially among its young. To buttress his economic development program, DiPrete persuaded the Democratic legislature to adopt what he described as an agenda for jobs. He succeeded in getting the legislature to pass a 16 percent cut in the state income tax and a restructuring of the state unemployment compensation system. He also repealed the state gift and estate tax as well as the highly controversial strikers' benefit statute—a provision that enabled union members to collect unemployment benefits while on strike. He also established a state Partnership for Science and Technology and increased funding for education, Head Start, and other children's programs. Using the national media, he ran ads in papers across the country saying, "If you want to talk business in Rhode Island, talk to a businessman, the governor." Sensitive to the state's poor image, he tried to use state money to help the University of Rhode Island expand its robotics laboratory in conjunction with private industry, and to help Brown University develop pharmaceutical products at its large medical school that could be marketed by commercial concerns. He also called for more research to bolster economic development, and more cooperation between public and private colleges.

With the state's economy growing and the unemployment rate well below the national average, political analysts observed that DiPrete's policies seemed to be working. His second-term program—more money for school textbooks, encouraging small businesses, implementing workfare incentives—has met with approval from Democrats as well as Republicans.

Seeking a third term in office in 1988, DiPrete was locked in a tough battle with Bruce G. Sundlun, the wealthy broadcasting executive he had defeated in 1986. DiPrete had been considered a sure bet for re-election until the disclosure that his family was involved in a land deal that netted $2 million in profits. Surviving a campaign beset by ethical questions, DiPrete squeaked out a narrow 51 percent–49 percent victory over his Democratic challenger.

Bibliography: Biographical information courtesy of governor's office; *The Chronicle of Higher Education,* 11–12–86; Michael Barone *et al., The Almanac of American Politics 1988* (New York and Washington, D.C., 1987); Jaques Cattell Press, *Who's Who in American Politics, 1985–1986* (New York, 1985); *The New York Times:* 9–11–84; 9–13–84; 11–6–84; 1–2–85; 9–15–85; 9–11–86.

Richard Wilson Riley (Courtesy of Governor Riley)

SOUTH CAROLINA

RILEY, Richard Wilson, 1979–1987

Born on January 2, 1933 at Greenville, South Carolina, the son of Edward Patterson and Martha (Dixon) Riley. A Methodist, Riley was graduated in 1954 from Furman University, receiving an A.B. with honors. He was operations officer on a minesweep control ship in the United States Navy from 1954 to 1956. On August 23, 1957, he married Ann Osteen Yarborough; they have four children—Richard W. Jr., Anne Y., Hubert D., and Theodore D. In 1959 Riley received an LL.B. from the law school of the University of South Carolina. That same year he became legal counsel for the Judiciary Subcommittee of the United States Senate.

Riley became a Democratic member of the South Carolina House of Representatives in 1963, and in 1967 he was elected to the South Carolina Senate. In the legislature he advocated judicial reform and local autonomy. In 1970 Riley pleaded for harmony in the face of an order requiring rapid school desegregation. He left his own children in the public schools during this period. He resigned from the legislature in 1975 to become Jimmy Carter's state campaign manager. In 1978 Riley placed second in the initial primary for governor, but he defeated Lieutenant Governor W. Brantley Harvey in the runoff primary. He ran as a reform candidate in the general election, defeating Edward Young, a former U.S. Congressman, by 385,016 votes to 236,946, taking every county in the state but Lexington.

As chief executive, Riley was prominent particularly as an environmentalist. He refused to permit the dumping of nuclear waste from the Three Mile Island nuclear generator in his state after the accident at that plant. Riley urged a federal solution to the difficulty. In 1980 President Carter named him to the Nuclear Waste Disposal Council. Riley and his wife received an award from conservationists in 1982, when they designed the grounds of the governor's mansion to be hospitable to wildlife.

Midway in Riley's term the state constitution was amended to permit a chief executive to succeed himself. Riley thus ran again in 1982; no one challenged him in the primary. Former Governor and then United States Secretary of Energy James Edwards initially considered opposing Riley in the general election, but Edwards decided that Riley was too popular to defeat. Ultimately, Riley ran against William Workman, a retired newspaper editor, whom he beat easily by 468,819 votes to 202,806.

In one important respect the Riley administration continued the policies of its predecessors: he maintained South Carolina's efforts to attract high wage jobs, and like governors before him, grappled with difficult problems of nuclear waste disposal. Although he failed to obtain the tax reform measure he had sought in 1983, he succeeded in 1984, putting through a thorough education reform package complete with higher taxes to pay for it. The program included merit pay and pay raises for teachers, a building program, remedial education, and cash bonuses to schools that improved. The bill passed after Riley convinced both businessmen and voters that the state needed a better educated workforce if it was to enjoy further economic growth.

Hailed as one of the nation's best governors, Riley retired from office after two terms with his popularity intact. He reportedly declined an opportunity to run for the U.S. Senate in 1984. He is presently a partner with the law firm of Nelson, Mullins, Riley and Scarborough in Columbia, South Carolina.

Bibliography: South Carolina Legislative Manual (1975); *The Washington Post:* 4–23–79; 11–24–79; 5–7–81; Jaques Cattell Press, *Who's Who in American Politics, 1985–1986* (New York, 1985); Michael Barone *et al., The Almanac of American Politics, 1984, 1986* (New York and Washington, D.C., 1983, 1985).

Carroll A. Campbell, Jr. (Courtesy of governor's office)

CAMPBELL, Carroll A. Jr., 1987–

Born in Greenville, South Carolina on July 24, 1940; the son of Carroll Ashmore Campbell and Anne Williams Campbell. An Episcopalian, Campbell married the former Iris Rhodes in 1959. The couple has two sons, Carroll and Richard.

Educated in the Greenville public schools, Campbell graduated from the McCallie School in Tennessee. He attended both the University of South Carolina and American University in Washington, D.C. on a part-time basis. At age 19 he was working in the real estate business when he and a partner founded Handy Park Company, a successful chain of parking facilities. In 1967 he was a principal in the formation of Rex Enterprises, which developed a chain of 13 Burger King restaurants before being sold in 1978. Campbell also became active as a breeder of Arabian horses, and owned and operated a farm near Fountain Inn, South Carolina for many years.

Campbell began his political career helping a friend run for public office in 1960, and through the years managed campaigns for others, including the campaign that elected the first Republican mayor of Greenville. He himself first sought political office in 1969, but was defeated in a special election. He ran successfully in 1970, elected to the South Carolina House of Representatives, winning re-election in 1972. In 1973 Campbell served as assistant minority leader, and was elected as the first Republican in a century to hold an office on a standing committee. He lost a close race for lieutenant governor in 1974, and in 1975–1976 served as executive assistant to Governor James B. Edwards, the first Republican governor in South Carolina since Reconstruction. He served in the South Carolina State Senate from 1976 to 1978, when he was elected to the U.S. Congress from South Carolina's fourth congressional district. The popular congressman served four terms before being elected governor in 1986. In Congress Campbell served on two powerful committees, the Appropriations and Ways and Means Committees. He also served for four years as a member of the Republican Policy Committee of the Textile Caucus. While in Congress, he received the Watchdog of the Treasury Golden Bulldog Award for fiscal responsibility, as well as the National Federation of Independent Business Award for support of the free enterprise system.

In 1986 Campbell sought the governorship upon the retirement of popular incumbent Richard Riley. Relinquishing a safe house seat to make the run, he waged an uphill battle to become only the second Republican to hold the statehouse in over a century. His opponent was Lieutenant Governor Michael Daniel, who in 1984 gained national attention for his efforts to cool racial tensions after two white men had burned down three rural black churches in Lancaster County. Daniel waged a defensive campaign, running on Riley's record and seeking to rebut Campbell's charges that the state was not doing well.

Campbell promised to throw out the "good ol' boy" system of entrenched state politicians. Stressing education, economic development, and political ethics, he called for cutting insurance rates, reorganizing state government, and lowering taxes. In the campaign, he seemed to be following a strategy developed in 1985 at a meeting of leading Republican governors, members of Congress, and political consultants. The group, convened by Governor Lamar Alexander of Tennesee, concluded that Republicans could not win state elections by running on the "Washington agenda" of foreign policy and social issues. Although the Republicans had won national elections by promising to restrain the role of the federal government, they had to recognize that people expected state government to be active and involved in solving their problems. Political analysts saw Campbell as a model of a new breed of Republican emerging in the modern South, a conservative who was actively seeking black votes. Campbell also benefitted from President Reagan's popularity in the state.

Campbell pulled out a narrow victory, 51 percent to 49 percent. His margins came in suburban areas, especially in his home base of Greenville. Profiting from a well-tuned and well financed party organization, he managed to withstand a vicious smear campaign by some Democratic activists. The controversy, which had been a lingering undercurrent in South Carolina politics for some time, dated back to his 1978 campaign for Congress. Critics suggested that he or his campaign organization was behind an attempt to make his Democratic opponent's Jewish faith an issue in the race, which Campbell won.

Sworn in on January 14, 1987 as the state's 112th governor, Campbell extended an olive branch to the Democratically controlled legislature, calling for an era of "unparalleled opportunity for all South Carolinians." In office, he stressed education reform and economic development. He also announced that ensuring the well being of the state's children would be a top priority of his administration. In the area of higher education, he proposed eliminating remedial courses at four-year institutions, using the savings to finance a research program linking the state's three major universities. He also wants the state's universities to help in the development of new jobs.

In the opinion of political observers, Campbell has been instrumental in building an effective Republican party in the state. The Republicans have done a better job in South Carolina than in other Southern states of generating candidates able to win local elections in all kinds of constituencies.

Because of his successes, Campbell has frequently been mentioned as a rising star in national Republican politics. His name appeared on a long list of contenders for a spot as George Bush's vice presidential running mate on the 1988 Republican ticket.

Bibliography: Biographical information courtesy of governor's office; Michael Barone *et al., The Almanac of American Politics, 1986, 1988* (New York and Washington, D.C., 1985, 1987); Jaques Cattell Press, *Who's Who in American Politics, 1985–1986* (New York, 1985); *The Chronicle of Higher Education:* 11–12–86; 2–18–87; *U.S.A. Today,* 6–7–88; *The New York Times:* 8–6–85; 9–4–86; 9–24–86; 11–6–86; 1–15–87.

William John Janklow (Credit: South Dakota Department of Education and Cultural Affairs)

SOUTH DAKOTA

Born on September 13, 1939 in Chicago, Illinois. A Lutheran, Janklow is married to the former Mary Dean Thom, a native of Flandreau, South Dakota. They have three children—Russell, Pamela, and Shonna.

In 1956 Janklow enlisted in the United States Marine Corps, serving in Southeast Asia from 1956 to 1959. Following his discharge he enrolled at the University of South Dakota, graduating with honors with a B.S. in business administration in 1964. He earned his J.D. from the University of South Dakota School of Law in 1966.

As a Legal Services attorney, Janklow was chief officer at the Rosebud Indian Reservation from 1966 to 1973. There he developed a reputation both as a trial lawyer and administrator, as he and his staff handled over 43,000 requests for assistance in seven years. He personally defended Indians accused of murder or manslaughter in 30 cases, winning all 30, and filed a major civil rights case leading to reform of the jury selection process. During his years with the reservation, Janklow won an anti-discrimination case against Winner, South Dakota.

In 1973 Janklow was appointed chief prosecutor of South Dakota. As the chief trial attorney in the attorney general's office, he quickly earned a reputation as a top trial lawyer in one of the most difficult periods of the state's history. South Dakota has one of the largest Indian populations in the nation, and when Indian militants erupted into violence at Wounded Knee in 1973, Janklow's vigorous law and order stance drew widespread attention. Prosecuting 22 persons, most of whom were associated with the American Indian movement, on charges of rioting and arson, the conservative Janklow drew the wrath of many Indian leaders and pro-Indian liberals. He became known for his opposition to the land claims of the American Indian movement, and was christened by political analysts as the "premier anti-Indian politician in the state." This reputation endeared him to many South Dakota voters, however, who were disenchanted with Indian demands and methods.

In 1974 the Republican State Convention nominated Janklow for attorney general. Campaigning on the theme, "a trial lawyer, not a politician," he pledged to clean up the "mess" in the attorney general's office and to reverse the state's rising crime rate. While Democrats captured most state offices that year, Janklow upset his former boss, Democratic Attorney General Kermit Sande, in a landslide that repudiated what he called Sande's "mudslinging, vicious campaign tactics." Sande, who was seeking a second term in office, had charged that Janklow had a criminal record, but he was unable to substantiate the accusation. Despite other inflammatory allegations by his opponent, Janklow won 67 percent of the vote and carried every county in the state.

As attorney general, Janklow continued to be active in the courtroom. He personally argued and won two cases before the United States Supreme Court, a first for a South Dakota attorney general. He also continued to attract publicity as Indian violence persisted in the state throughout the early 1970s. As the state's top law enforcement officer, Janklow even ordered that anyone found with dynamite should be detonated with it. Fortunately, the order never had to be carried out. When someone threw a firebomb into his home, Janklow let it be known that he was sleeping with an M-16 by his side, and that he would shoot to kill anyone trespassing on his lawn at night. The most famous of such colorful incidents came on July 4, 1976. Hearing that a man had taken hostages at the State Capitol, Janklow, working at home, grabbed his gun and went off to the rescue.

Justifiably labelled "flamboyant" by political observers on account of such episodes, Janklow was elected governor in 1978. After defeating State Senator Leroy Hoffman, a millionaire farmer, rancher, and former concert singer, and rancher Clint Roberts to gain the Republican gubernatorial nomination (the vote totals were 51 percent, 33 percent, and 16 percent, respectively), he then benefited from the discord plaguing South Dakota's Democrats. Three-term incumbent Richard Kneip had resigned to become United States Ambassador to Singapore, and his successor, Lieutenant Governor Harvey Wollman, was narrowly defeated by State Senator Roger D. McKellips in the Democratic primary. McKellips himself got into trouble because of his party's position in the Oahe Irrigation Project, a once-popular program endorsed by many Democrats but increasingly opposed by South Dakota voters. Janklow won the election with a solid 57 percent of the vote to McKellips' 43 percent.

Political commentators saw Janklow as highly intelligent, intense, and articulate, a man of high energy and with strong populist tendencies. A conservative, he balanced the state's books and avoided tax increases for several years through job attrition and a series of bookkeeping maneuvers. Janklow was a strong supporter of a constitutional amendment requiring the federal budget to be balanced. Indeed, he stated publicly in the national press that the time had come "to protect the future economy of the nation with a measure of this kind." Unopposed in the 1982 Republican primary, he won re-election to a second term overwhelmingly, defeating the Democratic nominee, State Senator Mike O'Connor, with 71 percent of the vote to O'Connor's 29 percent, the largest margin of victory for a governor in South Dakota history.

During his years as chief executive, Janklow's style continued to gain him a measure of notoriety. His decision to allow a San Francisco-based energy concern to siphon water from Lake Oahe and pipe it 260 miles west to the coal fields of the Powder River Basin near Gillette, Wyoming provoked outrage and court challenges from conservationists, the Sioux Indians, and several states downstream. Although Janklow defended his decision by arguing that it would bring the state hundreds of millions of dollars that could pay for badly needed projects to get more water into arid western South Dakota, the other states of the Missouri River basin feared that the deal presaged the extensive commercial exploitation of their primary water source. Under Janklow's direction South Dakota, which has no corporate or personal income tax and lower wages than surrounding states, also began an aggressive bid to attract businesses to the state. When almost 60 companies relocated to South Dakota from adjacent Minnesota, a high tax state, Janklow became the target of invective from neighboring governors. His public dispute with Minnesota Governor Rudy Perpich, which saw both men feuding over which state offered the better business climate, drew considerable attention. Both men appeared together on public television's "McNeil-Lehrer Report" and, in the words of a *New York Times* reporter, "verbally assaulted each other with considerable zeal." At times, Janklow's past returned to haunt him. In 1983 he sought to remove all copies of a book entitled *In the Spirit of Crazy Horse* from the shelves of South Dakota bookstores, because he believed the book libeled him. A biography of Leonard Peltier, a leader of the American Indian movement, the book contained passages critical of Janklow when he was an attorney on the Rosebud Indian Reservation.

As governor, Janklow focused hard on the state's ailing economy, especially in the agricultural sector that is deeply intertwined with federal farm policies. In 1985 he led the entire South Dakota legislature to Washington to lobby on behalf of the state's debt-ridden farmers. He changed South Dakota's banking laws to allow out-of-state banks chartered in South Dakota to acquire insurance companies, while freeing them from ceilings on interest rates for credit cards. His policies created thousands of new jobs in banking services and millions in investments by banks in parts of the state. He also was successful in attracting businesses from high-tax Minnesota over the line to low-tax South Dakota. He also got the state to buy 936 miles of Milwaukee Railroad tracks and lease them to Burlington Northern to hold down farmers' freight rates. He also launched a state hail insurance program, a coal operation, gas station chain, and a cement plant.

Janklow was constitutionally barred from seeking a third term in 1986. Political observers consider him to have been a tough and feisty leader whose policies and personality put a real stamp on state politics. He was considered a "hard, perhaps impossible" act to follow.

Despite his popularity, however, Janklow was unsuccessful in a bid for higher office upon the completion of his gubernatorial term. He was defeated in the 1986 Republican senatorial primary by incumbent James Abdnor. Although Abdnor had a rather conservative record in the senate and lacked a list of spectacular accomplishments, he remained personally popular. Voters could think of few reasons "to fire Jim Abdnor," a slogan that became the focus of his campaign. Janklow, by contrast, focused on the same theme that had marked his years as governor—that rural America was falling behind the rest of the nation, and that America was falling behind the world. In a state where most voters actually meet candidates, few Republicans really could find fault with the pleasant and hard working incumbent, and he defeated Janklow, 55 percent to 45 percent. Janklow carried Sioux Falls and the state's northeastern counties, where his policies had brought jobs, while Abdnor carried his home area west of the Missouri River overwhelmingly. In the general election, however, he was defeated by Democrat Thomas Daschle, an active legislator.

Janklow retired to his private law practice.

Bibliography: Rapid City (S.D.) Journal, 11–6–74; Michael Barone *et al., The Almanac of American Politics, 1978, 1982, 1986, 1988* (New York and Washington, D.C., 1977, 1981, 1985, 1987); *The New York Times:* 6–2–78; 6–1–82; 6–4–82; 8–11–82; 3–5–83; 4–7–83; 5–1–83; 6–1–86; *South Dakota Legislative Manual, 1979, 1985;* Molly Ivins, "It's Rarely Politics as Usual to South Dakota Governor," *New York Times Biographical Service* 11 (August 1980): 1123.

George Mickelson (Courtesy of Governor Mickelson)

MICKELSON, George, 1987–

Born in Mobridge, South Dakota on January 31, 1941, the son of George Theodore Mickelson, a former governor of South Dakota (1947–1951) and Madge Ellen Turner Mickelson. In 1963 he married the former Linda McCahren. The couple has three children: Mark, Amy, and David. Governor Mickelson is a Methodist.

Mickelson is a graduate of Washington High School, Sioux Falls; The University of South Dakota, Vermillion (1963); and the University of South Dakota School of Law (1965). He entered the U.S. Army in 1965, serving tours of duty in Fort Benjamin, Indiana; Fort Knox, Kentucky; Fort Lee Virginia; and Vietnam. He was honorably discharged in 1967 with a rank of captain.

An attorney in private practice since 1968, he began his public service career in 1970, working as Brookings County States Attorney from 1970 to 1974. A member of the South Dakota House of Representatives from 1975 to 1980, he was elected speaker pro tempore for two years and speaker of the house for two years. While in the legislature, he served on the Taxation, Judiciary, State Affairs and Intergovernmental Relations committees, as well as on a special committee studying personal property tax replacement. He also served for four years as chairman of the State Board of Pardons and Paroles.

A Republican, Mickelson defeated three other candidates, Clint Roberts, Lieutenant Governor Lowell Hanson, and Secretary of State Alice Kundert, to win his party's gubernatorial nomination in 1986. In the general election, he defeated Democrat Lars Herseth with 52 percent of the vote. He got his winning margin in the state's two biggest cities, Sioux Falls and Rapid City, where the banking programs of outgoing Republican Governor William Janklow had created hundreds of jobs and stronger economies than in other Farm Belt towns.

In office, Mickelson is stressing the need for more economic development and has proposed increasing the sales tax. He wants to use the surplus tax funds to finance a new $4.7 million research program for state universities, and to raise salaries of faculty members and other state employees. He also favors expanding vocational education programs and promoting contacts between universities and businesses.

Active in many community and civic organizations, Mickelson has been chairman of the Brookings United Way; has served the Boy Scouts from whom he received the Dacotah District Award of Merit; was fundraising chairman for the Olympic Committee; and is a board member and chairman of the personnel committee of the South Dakota Easter Seal Society. He has been a member of the Brookings Chamber of Commerce and state Chamber of Commerce, as well as a member of the Brookings Industrial Development Committee. As a veteran, he is a member of the

Veterans of Foreign Wars and American Legion. He has also been involved in a variety of professional organizations including the South Dakota Bar Association, the South Dakota Trial Lawyers Association, the American Bar Association, the American Trial Lawyers Association, and the American Judicature Society.

Bibliography: Biographical information courtesy of governor's office; Michael Barone *et al., The Almanac of American Politics 1988* (New York and Washington, D.C., 1987); *The New York Times,* 6-1-86; *The Chronicle of Higher Education:* 11-12-86; 2-18-87; Jaques Cattell Press, *Who's Who in American Politics, 1985–1986* (New York, 1985).

Lamar Alexander (Courtesy of Department of General Services, State of Tennessee)

TENNESSEE

ALEXANDER, Lamar, 1979–1987

Born on July 3, 1940 in Blount County, Tennessee, the son of Andrew and Flo Alexander, both of whom were teachers. (Andrew was also a principal.) A Presbyterian, Alexander married Leslee Kathryn "Honey" Buhler, a former aide to United States Senator John Tower, on January 4, 1969. He is the father of Leslee, Kathryn, Will, and Drew.

Alexander attended public schools and was graduated from Mary ville, Tennessee High School in 1958. The previous year, he had been selected "Governor" of the Tennessee American Legion Boys State, and heard Tennessee Governor Frank Clement predict that one of the delegates could one day become the "real governor." Alexander was graduated Phi Beta Kappa from Vanderbilt University and nominated twice for a Rhodes Scholarship. New York University eventually awarded him a Root-Tilden Scholarship, and he was graduated from its law school in 1965, after serving as an editor of the school's *Law Review*.

Alexander returned to Knoxville, and for a short time practiced with a firm before becoming a Clerk for the eminent Judge John Minor Wisdom of the United States Fifth Circuit Court of Appeals. A pianist of some talent, he supplemented his clerk's pay by appearing in a local club. In 1966 he was a campaign aide to Republican Howard Baker, and he became his Legislative Assistant when Baker was elected to the United States Senate. In 1969 Alexander became Executive Assistant to Bruce Harlow, President Richard Nixon's Congressional relations advisor. He also managed the successful campaign of Winfield Dunn for Governor of Tennessee in 1970.

A period in private law practice and work with groups devoted to revenue sharing and crime and deliquency control ended when Alexander ran for governor in 1974. An upset victor in the Republican primary, he lost to Ray Blanton in the general election, largely because of the Watergate scandals. Alexander then became political commentator for WSM, a Nashville television station, and joined Baker as special counsel when the senator became minority leader in 1977. Between January and July of 1978, Alexander, whom some had characterized as "too aloof" in his 1974 gubernatorial campaign, walked over 1,000 miles throughout the state. He easily won the Republican primary that year and went on to defeat Knoxville banker Jake Butcher in the general election by a vote of 661,959 to 523,495. Alexander took every part of the state, not only the traditionally Republican Appalachian region, by making particular use of the scandals of the administration of Ray Blanton and Butcher's lavish campaign spending.

Developments after election night, however, constitute one of the stranger stories in American politics. Blanton was the first Tennessee chief executive eligible for re-election to a consecutive term, but he had declined to run again. Earlier in his administration he had created a controversy by announcing that he would pardon Roger Humphries, the son of a former staff aide, who was in state prison for the murder of his ex-wife and her lover. Blanton then changed his mind when a public outcry ensued. Soon after the 1978 election, he granted clemency to a number of prisoners. The Federal Bureau of Investigation grew more suspicious, and Blanton chose to leave the country briefly in December 1978. He returned shortly before his term was to end on January 20, 1979. On January 15, 1979, Blanton granted executive clemency to 52 inmates, 24 of them murderers and including Humphries. Although under the Tennessee constitution a governor's power to grant clemency is absolute and personal, the Federal Bureau of Investigation had by now concluded that clemency was being sold. With Tennessee's government in disarray, Alexander was persuaded to take the oath of office on January 17, 1979. Blanton attempted to run the state for the next three days, but he was barred from his Capitol office.

Alexander's first term as governor was preoccupied with the scandals associated with Blanton's administration. Certain of Blanton's aides were sentenced for their role in selling clemency, and others were later freed when another Blanton aide, a star federal witness, admitted lying to the Federal Bureau of Investigation. Blanton's brother and uncle were indicted for mail fraud and bid rigging. Finally, in June 1981, Blanton was sentenced to three years in prison for selling liquor licenses while in office.

Tennessee managed to divert itself from these problems to some extent by staging the rather successful World's Fair at Knoxville in 1982. That same year Alexander ran for re-election against Knoxville Mayor Randy Tyree. While the incumbent governor was vulnerable on the issue of the state budget deficit, which had increased from $80 million to $150 million, Tyree focused his attack on President Ronald Reagan's economic program and high unemployment. Polls showed that Tennesseans were concerned about these issues, but they indicated that voters saw them as national and not state problems. Tyree did poorly throughout the state, even losing the Knoxville area by a margin of two to one. He was also defeated in the Memphis area, where Alexander made television commercials with *Roots* author Alex Haley and pledged to redevelop the region.

The final vote in the election was 737,963 for Alexander and 500,937 for Tyree.

Political analysts regarded Alexander's two terms in office as highly successful. Not only did he help the state maintain sound fiscal condition in difficult economic times, but he was willing to embrace courageous new stands for a Republican. He boasted of raising education spending and sought and received votes from blacks. Most important, his honesty, integrity, and devotion to public service provided a refreshing contrast to previous Democratic administrations, rocked by scandal and marred by a proclivity for wheeling and dealing.

His major achievement was his Better Schools program, which included a master teacher plan, an effort that predated the recommendations of various national educational commissions that issued similar proposals in 1983. Alexander's program foreshadowed the recommendations of these commissions—to reward outstanding teachers with additional pay and recognition, and to raise the status and standards of the profession. His sweeping educational changes made Tennessee the first state to offer incentive pay to teachers, an idea that later won the endorsement of the Reagan administration.

Another feather in Alexander's cap was his success in winning the competition to place a new $5 billion General Motors Saturn plant in Tennessee. The plant, designed to produce a low-cost compact to compete directly with Nissan's popular Sentra, was expected to bring 6,000 new jobs and untold millions in payroll and tax revenues to the state. Capital investment in Tennessee as a result of plant expansion or relocation grew to an average of $1.2 billion a year during Alexander's tenure, as compared with $500 million annually in the previous decade. Tennessee also attracted 12 percent of all Japanese capital investment in the United States.

Chairman of the National Governors' Association from 1985–1986, Alexander emerged as one of the most popular governors in the region, and a figure of rising stature in national Republican ranks. In August 1985 he invited a handful of leading Republican governors and congressmen to meet privately in Tennessee, to discuss ways to translate the party's successes at the national level into victories at the state and local levels. The session drew considerable attention both inside and outside the party. That same year, Alexander was appointed chairman of the President's Commission on Americans Outdoors, a 15-member panel charged with examining the nation's outdoor recreational needs in the twenty-first century. An avid hiker and outdoorsman who had waged his successful 1978 campaign by walking 1,000 miles across the state, Alexander made his last year in office a Tennessee Festival time, celebrating the state's traditions, highlighting its achievements, and building its pride.

In 1986 a poll commissioned by *Newsweek* magazine named Alexander as the nation's most effective Republican governor. Barred from seeking a third term, Alexander has been mentioned as a possible senatorial opponent for Democratic incumbent James Sasser, up for re-election in 1988. He also drew frequent mention as a possible vice presidential running mate for George Bush in the 1988 presidential campaign, with many political observers believing that Alexander's record could provide a strong counter to Democratic candidate Michael Dukakis' tales of a "Massachusetts Miracle" under his gubernatorial administration.

On July 1, 1988 Alexander was named president of the University of Tennessee system upon the retirement of long-term President Edward J. Boling. The appointment drew sharp protest from Democratic politicians, civil rights lawyers, and some faculty members. The Democratic legislature sharply criticized the selection, saying Alexander lacked academic credentials for the job and would use the post to advance his political career.

Bibliography: Biographical information courtesy of governor's office; *Nashville Tennessean:* 1–20–79; 11–3–82; Michael Barone *et al., The Almanac of American Politics 1984* (New York and Washington, D.C., 1983); Jaques Cattell Press, *Who's Who in American Politics, 1985–1986* (New York, 1985); "The Statehouses: Action and Innovation," *Newsweek* (March 24, 1986); *U.S.A. Today,* 6–7–88; *The Chronicle of Higher Education:* 1–27–88; 2–3–88; *The New York Times,* 8–4–85.

Ned McWherter (Courtesy of governor's office)

McWHERTER, Ned, 1987–

Born in Palmersville, Tennessee on October 15, 1930, the son of share-cropper parents Harmon R. McWherter and Lucille Smith McWherter. A Methodist, McWherter was married to the late Bette Jean Beck Mc-Wherter. He is the father of two children, Michael and Linda.

McWherter operated several small businesses and a farm headquartered in Dresden, Tennessee before entering political life in 1968. He also served 21 years in the Tennessee National Guard, retiring with the rank of captain.

A Democrat, McWherter began his career in state government in 1968 when he won a vacant Tennessee House seat. After just two terms, he was elected speaker of the House, a post he then went on to hold longer than anyone in Tennessee history. As speaker, McWherter fought for improved education, jobs, and economic development, better highways, a cleaner environment, and responsible management of state tax dollars. A pioneer of open government, he authored Tennessee's campaign financing disclosure law and supported legislation requiring all public officials to disclose their financial holdings. He also backed legislation to open all government meetings and records, as well as all proceedings of the House, to the public and the press. While McWherter was speaker, Tennessee consistently balanced its annual budget, attaining the highest bond rating of any state and keeping its taxes among the lowest in the nation.

Although never elected by a constituency larger than his state legislative district, McWherter proved himself adept at winning votes when he ran for the governorship in 1986. He defeated two serious candidates to win the Democratic gubernatorial nomination: Public Service Commissioner Jane Eskind, the Democratic nominee against Senator Howard Baker in 1978, who spent liberally on her campaign; and Richard Fulton, the long-time mayor of Nashville. McWherter garnered 42 percent of the vote in the three-way race, to his opponents' 30 percent and 26 percent, respectively.

In the general election he faced Republican Winfield Dunn, a former governor. Although McWherter ran behind the usual Democratic showings in the state's four largest cities, he ran ahead in rural areas and carried the far tip of eastern Tennessee, defeating Dunn with 54 percent of the vote.

As governor, McWherter has promised to build on the achievements of his Republican predecessor, Lamar Alexander, by building a better educational system, a modern transportation network, and providing more well-paying jobs for state citizens. Continuing his commitment to honest and open government, he has proposed a comprehensive public integrity and disclosure package for ranking officials serving in his administration. He has also proposed creating state merit scholarships to keep top high school students in the state, and increasing state support for agricultural research.

He did suffer a legislative setback in 1987, when the state senate selected as lieutenant governor the choice of a coalition of Republicans and conservative Democrats.

Bibliography: Biographical information courtesy of governor's office; Michael Barone *et al., The Almanac of American Politics 1988* (New York and Washington, D.C., 1987); *The Chronicle of Higher Education,* 11–12–86; Jaques Cattell Press, *Who's Who in American Politics, 1985–1986* (New York, 1985).

Mark White (Courtesy of Governor White)

TEXAS

WHITE, Mark, 1983–1987

Born in Henderson, Rusk County, Texas on March 17, 1940, the son of Mark Wells White and Sarah Elizabeth Wells White. In 1966, he married the former Linda Gale. The couple has three children: Mark, Robert, and Elizabeth.

White attended public schools in Houston and gradauted from Lamar High School in 1958. He worked his way through Baylor University where he received a degree in business administration in 1962 and a law degree in 1965. He was elected Lawyer of the Year by the Baylor Law Fraternity, Phi Alpha Delta, in 1977.

A Democrat, White began his public service career in 1966, when he served as an assistant attorney general of the Insurance, Banking and Securities Division. There he spent three years handling some of the first consumer protection investigations in the state's history, and representing state agencies in both trial and appellate cases. He was also in the 36th Infantry Division of the Texas National Guard during this time.

After practicing law for four years with the Houston law firm of Reynolds, Allen and Cook, he was appointed secretary of state by Governor Dolph Briscoe in 1973. During the nearly five years that he served as secretary of state, he supervised the first state-supported voter registration drive, including postage-free annually updated registration, which resulted in a record 6.3 million registered voters in 1976. He also streamlined operations in the office, improved communications between state agencies with publication of the *Texas Registrar,* and made his office more responsive to the public by installing 24-hour toll-free telephone service to answer questions on election laws, bilingual voter assistance, and other topics.

In 1978, White resigned his position as secretary of state to run for attorney general of Texas. Defeating James A. Baker, chief of staff and later Secretary of the Treasury in the Reagan White House, he was sworn in on January 1, 1979. As attorney general, he won more than 98 percent of his cases, modernizing the internal operations of the office through computerization and good management, increasing the hiring of minorities and women in administrative and policy-making positions, and publishing a voluntary Student Code of Conduct which was adopted by school districts throughout the state. In office he gained widespread publicity as a champion of law and order and as a protector of consumers.

White won the governorship in 1982, defeating incumbent William P. Clements, Jr. in a rancorous campaign. Polls indicated that voters were increasingly annoyed not only with Clements' gruff personal style, but also with his handling of the state's faltering economy. Although the Texas economy had been booming during most of his administration, the recession of the early 1980s hit Texas hard. Rising unemployment rates and depressed prices for oil and natural gas put Clements on the defensive. The Democratic platform attacked Clements for "callous," "shortsighted," and "morally bankrupt" leadership. White also criticized high utility rates, low teacher salaries, looming water shortages, prison overcrowding, and rising interest rates. Adopting a neopopulist stance, he made the issue of soaring utility rates the symbol of his attempt to link Clements, an oil man, to the wealthy and privileged.

Although outspent in the race, White defeated Clements by a large margin, 54 percent to 46 percent. He took more than 85 percent of the Hispanic vote, an increasingly important factor in Texas elections. With his victory, White became the youngest person elected governor of Texas in almost half a century.

White's administration was a troubled one. Political observers lamented his lack of a clear political philosophy. Although he had come up in Democratic politics as a moderate, he was elected governor on a liberal-studded ticket, and his policies alienated rural Texas. The hallmark of his administration was major educational reform. White took credit for raising teacher salaries; carrying out teacher testing programs; limiting class sizes; reducing teachers' paperwork; establishing a state-supported university research fund; and protecting university budgets from even bigger cutbacks. Yet he angered many teachers with his embrace of mandatory teacher testing programs, as well as with his support for a controversial "no pass, no play" law that was not well received in rural areas. The measure stipulated that high school students who failed any course during a six-week grading period could not take part in sports or extracurricular activities during the following six-week period.

White was also harmed by continuing problems with the state's economy. The huge surpluses that enabled Texas to cut state taxes in the 1970s disappeared in the 1980s, and the continued plunge in worldwide oil prices led to high unemployment and a state budget crisis. In a state that hates high taxes, White did the politically unthinkable, and called for a tax increase in an election year. It was the second tax increase for a politician who had promised he wouldn't raise taxes. Although some observers speculated that White's campaign for higher taxes gave him an opportunity to demonstrate leadership as well as to capture media attention, the move was highly unpopular.

With such problems, White was an underdog in his 1986 campaign for re-election. The race was a replay of his bitter battle with William Clements four years earlier. Clements, who had won the Republican nomination in a hotly contested primary, based his campaign on reviving Texans' memories of the boom years over which he had presided. Using the strategy of comparing his four years in office with White's, he assailed the incumbent, saying that since White took office unemployment had increased and the state had accumulated a deficit of at least $2.2 billion.

The contest drew national attention as a test of whether the Republican administration in Washington or local Democrats would be blamed for the collapse of the region's energy-dominated economy. Both candidates differed with the White House by calling for a fee on imported oil.

Clements' victory, with 52.7 percent of the vote to White's 46 percent, was seen as another historic breakthrough for the GOP. It was viewed as an additional sign of growing Republican vigor in a conservative state that until fairly recently was immune to two-party politics.

Bibliography: Biographical information courtesy of governor's office; *The Chronicle of Higher Education,* 10–22–86; Michael Barone *et al., The Almanac of American Politics, 1986, 1988* (New York and Washington, D.C., 1985, 1987); *The New York Times:* 6–9–85; 8–23–85; 9–4–86; 9–29–86.

William P. Clements, Jr. (Courtesy of governor's office)

CLEMENTS, William P., Jr., 1979–1983, 1987–

Born in Dallas, Texas on April 13, 1917. An Episcopalian, Clements and his wife Rita have two children.

After attending Southern Methodist University, Clements was a "roughneck" in the oil fields and a driller of oil rigs from 1937 to 1947. He founded Sedco, Inc., in 1947, a firm that manufactures oil drilling equipment. That venture made Clements a multi-millionaire. He worked as a deputy secretary at the United States Department of Defense from 1973 to 1977, receiving a Distinguished Public Service Award from the Defense Department in 1975. Clements was also awarded the Bronze Palm by President Gerald Ford in 1976.

The spread of prosperity in Texas throughout the 1970s, as well as a population boom and a large in-state migration from rural to urban areas, gradually altered the state's traditional voting patterns, and paved the way for Clements' election in 1978 as the state's first Republican governor since Reconstruction. Spending heavily in his first bid for elective office, the conservative Clements portrayed the election as a referendum on the policies of the Carter administration, which was highly unpopular in Texas. He easily defeated Dallas lawyer and former Texas Republican Chairman Ray Hutchinson in the primary, gaining 73 percent of the vote to Hutchinson's 24 percent (with a third candidate polling three percent). Clements then turned his attention to incumbent Democrat Dolph Briscoe, whom he attacked for not taking "an active role in Washington for the state." Clements' criticisms of Briscoe were premature, however, for in a startling upset the incumbent lost his own bid for the Democratic nomination to the liberal Attorney General John Hill in a bitter primary battle. Hill's victory gave Texans a choice that they had never really had before—a contest between a liberal Democrat and a *laissez-faire* Republican.

Presenting himself as a conservative businessman who believed in less government, Clements campaigned on a platform promising to reduce state spending and taxes, and to streamline the state's bureaucracy. Despite a staggering lead by the better known Hill in early polls, Clements came back to win a narrow victory, gaining 50 percent of the vote to Hill's 49 percent. Aided by his conservative views, the unpopularity of the Democratic administration in Washington, a high turnout in the affluent urban areas of the state, and a $7 million war chest, Clements gained national attention with his narrow victory. Unlike the retiring Governor Briscoe, he seemed a force to be reckoned with in national politics, as he boldly advocated policies to encourage free enterprise and to reduce the size of government on all levels. Clements was the first chief executive to endorse Ronald Reagan publicly in 1980, and during his term in office he attempted to make the Republican party a major force in state politics.

During his term Clements tried to cut the state payroll by five percent a year, and vetoed a record $250 million from the $21 billion biennial budget. He streamlined the bureaucracy, encouraged a tough, anti-crime stance in state government, and attempted to work out a plan with Mexico to curb the flood of illegal aliens across Texas borders.

Clements alienated many voters, however, with his outspoken views. For example, when during the campaign he was asked to express his opinion on the problems of Mexican-Americans, he replied gruffly that he was not running for governor of Mexico. In his campaign for re-election in 1982, much was made of this so-called "meanness issue," and of Clements' personal style. Although he easily overcame the challenge of Duke Embs, a San Antonio insurance broker, to win the Republican nomination with more than 90 percent of the vote, he was not as fortunate in the general election. Clements' opponent was the moderate Attorney General Mark White, a Democrat with strong name recognition around the state. In 1978 White had defeated James A. Baker, President Reagan's chief of staff, to become attorney general, and in that office he gained widespread publicity as a champion of law and order and as a protector of consumers.

The 1982 gubernatorial campaign was a rancorous one, with Clements attempting to portray White as a "bumbling incompetent" and White hoping to capitalize on the meanness issue, a charge revived when a Clements campaign tabloid ran a story about White's arrest for drunk driving almost 20 years earlier. Polls indicated that voters were dissatisfied not only with Clements' style, but also with his handling of the state's economy. Although the Texas economy had been healthy during most of his administration and unemployment, at 6.7 percent, was lower than in any other large state, the recession was beginning to hit Texas hard. Rising unemployment rates, that set records by Texas standards, soon put Clements on the defensive. With worldwide petroleum prices depressed, drilling for new gas and oil wells slowed dramatically, and nearly every state business depending on the oil industry was affected. The Democratic platform attacked Clements' lack of leadership. White also criticized high utility rates, low teacher salaries, looming water shortages, prison crowding, and rising interest rates. Adopting a neopopulist stance, he attempted to link Clements to the wealthy and privileged with the issue of soaring utility rates.

Although Clements raised and spent nearly $12 million in his re-election bid, possibly the largest campaign fund ever devoted to an American gubernatorial election, he lost to White by a rather large margin, 46 percent to 54 percent. The Democrats took more than 85 percent of the Hispanic vote, an increasingly important factor in Texas elections. This, said the neopopulist White, "was a victory of the people."

The election was closely watched by political observers because of the important role that Texas plays in national politics. Although Clements lost by 200,000 votes, most of the Republican strongholds in the state stayed that way, and in most areas he managed to poll as many votes as he had four years earlier. His defeat was attributed to a surprisingly high voter turnout, which has always favored the Democrats in Texas.

After he left office, Clements returned to his oil drilling equipment business. He was also asked by President Reagan to serve on two national commissions, one on America's policy in Central America and the other on strategic forces.

Clements was encouraged by a grassroots movement to seek the Republican nomination for governor again in 1986. Incumbent Mark White, who had thwarted Clements' re-election bid in 1982, had himself fallen on hard times, having had the misfortune of holding office during four of the most trying years in Texas history. The plunge in world oil prices had left the state's once booming energy industry in ruins, and White went into the election with unemployment at nine percent, well above the national average, and as high as 30 percent in some areas. He was forced twice to call for higher taxes and fees to keep up state services, and had sought a rise in the sales tax to overcome a $2.8 billion state deficit, the largest ever. Clements made the economy the focus of his campaign, charging that White had failed to provide the leadership to help Texas out of its troubles, and that he had allowed spending and taxes to run "out of control." Putting forth his own six-point employment plan, he contended that White, as a Democrat, was unable to deal with the Republican administration in Washington to help the state's economy recover.

White also gambled heavily with his highly touted program for the reform of Texas public schools. Pushing through measures that, among other things, barred failing students from playing sports and required competency testing of teachers, he alienated teachers and parents alike, as well as rural Texas constituents who were offended when star athletes were unable to perform.

The bitter race provided a measure of personal vindication for Clements, who relished in his 53 percent to 46 percent victory over the man who had defeated him four years earlier. Clements' victory drew national attention as a barometer of growing Republican strength in this once solidly Democratic state.

In office, Clements faced what many observers felt would be the most painful era in the state's history. Obstacles confronting him included a state budget deficit approaching $1 billion, high unemployment, an overcrowded prison system under federal court order to improve conditions, an outdated tax system, and legislative leaders who were determined to force him to break his promise not to raise taxes.

Battered by troubles in the oil industry, in 1987 he had no alternative but to endorse a compromise state budget that included new taxes. His anti-tax stand was widely regarded as unrealistic, especially in a state whose already low levels of funding for social services left little room for budget cuts to stave off an expected budget deficit.

Clements was also badly hurt by a scandal that rocked his administration in the early months of his second term. As chairman of the Southern Methodist University Board of Governors from 1967 to 1973 and again from 1983 to 1987, Clements admitted that he and other board members had approved improper payments to student athletes, a practice that continued even after the NCAA had placed the school on probation in 1985. Attempting to profit from the governor's troubles, state Democrats seized the opportunity to scuttle Clements' plans to cut state spending on education and welfare as an answer to the budget crisis. Some Texas lawmakers even called for his impeachment as efforts to resolve the budget crisis became mired in the college football scandal and resulting political infighting.

Clements has already announced that he does not plan to seek re-election upon the expiration of his current term.

Bibliography: Biographical information courtesy of governor's office; *The Chronicle of Higher Education:* 11–12–86; 7–1–87; *Dallas Morning News,* 8–1–87; "Ups and Downs of the Newest Governors," *U.S. News and World Report* (September 24, 1979); "Texas: Jobs vs Competence," *Newsweek* (October 4, 1982); "Did Money Talk? Sometimes," *Newsweek* (November 15, 1982); "Playing for Pay in Texas," *Newsweek* (March 16, 1987); *The New York Times:* 3–26–78; 5–4–78; 8–18–78; 11–8–78; 1–17–79; 9–23–79; 6–29–80; 9–9–81; 9–22–81; 4–29–82; 5–3–82; 5–28–82; 6–16–82; 9–13–82; 10–12–82; 10–14–82; 10–31–82; 11–3–82; 1–19–83; 9–29–86; 10–8–86; 11–1–86; 11–5–86; 11–6–86; 1–21–87; 2–4–87; 3–5–87; 3–6–87; 3–11–87; 4–6–87; 4–22–87; 5–15–87; 6–2–87; 6–24–87; 7–17–87.

Scott Milne Matheson (Credit: Busath Photography, Salt Lake City)

UTAH

MATHESON, Scott Milne, 1977–1985

Born on January 8, 1929 in Chicago, Illinois, the son of Scott Milne and Adele (Adams) Matheson. A Mormon, Matheson is married to the former Norma Louise Warenski. They have four children—Scott Milne III, Mary Lee, James, and Thomas.

Matheson spent his early years in southern Utah and was graduated from Salt Lake City's East High School in 1946. He was graduated with honors in political science from the University of Utah in 1950, and took his law degree from Stanford University in 1952. A city attorney in Parowan, Utah and a deputy attorney with Iron County, Utah from 1953 to 1954, he was a law clerk with a United States District Court judge in Salt Lake City between 1954 and 1956, before entering private practice with a Cedar City firm. Matheson joined the legal department of the Union Pacific Railroad in 1958, eventually becoming solicitor general for the company. Except for a brief period (1969–71) during which he served as assistant general counsel for Anaconda Copper Company, he worked continuously for the Union Pacific Railroad until his election as governor of Utah in 1976.

Matheson had been a long-time Democratic fund-raiser in Utah and was well known in legal circles, having served as president of the Utah State Bar Association from 1968 to 1969, but except for a youthful post as president of the University of Utah Young Democrats in 1948, he had never before held a political or politically related office. Yet his candidacy was personally endorsed by retiring Democratic Governor Calvin Rampton, who had held office since 1964 and who remained immensely popular in the state. Political observers agreed that Rampton would probably have been re-elected with more than 70 percent of the vote had he chosen to run again in 1976. With his support, Matheson defeated John Preston Creer, 59 percent to 41 percent, to win the Democratic gubernatorial nomination. Advocating a "preparedness growth plan" and exuding an attitude of competence and efficiency, Matheson was able to defeat a better known opponent in the general election, Republican Attorney General Vernon Romney, by a margin of 53 percent to 47 percent. Unopposed in the 1980 Democratic primary, Matheson easily won his bid for a second term. Despite Republican gains elsewhere in the state and nation in 1980, he handily defeated Republican Bob Wright, 55 percent to 44 percent.

During his years in office, Matheson acquired a reputation as being possibly the best of all the governors in the West. Under his leadership, a record $1 billion appropriations bill was passed by the Utah Legislature, and state sales taxes on electricity, natural gas, coal, and fuel oil were reduced. He gained extensive publicity as the leading spokesman for a group of western governors who were demanding and building a new kind of partnership with the federal government on issues of water conservation, energy development, and the use of western land. The hardworking, "70-hour-a-week" governor had a "passion" for what he called "returning the state of Utah to traditional federalism, Henry Clay federalism, full partnership" with the national government on these matters. Political observers called him a "technician . . . with a real enthusiasm for the arcane tedium of working out inter-governmental relations."

Matheson became interested in this problem early in his first gubernatorial term, when fellow Democrat Jimmy Carter tried to cancel a key portion of a central Utah water project without consulting state officials in 1977. Matheson forced the Carter administration to restore the funding, and after that worked to ensure that states and their elected officials had a voice in such national planning. Speaking for a group of western governors, he disagreed publicly with the Reagan administration, eventually getting Interior Secretary James Watt to agree to broad changes in federal coal leasing regulations. Outside of Utah, he was best known for his efforts in bringing the federal government to admit the probable connection between southern Utah's abnormally high cancer rates and the nationally sanctioned atomic testing programs in nearby Nevada during the 1950s. Matheson also led his state in questioning the benefits of its selection as a site for the MX intercontinental ballistic missile system, going to Washington, D.C. to testify before congressional committees as to the system's effect on health, grazing, mining, and the regional economy.

As chairman of the National Governors' Association in 1982–83, Matheson called on the federal government to reduce the growth of military spending, to maintain the current level of social welfare appropriations, and to consider raising taxes to slash the federal budget deficit over the next five years. He also served as chairman of the Agenda for the 80s Task Force of the National Governors' Association in 1982, and was president of the Council of State Governments in 1982–83. Matheson was the first chairman of the Subcommittee on Water Management of the National Governors' Association from 1977 to 1982, and is a former chairman of the Four Corners Regional Commission (1978–79) and of the Western Governors' Policy Office (1979–80). In 1977 he was one of four chief executives named by former Secretary of the Interior Cecil Andrus to serve on the Intergovernmental Task Force on Water Policy; in 1983 he was named by President Ronald Reagan to the Advisory Council on Intergovernmental Relations.

Matheson was considered to have been one of the most popular public officials in state history. Public opinion polls conducted in 1982 showed him enjoying a popularity rating of 85 percent in a predominantly Republican and conservative state. In the opinion of political analysts, one of Matheson's greatest strengths was that he had never been a politician before becoming governor and was not particularly concerned whether he would continue to be one. His attitude was revealed by his favorite political dictum—"You get in, you give it your best shot, and then you get out again."

In keeping with these views on public service, Matheson chose not to run for a third term. His surprise announcement stunned the state, threw its political season into turmoil, and profoundly disappointed many supporters. Yet he defended his position: "I feel so strongly on a personal basis about non-career politics that it would be unseemly for me not to practice what I preach." His decision opened a door for state Republicans, who had not held the governorship in 20 years.

Upon his retirement from office, Matheson took a position as an attorney with the firm of Parsons, Behle and Latimer in Salt Lake City. He practices primarily natural resources, railroad, and corporate law. In 1985 he was elected to the Board of the Williams Companies (Tulsa, Oklahoma), American Savings and Loan Association (Salt Lake City), and the Lincoln Institute of Land Policy (Cambridge, Massachusetts). In 1987 he was elected to the Board of Bonneville Pacific Corporation (Salt Lake City).

An expert on land use and water rights issues, he is the author of numerous books and articles on this topic. He has honorary degrees from the University of Utah, Brigham Young University, Weber State College, and Southern Utah State College.

In retirement, Matheson has retained his political interests. Appointed chairman of the Democratic National Policy Commission in 1985, he declined to run for the U.S. Senate against popular Republican incumbent Jake Garn in 1986, figuring that the extremely popular Garn would be tough to beat. Although political observers had predicted that he might challenge Republican incumbent Orrin Hatch for the U.S. Senate in 1988, the run never materialized.

Matheson is a fiscal conservative who has taken some nonconservative positions, including support for the ERA and opposition to restrictions on legalized abortion. Democrats consider him one of the strongest in their ranks in the Rocky Mountain region, where Republicans have been on the ascendancy for some time.

Bibliography: Biographical information courtesy of Governor Matheson; *Newsweek,* 5–18–87; Michael Barone *et al., The Almanac of American Politics, 1978, 1982* (New York and Washington, D.C., 1977, 1981); *The New York Times:* 5–27–79; 3–14–80; 11–5–80; 2–24–81; 11–6–81; 2–18–82; 8–11–82; 11–22–82; 11–23–82; 1–1–83; 2–28–83; 3–1–83; 4–2–83; 2–11–84; 2–28–84; 3–1–84; 5–6–84; 11–8–84; 10–15–85.

Norman H. Bangerter (Courtesy of governor's office)

BANGERTER, Norman H., 1985–

Born in Granger, Utah on January 4, 1933. Married to the former Colleen Monson, he and his wife have six children, one foster son, and nine grandchildren.

After graduating from Brigham Young University, Bangerter began a career as a builder that has continued to the present. A building contractor and 25-year veteran of Utah's homebuilding and real estate development industries, he is past president of NHB Construction. A Korean War veteran, he has given his time and talents to various business and labor-oriented activities. He has been a past member of the advisory board of Utah Technical College, Salt Lake, a member of the State Constitutional Revision Commission, and former chairman of the advisory board for Latter Day Saints Social Services in Utah. He has also served on Utah's Job Training Council, the task force formed to recommend the proper distribution of Utah's federal oil lease money, and as Utah chairman of the apprenticeship program for the Home Builders of America.

A Republican, Bangerter made his first run for public office in 1974 when he won a seat in the Utah House of Representatives from the burgeoning middle class suburbs west of Salt Lake City. Four years later he was elected majority leader by house Republicans and two years later ascended to the speakership. As a prominent Mormon, however, Bangerter was familiar with public life even before his first political campaign. The Mormons, who believe in the priesthood of all male members, quickly promote church activists to positions that require public speaking and public administration of the church's extensive social and political activities. Bangerter had been a Ward Bishop of the church, equivalent to the head of a congregation, and Stake President, head of a parish.

As a state legislator, Bangerter was recognized by President Reagan for his leadership. He is listed in *Who's Who in Politics* and *Who's Who in the West*. In 1983 he was named as one of the top 10 legislators in America by the National Republican Party.

Bangerter entered the race for governor in 1984, a race that had suddenly been thrown wide open by the surprise retirement of long-time incumbent Scott Matheson. He was an upset winner in his party's August primary, defeating Congressman Dan Marriott with 56 percent of the vote. Marriott, a four-term incumbent, had given up a safe seat in the U.S. House of Representatives to make the run.

In the general election Bangerter faced Democrat Wayne Owens, a former congressman. Although Owens repeated a campaign tactic that he had used successfully before—walking the breadth of the state—he faced formidable obstacles in the race: his reputation as a liberal in this conservative state, and the opposition of the Democratic leadership. He was forced to campaign without the endorsement of a majority of party leaders, whom he had alienated through a series of political maneuvers a decade ago, when he was a freshman congressman.

During the campaign, Bangerter promised to limit the role of his administration to helping Utahans help themselves—a characteristic message of self-reliance and governmental restraint from the conservative Republican. He pledged the following: to help make the state's public school students "understand that they are ultimately responsible for their own learning and destiny"; to redouble efforts to foster a strong pro-business climate; and to streamline the state bureaucracy. He also promised to hold the line on taxes for at least two years—a pledge made possible by a budget surplus of almost $100 million left by outgoing Governor Matheson.

The sharpest point of difference between the two candidates was over the state's response to federal exploration of a southern Utah site as a dump for high-level radioactive waste from nuclear power plants. Although Bangerter had taken a wait-and-see attitude during the race, after his victory he declared his opposition to the nuclear depository.

Bangerter won the election with 56 percent of the vote. The victory was an important one for Republicans, since Democrats had held the governorship for 20 years, 12 under Calvin L. Rampton and eight under Matheson.

In office, Bangerter faced tremendous challenges and opportunities. The state's economy was recovering steadily from the recession but it still lagged behind other states in the region. Its wealth in natural resources is immense, but markets are distant and demand weak. Finally, although Utah's people are among the best educated in America, their per capita income is next to the lowest. Consequently, Bangerter has focused on the practical problems of educational and economic development.

In office, Bangerter has not proven to be a dogmatic supporter of minimalist government. On the contrary, he proposed that the state absorb the windfall revenue from the 1986 tax reform act, and in early 1987 urged the biggest tax increase in Utah's history to replace revenue lost from the slowdowns in the state's mineral economy. Defending the increase, he explained that conservatism, in his view, "is facing up to our responsibilities and paying our bills." Increased revenues, he explained, would go toward the most important and basic functions of government: education and infrastructure. Bangerter proposed the combination of new and higher taxes to raise $206 million for public schools and higher education.

Bangerter has been praised for his leadership style, the hallmark of which is delegating initiative. He believes in letting others make the first move and then reacting. In the opinion of political observers, his easy accommodating nature, given to compromise and coalition building, has served him well.

In office, Bangerter has served both as chairman and vice-chairman of the Western Governors' Association, a group of governors of the 16 western states, two territories, and one commonwealth. The association provides a vehicle for members to unite in their efforts to protect regional fiscal interests, enhance gubernatorial participation in federal/state decisionmaking, and develop policies affecting the West. In his leadership roles, Bangerter's agenda included economic development, international trade, educational excellence, natural resources, and emphasis on western leadership. Bangerter has also served as vice-chairman of the National Governors' Association School Facilities Subcommittee for the Education 1991 Project. In 1987 he was elected to the Executive Committee of the NGA.

In his 1988 campaign for re-election, Bangerter staved off an aggressive challenge from former Salt Lake City mayor, Ted Wilson. He won 40 percent of the vote in a three-way race, with Wilson gaining 38 percent and anti-tax third party candidate Merrill Cook drawing 21 percent.

Bibliography: Biographical information courtesy of governor's office; Jaques Cattell Press, *Who's Who in American Politics, 1985–1986* (New York, 1985); Michael Barone *et al., The Almanac of American Politics, 1986, 1988* (New York and Washington, D.C., 1985, 1987); *The Chronicle of Higher Education,* 2–18–87; *The New York Times:* 5–6–84; 8–22–84; 8–23–84; 11–8–84; 1–6–85; 1–8–85.

Richard Arkwright Snelling (Credit: Office of the Governor, Vermont)

VERMONT

Born on February 18, 1927 in Allentown, Pennsylvania, the son of Walter Otheman, a doctor, and Marjorie (Gharing) Snelling. A Unitarian, Snelling married Barbara Weil in 1947; he is the father of Jacqueline Taylor, Mark Hornor, Diane Bryant, and Andrew Preston Snelling.

Snelling attended Lehigh University and the University of Havana in Cuba; he received an A.B. *cum laude* from Harvard University in 1948. After entering the United States Army as a private in 1944, he served in the infantry in the European theater of operations from 1945 until his discharge in 1946. Snelling served as a member of the Vermont Development Commission from 1959 to 1961, and as a delegate to the Republican National Convention in 1960 and 1968. The president of Shelburne Industries, Inc. of Shelburne, Vermont since 1959, he was also president and chairman of the Executive Committee of the Greater Burlington Industrial Corporation from 1961 to 1964. Snelling was a member of the Vermont State Republican Executive Committee from 1963 to 1966, and he has been on the Vermont State Republican Committee since 1970.

Although he was an unsuccessful candidate for lieutenant governor of Vermont in 1964 and for governor in 1966, Snelling did serve as a member of the Vermont House of Representatives between 1973 and 1977. As the Republican gubernatorial candidate following his victory over William G. Craig in the primary, Snelling was elected governor of Vermont on November 6, 1976, when he defeated the Democratic candidate, Stella B. Hackell, by a vote of 99,268 to 75,262. He was inaugurated in January 1977. Snelling's first term was marred by a dispute over the selection of a lieutenant governor, after the Vermont Legislature was required to consider the matter because no candidate had received a majority in the general election.

In the 1978 gubernatorial contest Snelling overcame light opposition in the primary and defeated Edwin C. Granani, a member of the State Legislature, by a vote of 78,181 to 42,482 in the general election. By virtue of his victory, Snelling became the only Republican to win a governor's seat that year in New England. Snelling's second term was marked by a serious secession movement involving residents of the islands located in

Lake Champlain, who had become bitter over the elimination of a state attorney's office in the county that held jurisdiction over the island.

In 1980 Snelling suggested to Canadian officials that they speed up construction of Canada's hydroelectric projects and sell any surplus electricity to New England. In that year's primary election he overwhelmed Clifford Thompson and then went on to defeat Jerome Diamond, an old political foe and state attorney general, by 123,229 votes to 77,363 in the general election. Snelling became chairman of the National Governors' Conference in 1981. Meanwhile, Vermont established a five-year transportation plan to cope with the loss of federal funds incurred during the Reagan administration. In 1982 the governor vetoed a bill which would have raised the drinking age to 19.

Although Snelling had announced that he would not seek a fourth term, he eventually changed his mind and defeated Lieutenant Governor Madeleine Kunin in the 1982 general election by a vote of 93,111 to 74,394. Kunin, who had promised to raise the drinking age to 19, contended that the governor had ignored the safety of Vermonters by permitting certain nuclear waste shipments to pass through the state. Snelling responded by pointing to the influx of jobs and businesses into Vermont. He was a prominent member of the National Governors' Association, using that forum and others to make his case that the individual states could not provide services lost through federal budget cuts. An expert on federalism, he became a national spokesman on that issue and a stern critic of Reagan administration proposals.

In January 1984, Snelling surprised the legislature by announcing he had chosen not to seek re-election to a fifth term. He planned instead to devote himself to finding a solution to the state's fiscal problems.

Retired from public life for two years, Snelling sought to make a political comeback in 1986 by challenging incumbent Democrat Patrick J. Leahy for the U.S. Senate. Both men were popular among voters who, in the words of one political observer, were being asked to choose "the better of two goods."

Snelling tried to charge Leahy with being a big spender and with not showing up at hearings of the Senate Committee on Agriculture, Nutrition and Forestry, of which he was a member. The moderate Snelling also tried to portray Leahy as being too liberal for state voters. Political observers feel that Snelling's negative campaign backfired. In his defense, Leahy was able to counter that he would become chairman of the Senate Agricultural Committee if the Democrats regained control of the Senate. In a race which voters began with positive feelings about both candidates, a consensus quickly developed for Leahy, and he won by 63 percent to 35 percent carrying all the state's counties and all but 10 of Vermont's towns.

In the wake of Snelling's defeat, the state Republican party planned to recast its image in a new, more liberal light. The need to do so was brought home not only by Leahy's overwhelming victory but also by Democratic Governor Madeleine Kunin's re-election to a second term.

Bibliography: Michael Barone *et al., The Almanac of American Politics, 1986, 1988* (New York and Washington, D.C., 1985, 1987); *The New York Times:* 11–3–76; 1–4–77; 1–14–79; 1–6–84; 11–8–84; 9–9–86; 11–15–87; Bob Hollingsworth, ed., *Facts on File Yearbook, 1976* (New York, 1977).

Madeleine May Kunin (Courtesy of governor's office)

KUNIN, Madeleine May, 1985–

Born in Zurich, Switzerland on September 28, 1933, the daughter of Ferdinand May and Renee Bloch May. As a Jew, she fled Zurich with her widowed mother and brother Edgar in 1940. The Nazis later killed five other members of her family. The family settled in Forest Hills, New York and later moved to Pittsfield, Massachusetts. Working her way through the University of Massachusetts as a waitress, she earned a B.A. in history in 1957. She also holds an M.A. in journalism from Columbia University and an M.A. in English literature from the University of Vermont. Turned down for a reporting job at the *Washington Post,* she took a position with the *Burlington (Vt.) Free Press.* In Burlington, she met her husband, Dr. Arthur Kunin, a kidney specialist who teaches at the University of Vermont Health Center. The couple has four children: Julia, Peter, Adam, and Daniel.

A Democrat, Kunin began her political career in 1972 with election to the state House of Representatives. She served three two-year terms and chaired the Appropriations Committee, 1977–1978. In the legislature, she developed a reputation as a liberal concerned with issues of poverty, environment, and education. She was elected the state's lieutenant governor in 1978 and re-elected in 1980.

Making her first run for the governorship in 1982, she was defeated by popular incumbent Richard Snelling. She then spent some time as a fellow at the Institute of Politics at the Kennedy School of Government, Harvard University.

Her unsuccessful 1982 campaign, however, had given her the stature to lead the list of potential candidates upon Snelling's retirement in 1984. More aggressive as a campaigner in 1984, she forcefully promoted her experience as lieutenant governor and in the legislature. She proposed a toxic waste cleanup fund, as well as stronger rules for reviewing the impact of ski area development. Her Republican opponent, Attorney General John J. Easton, Jr., was best known outside the state for directing a raid on a religious community in Island Pond, responding to charges of child abuse there. The election was the closest state gubernatorial contest in 22 years, with Kunin escaping a legislative runoff by only 60 votes. With her victory, Kunin became the first woman to govern Vermont and only the third Democrat to hold the office in 130 years. She was the fourth woman in U.S. history to be elected governor in her own right, after Dixy Lee Ray of Washington, Ella Grasso of Connecticut, and Martha Layne Collins of Kentucky.

In her first term, Kunin focused on three areas: retiring the state's record $35.8 million deficit, a debt inherited from the previous administration; improving the quality of education; and enacting strong environmental protection legislation.

Seeking re-election in 1986, she defended her fiscally cautious, moderately liberal record against two candidates: Lieutenant Governor Peter P. Smith, a Republican, and independent candidate Bernard Sanders, the socialist mayor of Burlington. While Kunin drew 47 percent of the vote in the three-way contest (with her opponents garnering 38 percent and 15 percent respectively), political analysts predicted that the closeness of the vote would make a second Kunin term harder than the first.

Kunin has made education reform one of the top priorities of her second term. She has supported more interaction between higher education and the public schools, and has encouraged colleges to help small businesses. One of her chief accomplishments has been to equalize education spending across the state.

In 1988 she exhorted a joint session of the legislature to grapple with the issue of uncontrolled growth, hoping to strike a balance between economic development and the rustic quality of life that has long been the state's hallmark. She appointed a highly visible commission to study the problem and come up with an agenda for action. A liberal Democrat who has been called "a symbol of the new Vermont," Kunin has also argued that state government can't afford more taxes or great increases in services.

A member of the National Governors' Association Executive Committee, Kunin serves as a member of the NGA's Environment and Energy and Agriculture Committees. Chairman of the New England Governors' Conference, she also serves on the Executive Committee of the Democratic Governors' Association.

Although political observers speculated that Kunin might make a race for the U.S. Senate in 1988, she chose instead to seek re-election to a third term. Winning 56 percent of the vote, she easily defeated Michael Bernhardt, State House Minority Leader.

Bibliography: Biographical information courtesy of governor's office; James Howard Kunstler, "The Selling of Vermont," *The New York Times Magazine* (April 10, 1988); Jaques Cattell Press, *Who's Who in American Politics, 1985–1986* (New York, 1985); Michael Barone *et al., The Almanac of American Politics, 1984, 1986, 1988* (New York and Washington, D.C., 1983, 1985, 1987); *The Chronicle of Higher Education,* 11–12–86; *The New York Times:* 3–6–84; 9–3–84; 9–9–84; 11–8–84; 11–14–84; 12–11–84; 1–11–85; 11–4–86; 11–6–86; 1–13–88.

Charles Spittal Robb (Courtesy of governor's office)

VIRGINIA

ROBB, Charles Spittal, 1982–1986

Born in Phoenix, Arizona on June 26, 1929, the son of James Spittal and Francis Howard (Woolley) Robb. An Episcopalian, Robb attended Cornell University in 1957 and 1958; he then transferred to the University of Wisconsin, which granted him a B.A.A. in 1961. While a member of the United States Marine Corps, Robb married Lynda Bird Johnson, the daughter of President Lyndon B. Johnson, in a White House ceremony on December 9, 1967. The ceremony was the first White House wedding in 53 years. The Robbs are the parents of Lucinda Desha, Catherine Lewis, and Jennifer Wickliffe.

A few months after his marriage, Robb left for Vietnam. He was discharged from the Marines in 1970, and entered the University of Virginia Law School. While there, he became a director of the LBJ Company. In 1973, the year in which President Johnson died, Robb was graduated from law school and was admitted to the Virginia bar. After serving as a law clerk for Judge John D. Butzner, Jr. of the United States Court of Appeals, in 1974 he joined the staff of the Washington law firm headed by Edward Bennett Williams (the noted criminal lawyer and president of the Washington Redskins professional football team), John Connally (the former governor of Texas), and Joseph Califano (the former Secretary of Health and Human Services).

Robb quickly became active in civic organizations in the District of Columbia and in northern Virginia. By 1976, he had become deputy general counsel and assistant parliamentarian for the Democratic National Committee's Platform Committee. He was elected to the post of lieutenant governor of Virginia in 1977 despite the fact that a Republican, John Dalton, won the gubernatorial race that year. In 1981 Robb ran as a Democrat for governor and defeated Virginia Attorney General J. Marshall Coleman by a vote of 760,357 to 659,398. President Ronald Reagan had campaigned actively for Coleman, but Robb defended himself from charges that he believed in lavish public spending and projected a conservative image similar to that of Coleman. Agreeing with the need for the Reagan administration's budget cuts in domestic spending, Robb portrayed his opponent as soft on drug pushers, and managed to fend off negative campaign advertising by the opposition. In the election Robb took most of Virginia handily. He captured his home territory, the usually Republican Fairfax County, and won the rest of the state except for Coleman's home base in the Shenandoah Valley. Robb's victory marked the first time that a Virginia governor from the northern part of the state had been elected. He was also the first Democrat elected to the post since 1965.

During Robb's administration Virginia raised the interest ceiling on credit card transactions, and provided for "no-fault" divorces after a six-month waiting period. At the national NAACP convention in 1983, he characterized the state as a leader in racial progress. He demonstrated his commitment to the ideal of racial integration by sending his own children to predominantly black public schools. He also championed economic development, increased financing for education, and a larger role for women and minorities in state government.

Constitutionally barred from succeeding himself in office, Robb was given much credit for reversing the political fortunes of state Democrats. Clinging to Robb's coattails, Democrat Gerald L. Baliles followed his friend and associate into office, promising to continue the Robb record of fiscal conservatism and social moderation.

Upon leaving office, Robb joined the 300-member law firm of Hunton and Williams. But he remained active in national Democratic politics, emerging as a major spokesman for the party's centrist forces which sought to rescue the Democrats from their leftward drift. Robb is currently chairman of the Democratic Leadership Council, a group of centrist and conservative Democrats, primarily elected officials from the South and West, who are attempting to move the national Democratic party closer to its constituency and ideals. Although many analysts had speculated that he would be a leading contender for the Democratic presidential or vice presidential nomination in 1988, Robb chose instead to run for the U.S. Senate. Seeking the post held by retiring Republican Paul S. Trible, Jr., he faced black businessman and former Democrat Maurice Dawkins in the general election. Drawing on the record and popularity he has established over the past decade in state politics, Robb was a heavy favorite to win the Senate seat. Drawing 71 percent of the vote, the popular Robb became the first Democrat elected to the Senate from Virginia in 22 years, and political observers quickly targeted him as one of the faces to watch in future national Democratic politics.

Bibliography: Biographical information courtesy of governor's office; *The Washington Post:* 11–4–81; 7–1–82; 7–12–83; *The New York Times:* 12–10–67; 12–12–85; 4–13–86; 4–30–87; 11–7–87; 11–12–87; 6–12–88; Michael Barone *et al., The Almanac of American Politics, 1986* (New York and Washington, D.C., 1985).

Gerald L. Baliles (Courtesy of governor's office)

BALILES, Gerald L., 1986–

Baliles was born on July 8, 1940 in a mountain farming community in Patrick County, Virginia. Graduating as the leader of the Cadet Corps from Fishburne Military School in Waynesboro, Virginia, 1959, he went on to earn his undergraduate degree at Connecticut's Wesleyan University in 1963. He received a J.D. from the University of Virginia in 1967. From 1967 to 1975, he worked in the state attorney general's office as an assistant attorney general and then deputy attorney general, where he developed a reputation as an expert in environmental law. Joining a private law firm in 1975, he also began his political career that year. Defeating the incumbent in an upset, he won a seat in the state House of Delegates, where he served from 1976 until 1982. During his first term in office, he was voted one of the most effective members of the legislature in a survey by the *Virginian-Pilot* newspaper.

In 1981, Baliles was elected state attorney general, part of a Democratic sweep that year of the offices of governor, lieutenant governor, and attorney general. As attorney general, he served as chairman of the Southern Association of Attorneys General. In 1985, he was selected as the most outstanding attorney general in the nation by his peers in the National Association of Attorneys General.

Baliles sought the governorship in 1985, looking to succeed his friend and political mentor Charles Robb, constitutionally barred from succeeding himself. Forging a coalition of blacks and whites, he defeated Lieutenant Governor Richard Davis in the state party convention to win the Democratic gubernatorial nomination. In the general election he faced Richmond lawyer Wyatt B. Durrette, a former state legislator who had lost races for lieutenant governor in 1977 and attorney general in 1981.

In the campaign, Baliles worked hard to establish an identity for himself separate from that of the Robb administration of which he had been a part, and whose policies of fiscal conservatism and social moderation he pledged to continue. Because the ideological differences between the two candidates were not great, Baliles emphasized that he had more state government service and leadership experience than his opponent.

Baliles' victory, with 55 percent of the vote, was an historic sweep in a state long considered to be a conservative stronghold. The race drew national attention because of the nature of the Democratic ticket: Baliles' successful running mates included a black candidate for lieutenant governor, L. Douglas Wilder, and a female candidate for attorney general, Mary Sue Terry.

In office, Baliles has been highly successful in working his programs through the legislature. His achievements include a $12 billion transportation program for the improvement of roads, seaports, airports, and mass transit, programs to fight illiteracy, and continued efforts to end pollution of the Chesapeake Bay. He has also placed a special emphasis on international trade and educational reforms to promote competition in world markets. He has also initiated several new programs intended to improve both the image of the state and to strengthen the effectiveness of its high technology training.

Regarded by political observers to be a tough, intelligent, and shrewd politician, he is viewed as one of the brightest stars in the nation's gubernatorial corps. Past chairman of the International Trade Committee of the National Governors' Association, chairman of the Southern States Energy Board, and chairman of the Advisory Council for International Education in the Southern Governors' Association, he served as vice-chairman of the National Governors' Association from 1987 to 1988. In July 1988, he succeeded to the chairmanship, agreeing with his predecessor John Sununu (R-N.H.) on the need for less federal regulation and more state authority.

Baliles is married to the former Jean Patterson. The couple has two children, Laura and Jonathan.

Bibliography: Biographical information courtesy of governor's office; Michael Barone *et al., The Almanac of American Politics 1986, 1988* (New York and Washington, D.C., 1985, 1987); *The New York Times:* 11–5–85; 11–6–85; 1–12–86; 7–29–87; 3–22–88.

John Dennis Spellman (Courtesy of governor's office; Credit: Washington State Library)

WASHINGTON

Born in Seattle, Washington on December 29, 1926, the son of Sterling B. and Lela (Cushman) Spellman. A Roman Catholic, Spellman is married to the former Lois Elizabeth Murphy, by whom he is the father of Margo, Bart, David, Jeffrey, Theresa, and Katherine.

Spellman is a graduate of Seattle University, where he was valedictorian of his class. After serving in the United States Navy during World War II, he completed his education at Georgetown University, where he received his law degree in 1953. Spellman, a Republican, was a practicing attorney in Seattle for 13 years before embarking on a career in public service. After an unsuccessful campaign for mayor of Seattle in 1965, he was a King County Commissioner from 1967 to 1969, and was elected King County Executive in 1969. Re-elected in 1973 and 1977, he won wide acclaim for completing Seattle's domed stadium, the Kingdome, with no cost overruns. During his tenure as county executive, Spellman also served as first vice president of the National Association of Counties, chairman of the King-Snohomish Manpower Consortium, and chairman of the Statewide Citizens Committee for Revenue Sharing. He made his first bid for statewide office in 1976 when, as the Republican candidate for governor, he was defeated by Dixy Lee Ray, who gained 53 percent of the vote to his 44 percent. The key to her victory, political observers believed, was the fact that she was able to attract votes from conservative Republicans who were dissatisfied with the more moderate Spellman.

Conservative opposition to Spellman continued, and when he again sought his party's gubernatorial nomination in 1980, he captured barely 41 percent of the vote to Duane Berentson's 39 percent and Bruce K. Chapman's 18 percent, but his margin was enough to make him the Republican candidate. Although he had acquired a reputation as a competent but rather colorless administrator, Spellman was helped during the campaign by tension within the Democratic ranks. When the tempestuous Governor Ray was rejected by her own party, with Washington Democrats choosing instead State Senator James McDermott, a liberal Seattle psychiatrist, as their gubernatorial candidate, more traditional and conservative Democrats defected to Spellman. This development allowed the Republicans to capture the statehouse, with Spellman receiving 57 percent of the vote to McDermott's 43 percent.

As governor, Spellman was chairman of the National Governors' Association Task Force on Export Finance, vice-chairman of the National Governors' Association Committee on International Trade and Foreign Relations, founding co-chairman of the business and labor Coalition for Employment Through Exports, and national state government chairman for the United States Savings Bonds Campaign. In 1981 he was awarded an honorary LL.D. by his alma mater, the University of Seattle.

In the November 1984 gubernatorial race, Spellman unexpectedly lost his bid for re-election against the Democrat Booth Gardner, heir to the Weyerhauser lumber fortune. Despite Ronald Reagan's landslide Presidential victory that year, Gardner attracted 53 percent of the vote compared with Spellman's 47 percent. Political observers attributed Spellman's loss to problems associated with the condition of the state's Public Power Supply System. The WPPSSS had provided cheap public hydroelectric power to most of the Pacific Northwest for years but, by the 1960s, when the state had exhausted most of its hydroelectric capacity, the agency was forced to find new ways to meet the power needs of the region. Its decision to go nuclear spawned numerous problems—delayed construction, sloppy management, vast cost overruns—that had dismal effects on the Northwest's long-term economic development. The state also suffered greatly from a lingering recession in the logging and lumber industries. Although Spellman reaped major newspaper endorsements, he lost support by charging that Gardner had sold out to organized labor.

With his defeat, Spellman retired to private law practice.

Bibliography: Biographical information courtesy of governor's office; Michael Barone *et al., The Almanac of American Politics, 1982, 1984* (New York and Washington, D.C., 1981, 1983); *The New York Times:* 11–6–84; 11–8–84.

Booth Gardner (Credit: Washington State Library)

GARDNER, Booth, 1985–

Born in Tacoma, Washington on August 21, 1936, the son of Bryson Gardner and Evelyn Booth Gardner. Married to the former Jean Forstrom, he has two children, Doug and Gail.

Gardner received a B.A. in business from the University of Washington in 1958 and an M.B.A. from Harvard University in 1963. Prior to beginning his political career he served as assistant to the dean at the Harvard Business School from 1966 to 1967, and as director of the School of Business and Economics at the University of Puget Sound from 1967 to 1972. A Democrat, he was first elected to public office in 1970 when he became a state senator from the 26th District. Serving one term, he chaired the Education Committee in addition to serving on the Manufacturing and Development and Commerce and Regulatory Committees.

He left the senate in 1973 to devote time to his posts as president of the Laird Norton Company, a national building supply firm, and as a member of the Board of Directors of the Weyerhauser Company, the family timber giant to which he is heir. Before returning to public life, he also taught economics and held an administrative job at Pacific Lutheran University in Tacoma.

In 1980 Gardner was elected as the first county executive of Pierce County, the state's second most populous. As county executive, he was credited with turning a $4.7 million county deficit into a $4 million surplus by the time of his accession to the governorship.

Seeking the governorship in 1984, he upset State Senator Jim McDermott to win his party's nomination. McDermott had been defeated four years earlier by Republican John Spellman, the incumbent whom Gardner sought to unseat.

In the campaign, Gardner presented himself as an outsider with a fresh approach to government. As a business executive himself, he promised to bring better management to government and to deal effectively with the state's economic problems. As a political moderate, he drew considerable support from conservatives and independents. He also enjoyed the benefits of his vast personal fortune, which he tapped to help finance his campaign. Gardner defeated the incumbent with 53 percent of the vote.

Political observers see Gardner as an extremely effective governor, the first, in the opinion of some, to establish real command over state government since Daniel Evans retired in 1976. He has made economic development the centerpiece of his administration, stressing the need for Washington to compete economically with other portions of the Pacific Rim. In 1987 he proposed extending the state sales tax to services to pay for an educational excellence program, and also pushed for workfare-type welfare reforms. Another of his efforts in the statehouse was legislation to permit schooling at home.

Gardner has achieved national recognition as vice-chairman of the Western Governors' Association and of the National Governors' Association Committee on Foreign Trade. A strong candidate for re-election in 1988, Gardner defeated State Senator Bob Williams, an evangelical conservative, with 63 percent of the vote. With his convincing victory, Gardner bucked a trend in the state, which had not re-elected a governor since 1972.

Bibliography: Biographical information courtesy of governor's office; Jaques Cattell Press, *Who's Who in American Politics, 1985–1986* (New York, 1985); Michael Barone *et al., The Almanac of American Politics, 1986, 1988* (New York and Washington, D.C., 1985, 1987); *The New York Times:* 9–16–84; 11–8–84; 1–17–85.

John Davison Rockefeller (Courtesy of Senator Rockefeller)

WEST VIRGINIA

ROCKEFELLER, John Davison ("Jay"), IV, 1977–1985

Born on June 16, 1937 in New York, New York, the son of John Davison, III, a philanthropist, and Blanche Ferry (Hooker) Rockefeller. Jay Rockefeller is the great-grandson of John D. Rockefeller, founder of the Standard Oil Company, and nephew of Winthrop Rockefeller, who was a governor of Arkansas, and Nelson A. Rockefeller, who was a governor of New York and vice president of the United States. A Baptist, he is the brother of Sandra, Hope, and Alidra. Rockefeller married Sharon Percy, the daughter of United States Senator Charles Percy of Illinois, on April 1, 1967; he is the father of Jamie, Charles, Valerie, and Justin Rockefeller.

After graduating from Phillip Exeter Academy in 1954, Rockefeller received an A. B. degree from Harvard in 1961. He was also a student at International Christian University in Tokyo in 1957, and did post-graduate work at the Yale University Institute of Far Eastern Languages. Appointed a member of the National Advisory Council of the Peace Corps in 1961, Rockefeller served as special assistant to the director of the Peace Corps in 1962. He was an operations officer in charge of work in the Philippines until 1963, an assistant to the assistant secretary of state for Far Eastern Affairs, and desk officer for Indonesian affairs in the State Department's Bureau of Far Eastern Affairs in 1963. Rockefeller served as a consultant on the President's Commission on Juvenile Delinquency and Youth Crime in 1964, was employed as a field worker in the Action for Appalachian Youth Program beginning in 1964, and sat as a Democratic member of the West Virginia House of Delegates from 1966 to 1968. After serving as West Virginia Secretary of State from 1968 to 1972, he spent two years, from 1973 to 1975, as president of West Virginia Wesleyan College. Rockefeller has also served as a trustee of the University of Chicago from 1967 until the present.

Rockefeller lost his initial bid for the West Virginia governorship in 1972, when he was defeated by the Republican Arch A. Moore by a vote of 423,817 to 350,462. Following his defeat, he retired from public view for a time, becoming president of West Virginia Wesleyan College. In 1976 he again became the Democratic Party's gubernatorial candidate, and this time defeated his Republican opponent, former West Virginia Governor

Cecil H. Underwood, by a popular vote of 495,661 to 253,420 on November 2, 1976. Rockefeller was inaugurated on January 17, 1977.

During his first term Rockefeller devoted much of his attention to the nation's energy problems. The energy crisis had led to a renewed interest in West Virginia as a source of fossil fuels, and wildcatting for oil and natural gas in the state was frequent and at times successful. In 1978 West Virginia sought to condemn land in Mingo County owned by a development corporation, in order to relocate residents who were living in an area that experienced persistent flooding. West Virginia also took title that year to a 52-mile branch line of the Chessie System, at the time probably the largest purchase of a non-commuter rail line by a state. West Virginia sought to become the site of the first commercial plant to extract synthetic fuel from coal in 1979; the same year, Rockefeller appealed to the United States Civil Aeronautics Board to protest cuts in air service to the state.

Challenged in the 1980 Democratic primary by John Rogers, Rockefeller defeated his opponent by a margin of about four to one. An acrimonious battle followed with the Republican candidate, former Governor Arch Moore. Moore criticized Rockefeller's lavish campaign spending, which came to over $11.7 million, a considerable amount even for a man with a net worth estimated at $90 million. Rockefeller replied that the spending was needed in order to overcome Moore's lead in the polls. Attempting to depict himself as an expert on coal, which he saw as the energy source of the future, Rockefeller also took advantage of the fact that Moore had been tried for extortion during his administration from 1969 to 1977. Though Moore had been acquitted on that charge, an aide's admission early in 1980 that he had accepted kickbacks from the liquor industry and channeled the money into Moore's campaign also weakened his candidacy. Rockefeller eventually won the general election by a vote of 401,863 to 337,240, becoming the state's first Democrat to serve two consecutive terms as governor. His victory fueled speculation that he would run for president in 1984 and that his wife Sharon, who became chairwoman of the Corporation for Public Broadcasting in 1981, would seek the West Virginia governorship.

As governor, Rockefeller made honest government a hallmark of his administration, an important achievement in a state with a history of political scandal and cronyism. He concentrated on finding ways to help industries modernize, and also worked to help West Virginia companies sell their coal mining equipment to China. He also devoted his efforts to upgrading the state's road system, a major undertaking in a mountainous state whose chief roadway, the West Virginia Turnpike, was still just two lanes wide in some places.

Barred from seeking a third consecutive term in 1984, Rockefeller entered the U.S. Senate race, looking to succeed retiring Democratic Senator Jennings Randolph. He defeated Republican rival John Raese, a millionaire businessman from Morgantown, by a margin of 370,762 votes to 339,871 votes. His election came after a characteristically expensive campaign: he reportedly spent over $9 million to defeat Raese, including $6.9 million of his own money.

Political commentators have widely assumed that after spending some time in the Senate, Rockefeller will attempt to play some role on the national political scene. With seats on the Commerce, Energy, and Finance Committees, he has an opportunity to make an impact in the Senate. His expertise in Asian affairs should also assist him in making his mark on international trade legislation.

Bibliography: Peter Collier and David Horowitz, *Rockefellers* (New York, 1976); *The Washington Post:* 7–29–78; 10–13–78; 3–24–79; 12–4–80; 1–10–82; *Charleston Gazette,* 11–5–80; *The New York Times:* 11–3–76; 1–13–77; 4–29–84; 6–2–84; 6–6–84; 9–26–84; 11–7–84; 11–8–84; 1–15–85; Michael Barone *et al., The Almanac of American Politics, 1986, 1988* (New York and Washington, D.C., 1985, 1987).

Arch A. Moore, Jr. (Courtesy of governor's office)

MOORE, Arch A., Jr., 1969–1977, 1985–

Born in Moundsville, West Virginia on April 16, 1923; the son of Arch A. Moore and Genevieve Jones Moore. A Methodist, he married Shelley S. Riley in 1949. The couple has three children, Arch, Shelley, and Lucy.

Moore was educated in the public schools of Marshall County. He enrolled at Lafayette College in 1941, but left to join the U.S. Infantry during World War II, going on to win several combat decorations. He completed his education after the war, graduating from West Virginia University with an A.B. in political science in 1941 and from the West Virginia University College of Law with a J.D. in 1951.

A dominant figure in West Virginia public life for more than three decades, Moore was the first governor in the state's modern history to be re-elected to a four-year term, and the first governor in state history to be elected to three four-year terms. His victories have been all the more impressive since he is a Republican in a state where Democrats dominate by more than two to one.

Moore began his political career in 1952, winning a seat in the West Virginia House of Delegates. In 1956 he was elected to the U.S. House of Representatives, winning re-election by impressive margins in 1958, 1960, 1962, 1964, and 1966. He chose to leave his safe congressional seat to seek the governorship in 1968, winning the state house by a narrow margin in a year when his party's candidate for president failed to carry the state. A popular governor, he won a change in the state constitution that allowed him to run for—and win—a second consecutive term in 1972. Four years later, he made plans to seek a third term, contending that since the constitution had been revised while he was in office, his second term could be counted as his first. The state supreme court, however, rejected this argument, and he was forced to step down after the completion of his second term in 1977.

A self-made man with a booming voice and a no-nonsense manner, Moore was a popular governor. In fact, his career was so successful that one faction of the dominant party became known as "Arch Moore Democrats," those who stuck with the Democratic ticket unless Moore was running. Even Democrats conceded that Moore had a unique talent for winning compromises from union members and management whose differences seemed irreconcilable. In his first two terms in office he also became a prominent leader among the nation's governors. In 1971 he became the first and only West Virginia governor to be elected chairman of the National Governors' Association. He also served as co-chairman of the Appalachian Regional Commission in 1971, president of the Council of State Governments in 1972–1973, and national chairman of the Republican Governors' Association in 1976. An educationally oriented governor, he served as president of the Education Commission of the States from 1974 to 1976. He also made an impact in the international arena. In 1974 he was one of the first governors to be invited to visit the People's Republic of China. In 1976 he served as the special representative of President Ford and formally opened the Bicentennial Exposition of the "World of Franklin and Jefferson" in Warsaw, Poland.

Despite these successes, Moore's future seemed uncertain after he was indicted on extortion charges in 1976, the final year of his second term. Although acquitted of charges that he had extorted $25,000 from a financier seeking a state bank charter, the indictment seemed to affect the voters' attitude. He lost races for the U.S. Senate and for the governorship in 1980, the first defeats in his political career.

In 1984 Moore struggled with a decision to seek either the governorship or the U.S. Senate seat being vacated by retiring incumbent Jennings Randolph. Rather than face his old nemesis Jay Rockefeller—the man who had defeated him for the governorship in 1980—Moore decided to seek a third term as governor rather than run for the Senate against Rockefeller. Unopposed in the Republican primary, he defeated Democrat Clyde M. See, Jr., speaker of the State House of Delegates, with 53 percent of the vote to win an unprecedented third term in the statehouse. In the campaign, he pledged to enact "the most revolutionary economic development program ever put before a legislative body." He also promised not to raise taxes.

Moore faced serious economic challenges during his third term, and entered office with state voters in a bleak mood. The state suffered from the highest unemployment rate in the nation and, dependent as it was on basic industries, had yet to show solid progress toward recovery from the recession of the early 1980s. As his term drew to a close, however, Moore was claiming credit for $1 billion worth of new jobs, for tax cuts, and for placing new emphasis on higher education, an area where West Virginia has traditionally trailed most Southern states.

In 1988 Moore officially announced that he would be seeking an unprecedented fourth term as governor, ending months of speculation that he would challenge incumbent Robert Byrd for the U.S. Senate. He won renomination only after a bitter primary fight with businessman John Raese. His opponent in the November 1988 general election was Democrat Gaston Caperton, an insurance executive whose primary victory in a seven-candidate field left the party bitter and divided. Depicting Moore as an old style politician and blaming him for the state's high unemployment rate, Caperton ousted the legendary Moore from office, winning 59 percent of the vote to the incumbent's 41 percent.

Bibliography: Biographical information courtesy of governor's office; Jaques Cattell Press, *Who's Who in American Politics, 1985–1986* (New York, 1985); Michael Barone et al., *The Almanac of American Politics, 1986, 1988* (New York and Washington, D.C., 1985, 1987); *The New York Times:* 3–25–84; 4–29–84; 11–6–84; 1–15–85; 4–1–87; 4–8–87; 12–3–87; 1–12–88; 5–10–88; 5–12–88.

Anthony S. Earl (Courtesy of Governor Earl)

WISCONSIN

EARL, Anthony S., 1983–1987

Born in Lansing, Michigan on April 12, 1936, Earl grew up in St. Ignace in Michigan's Upper Peninsula. A Roman Catholic, he married Sheila Coyle of Chicago in August 1962. The couple has four daughters: Julia, Anne, Mary, and Catherine.

Earl received his B.A. in political science from Michigan State University at East Lansing in 1958, and his J.D. from the University of Chicago in 1961. From 1962 to 1965 he served with the U.S. Navy. During his active duty years, he was admitted to practice before the U.S. Court of Military Appeals and the U.S. Supreme Court. Upon his release from the Navy, he was appointed assistant district attorney for Marathon County, Wisconsin. One year later, he was selected to be the first full-time city attorney for the city of Wausau.

A Democrat, Earl began his political career in 1969, running successfully for the state assembly seat vacated by Democrat David Obey, who had won a special election to the U.S. House of Representatives. Re-elected to a full assembly term in 1970, he was named to the Joint Committee on Finance, and in 1971, selected by his colleagues in the Democratic caucus to serve as majority leader. He held that position until he left the legislature in January 1975. While serving in the legislature, Earl was also a partner in the Wausau law firm of Crooks, Low, and Earl.

In 1974, Earl ran unsuccessfully for state attorney general. After his defeat, he was appointed to the cabinet of Governor Patrick Lucey and served as secretary of the Department of Administration for one year. In 1975 the state Natural Resources Board appointed Earl secretary of the Department of Natural Resources. He served as Wisconsin's chief environmental officer from December 1975 until 1980, when he returned to private law practice as a partner in the firm of Foley and Lardner.

In 1982 Earl narrowly won a three-candidate Democratic primary to win his party's gubernatorial nomination. Facing Representative Terry Kohler in the general election, he ran explicitly on a platform of big government and more taxes, yet won the election with ease. His margin of 57 percent to 42 percent was one of the largest in the history of Wisconsin gubernatorial politics.

Earl was inaugurated on January 3, 1983. One of the nation's most liberal governors, he believed that the services government performs for constituents are worth the cost, and he derided the notion that the state needed to lower tax rates to attract new jobs. As governor, Earl held national posts including the chairmanship of the National Governors' Association Standing Committee on Energy and the Environment, and membership on the Democratic National Committee's Fairness Commission and Policy Commission. From 1983 to 1985 he was chairman of the newly formed Council of Great Lakes Governors, an organization he helped to establish. He also played a major role in the creation of the National Alliance for Acid Rain Control.

In 1986 Earl faced a difficult choice: seeking re-election or opting for a challenge against Republican Senator Bob Kasten. Working against a Senate candidacy was the size of the potential field in the Democratic primary, and Earl made the race for re-election. Although he easily won renomination, he was defeated in his re-election bid by Republican Tommy Thompson, a state legislator and fiscal conservative. Earl lost by 100,000 votes in a year when most incumbent governors did very well. Despite his competence, he seemed to suffer from a rightward drift among the electorate, many of whom were concerned that the state's high taxes were stifling growth. He was also hurt by his support of homosexual rights and a new prison in Milwaukee, by his opposition to the 21-year-old drinking age, and by his off-the-cuff remark that he'd rather strike than take the 15 percent pay cut offered to Oscar Mayer employees. Others attributed his loss to an inability to get his message out, and his reliance on an overly tight-knit staff.

Earl made an unsuccessful comeback attempt in 1988, seeking a U.S. Senate seat.

Bibliography: Biographical information courtesy of Governor Earl; Michael Barone *et al., The Almanac of American Politics 1986* (New York and Washington, D.C., 1985); *The New York Times:* 9–11–86; 12–12–86.

Tommy G. Thompson (Courtesy of governor's office)

THOMPSON, Tommy G., 1987–

Born in Elroy, Wisconsin on November 19, 1941; the son of Allan Thompson and Julie Dutton Thompson. A Catholic, Thompson married Sue Ann Mashak in 1969. The couple has three children, Kelli, Tommi, and Jason.

Thompson graduated from the University of Wisconsin-Madison in 1963 with a degree in history and political science. In 1966 he received a law degree from the same university. A Republican, his interest in politics came early. In 1964 he was vice-chairman of Wisconsin Collegians for Goldwater, and from 1964 to 1966 he was a legislative messenger in the Wisconsin State Senate. Elected to the State Assembly in 1966, he served as assistant minority leader from 1972 to 1981, and as Republican Floor Leader from 1981 until his accession to the governorship. In the assembly, he served on numerous committees: Assembly Organization, Legislative Council, Rules, the Strategic Development Commission, the Select Committee on the Future of the University System, and joint legislative commissions on Employment Relations and Legislative Organization. During his years in the legislature, he also worked as an attorney in private practice with the firm of Elroy and Mauston, and as a real estate broker.

In 1986 Thompson challenged Democratic incumbent Anthony Earl for the statehouse. Although Earl had a reputation as one of the most liberal governors in America, Wisconsin had long been known as a liberal state, and political observers were surprised at his defeat by the conservative Thompson. Thompson's victory was even more surprising because most incumbent governors did fairly well in the 1986 elections. Despite his record of comptence, Earl's loss was attributed to his inability to get his message out, and to his reliance on an overly tight-knit campaign staff. The electorate also seemed concerned that the state's high tax policies—which Earl defended—were stifling economic growth. Thompson, on the other hand, based his campaign on a ringing call to cut both taxes and welfare. He defeated Earl by 100,000 votes, garnering 53 percent of the vote to the incumbent's 47 percent.

Once in office, Thompson appeared more willing to compromise with the Democratically controlled legislature than many had expected. He backed a small tax increase, insisted on no major cuts in welfare spending, authorized the building of a controversial state prison, and accepted a mandatory seat belt law. Pointing out that his responsibilities as governor were different from those of a minority party leader in the legislature, he began a campaign to boost state pride, praising its environment and work ethic. He angered many in the higher education community, however, by his policy of across-the-board budget cuts for all state agencies. He planned to raise tuition at state colleges, to expand student aid, and to limit enrollment at the University of Wisconsin so that the state could decrease its financial support.

In the late 1988 presidential campaign, Thompson also engendered a bit of controversy by denying rumors that he had encouraged Republican voters to cast cross-over votes in the April 5 Democratic primary. In a state with one of the oldest and most wide open primaries in the nation, Thompson was charged with encouraging Republicans to vote for Jesse Jackson in the belief that he would be a sure loser in the general election.

Bibliography: Biographical information courtesy of governor's office; Michael Barone *et al., The Almanac of American Politics 1988;* Jaques Cattel Press, *Who's Who in American Politics, 1985–1986* (New York, 1985); *The New York Times:* 1–6–87; 3–31–88; *The Chronicle of Higher Education:* 11–12–86; 12–17–86; 3–11–87.

Edgar J. Herschler (Credit: Peterson's Portrait Studio)

WYOMING

HERSCHLER, Edgar J., 1975–1987

Born on October 27, 1918 on his grandfather's pioneer homestead in the Fontenelle Creek region of Lincoln County, near Kemmerer, Wyoming. The son of Edgar F. and Charlotte (Jenkins) Herschler. Herschler married Kathleen ("Casey") Colter in 1944; he has two children, Kathleen and James. Herschler is an Episcopalian.

A product of Kemmerer public schools, Herschler was graduated in 1941 from the University of Colorado as a pre-law student; he received an LL.B. from the University of Wyoming Law School in 1949. During World War II he served with the United States Marine Corps in the South Pacific. Wounded in action, he received both the Purple Heart and the Silver Star.

Herschler's political career began soon after his graduation from law school. Serving as Kemmerer town attorney from 1949 until his election as governor in 1974, he was also the Lincoln County prosecuting attorney from 1951 to 1959 and a member of the Wyoming House of Representatives from 1959 to 1969. He was a member of the State Parole Board from 1972 to 1974.

Despite an unsuccessful attempt to become the Democratic candidate for a United States congressional seat in 1970, Herschler decided in 1974 to try and succeed Wyoming's popular Governor Stanley Hathaway, a Republican who had resigned to become United States Secretary of the Interior. After defeating Harry E. Leimback and John J. Rooney in the Democratic primary (where he captured 47 percent of the vote), Herschler faced conservative State Senator Dick Jones of Cody in the general election. One of the major issues in the race was the construction of a slurry pipeline—a device to mix coal with water and pipe it out of state to market. Outgoing Governor Hathaway favored the plan, as did Jones, but Herschler opposed it on the grounds that the pipeline would deplete Wyoming's scarce water resources. The voters obviously agreed. Herschler carried the traditionally Democratic southern counties of the state by large margins and ran almost even with Jones in the usually Republican north, where farmers and ranchers feared coal companies would bid up the price of water should the pipeline become a reality. Losing significantly only in Casper (because of his opposition to transforming a local junior college into a four-year school), Herschler won the election with 56 percent of the vote to Jones' 44 percent. He thereby became Wyoming's first Democratic governor since 1963, and the first actually elected to the position since 1958.

During his first term in office, Herschler identified the energy shortage, environmental protection, drought assistance, water development, aid to farmers and ranchers, and problems associated with industrial impact as the most important issues facing Wyoming. He favored an increase in the mineral severance tax and emphasized states' rights in regard to water, public land, and mining laws, and tried to make himself and his office more accessible to Wyoming citizens. Despite these accomplishments, Herschler barely retained his office in his 1978 bid for re-election. He was caught in the backlash of scandals coming out of Rock Springs, one of the major mineral boom towns of the state. The site of much prostitution and gambling, some of it apparently controlled by organized crime interests, the town and its problems were featured on the CBS television show "60 Minutes," where one of the state's leading investigators charged that Herschler himself was involved in the improprieties. Several of his political associates were also implicated. A grand jury investigating Rock Springs indicted Attorney General Frank Mendecino, a Herschler appointee, and there were charges that Don Anselmi, a Rock Springs hotel owner and state Democratic chairman, was involved in corruption. In 1978 the Rock Springs police chief shot and killed an undercover agent who was looking into crime in the area.

Although few voters thought that Herschler himself was guilty of wrongdoing, his Republican gubernatorial opponent, State Senator John Ostlund of Gillette, criticized Herschler's failure to do anything about the widening scandal. After his own re-nomination was secured with a victory over Margaret McKinstry in the Democratic primary by a margin of 65 percent to 35 percent, Herschler responded by firing Mendecino and obtaining Anselmi's resignation. He also shifted the focus of the campaign to his proposal to increase Wyoming's severance tax on minerals by five percent and to use the proceeds to reduce state property taxes, a move opposed by Ostlund. This allowed Herschler to charge that his opponent was a "mouthpiece" for the big mining companies, a charge that seemed to ring true when it was revealed that Ostlund had had profitable business dealings with at least one of the companies. The contest was a real cliffhanger, with Herschler re-elected by a margin of 51 percent to 49 percent, or less than 2,400 votes. With his re-election, Herschler became the first Democratic chief executive of Wyoming to serve more than one term since Governor Lester C. Hunt's tenure from 1943 to 1949.

During his second term Herschler obtained widespread publicity as a spokesman for the increasingly alienated West. He has angrily informed federal officials of his opposition to Wyoming's becoming the "energy breadbasket of the nation" or an "energy colony of the nation," speaking up against an amendment that would weaken federal environmental curbs on the strip mining of coal. Because the federal government owns vast tracts of land in Wyoming, Herschler has also bitterly denounced federal red tape and bureaucratic regulations that reflect ignorance of the realities of Wyoming life.

With his ability to balance the requirements of growth and environmental protection, Herschler was easily re-elected to a third term in 1982, defeating Republican Warren Morton, a former speaker of the Wyoming House, with 63 percent of the vote. During his administration, he served as chairman of the Interstate Oil Compact Commission, chairman of the Western Governors' Policy Office, chairman of the Western Governors' Conference, co-chairman of the National Governors' Association Subcommittee on Range Resources Management, and chairman of the Subcommittee on Coal. He also served as chairman of the Corrections Project of the Education Commission of the States and co-chairman of the Old West Regional Commission. He was known as a staunch supporter of the Reagan administration's plan to deploy the MX missile system in his state.

During his third term, a survey by the Wyoming Heritage Society showed him to be the most popular political figure in the state. Because of his popularity, his 1984 announcement that he would not seek a fourth term in office shocked political observers across the state. The unexpected announcement came almost three years before the end of his third term. Although Herschler explained that he wanted to give those seeking to succeed him plenty of time to organize, more immediate considerations may have helped him decide. By the middle of his third term, Wyoming's mineral-based economy was in a slump, state revenues were tight, and Republicans in the legislature were threatening to challenge his budget appropriations for the first time in recent years.

He also faced some personal difficulties. In 1985 he filed for bankruptcy, listing liabilities that exceeded assets by nearly $2 million. A large portion of his debt was associated with the million-acre Yellowstone Ranch which he and three partners purchased in 1977. With the filing, Herschler became the state's first governor to declare bankruptcy.

Although Herschler has frequently been mentioned as a possible candidate for the U.S. Senate, he has shown no inclination to make the run.

Bibliography: Biographical information courtesy of governor's office; Michael Barone *et al., The Almanac of American Politics, 1978, 1982, 1984, 1986* (New York and Washington, D.C., 1977, 1981, 1983, 1985); *The New York Times:* 3–18–79; 8–20–80; 9–19–82; 11–23–82; 2–28–84; 9–15–85; "The Angry West vs. the Rest," *Newsweek* (Sept. 17, 1979).

Mike Sullivan (Courtesy of governor's office)

SULLIVAN, Mike, 1987–

Born in Omaha, Nebraska on September 22, 1939, the son of J.B. Sullivan and Margaret E. Sullivan. He was raised in Douglas, Wyoming, where he graduated from Converse County High School in 1957. He followed both his parents to the University of Wyoming, where he received a B.S. in petroleum engineering in 1961 and a J.D. in 1964. Following his graduation from law school, he practiced law continuously in Casper, specializing in trial work.

A life-long Democrat, Sullivan rode a distinguished career in law and years of varied civic interests to the state's highest office. Over the years he served in many civic organizations, including the Casper Rotary Club (of which he was president), Natrona County United Fund, Board of Directors of the Shepherd of the Valley of Nursing Home, Board of Directors of the University of Wyoming Alumni Association, Board of Trustees of Natrona County Memorial Hospital (of which he was chairman), Board of Trustees of St. Joseph's Children's Home in Torrington, and Board of Directors of Norwest Bank, West Casper. In 1986 he served as co-chairman of the "We Are Wyoming" fund which raised funds throughout central Wyoming for victims of Cheyenne's 1985 flood.

The 1986 race for governor was wide open due to the unexpected retirement of three-term incumbent Ed Herschler. Most political observers predicted victory for Republican Pete Simpson, brother of U.S. Senator Alan K. Simpson and winner of a divisive party primary. But the Republican candidate proved less than adept as a campaigner, paving the way for Sullivan's 54 percent to 46 percent victory. During the race, Sullivan called for more economic diversification, and impressed voters with his optimistic attitude and record of competent achievement.

Taking office as the state's 29th governor on January 5, 1987, he set the tone for his administration: "Confidence must replace uncertainty," he urged in his inaugural address, "courage must replace our fear of the future, and creativity tempered with common sense must guide our thoughts."

In office, Sullivan has favored expanding the University of Wyoming's economic development efforts, and has opposed the creation of any new four-year colleges.

Bibliography: Biographical information courtesy of governor's office; Michael Barone *et al., The Almanac of American Politics 1988* (New York and Washington, D.C., 1987); *The Chronicle of Higher Education,* 11–12–86; *The New York Times,* 1–6–87.

APPENDIX

First Time U.S. Governors Elected Fall 1988:

Indiana	Evan Bayh (term expires Jan. 1993)
Montana	Stan Stephens (term expires Jan. 1993)
New Hampshire	Judd Gregg (term expires Jan. 1991)
West Virginia	Gaston Caperton (term expires Jan. 1993)

INDEX

A

B

C

D

E

G

H

J

K

L

Lamm, Richard David, Colorado, 49

M

Mabus, Ray, Mississippi, 197
Martin, James G., North Carolina, 251
Martinez, Robert, Florida, 81
Matheson, Scott Milne, Utah, 337
McKernan, John R., Jr., Maine, 161
McWherter, Ned, Tennessee, 323
Mecham, Evan, Arizona, 27
Mickelson, George, South Dakota, 313
Mixson, John Wayne, Florida, 77
Mofford, Rose Perica, Arizona, 33
Moore, Arch A., Jr., West Virginia, 375

N

Nigh, George Patterson, Oklahoma, 267

O

Olson, Allen Ingvar, North Dakota, 255
O'Neill, William Atchinson, Connecticut, 59
Orr, Kay Stark, Nebraska, 219
Orr, Robert D., Indiana, 111

P

Perpich, Rudy, Minnesota, 183

R

Riley, Richard Wilson, South Carolina, 299
Robb, Charles Spittal, Virginia, 356
Rockefeller, John Davison ("Jay"), IV, West Virginia, 371
Roemer, Charles ("Buddy"), 153
Romer, Roy, Colorado, 55